D0220830

David Hare is one of the most important playwrights to have emerged in the UK in the last forty years. This volume examines his stage plays, television plays and cinematic films, and is the first book of its kind to offer such comprehensive and up-to-date critical treatment. Contributions from leading academics in the study of modern British theatre sit alongside those from practitioners who have worked closely with Hare throughout his career, including former Director of the National Theatre Sir Richard Eyre. Uniquely, the volume also includes a chapter on Hare's work as journalist and public speaker; a personal memoir by Tony Bicât, co-founder with Hare of the enormously influential Portable Theatre; and an interview with Hare himself in which he offers a personal retrospective of his career as a film maker which is his fullest and clearest account of that work to date.

A complete list of books in the series is at the back of this book.

THE CAMBRIDGE
COMPANION TO
DAVID HARE

EDITED BY
RICHARD BOON
University of Hull

CAMBRIDGE UNIVERSITY PRESS
Cambridge, New York, Melbourne, Madrid, Cape Town, Singapore, São Paulo, Delhi

Cambridge University Press
The Edinburgh Building, Cambridge CB2 8RU, UK

Published in the United States of America by Cambridge University Press, New York

www.cambridge.org
Information on this title: www.cambridge.org/9780521615570

First published 2007

Printed in the United Kingdom at the University Press, Cambridge

A catalogue record for this publication is available from the British Library

ISBN 978-0-521-85054-4 hardback
ISBN 978-0-521-61557-0 paperback

For Minnie Francesca,
her parents and uncles

CONTENTS

CONTENTS

NOTES ON CONTRIBUTORS

PETER ANSORGE was a producer at the BBC and Head of Drama at Channel 4, where he commissioned a series of award-winning productions including *A Very British Coup, Traffik, GBH, Tales of the City* and David Hare's *Licking Hitler*. He is the author of *Disrupting the Spectacle* and *From Liverpool to Los Angeles*. He is currently commissioning editor for film at Inspired Movies.

TONY BICÂT is a writer, director and lyricist who has worked extensively in film, television and theatre. He was co-founder, with David Hare, of Portable Theatre. He is the author of two books about screenwriting, *Creative Screenwriting* and *Creative TV Writing* (www.crowood.com). He runs workshops in screenwriting, screen acting and directing both in the UK and abroad.

RICHARD BOON is Professor of Drama at the University of Hull. He has published widely in the area of modern British political theatre, and is the author of *Brenton the Playwright* (1991) and *About Hare* (2003). He is also co-editor of the 'Playwright and the Work' series on modern British and Irish dramatists, and has co-edited, with Jane Plastow, *Theatre Matters* and *Theatre and Empowerment* for Cambridge University Press's 'Studies in Modern Theatre' series.

JOHN BULL is Professor of Film and Theatre at the University of Reading. He has published extensively in the field of drama, particularly modern and contemporary drama, including *New British Political Dramatists, Stage Right: Crisis and Recovery in British Contemporary Mainstream Theatre* and *Vanbrugh and Farquhar*. He is editor of the ongoing series of volumes, 'British and Irish Playwrights Since World War II'.

RICHARD EYRE is a theatre, film and TV director. He was the Artistic Director of the Royal National Theatre for ten years. His work as a theatre director has included numerous classics and premières of new plays, including six by David Hare. He is author, with Nicholas Wright, of *Changing Stages: A View of British Theatre in the Twentieth Century*.

MICHAEL MANGAN is Chair of Drama at Exeter University. He has also worked as a playwright, a director, a literary manager, a dramaturg and an actor. His primary research interests lie in the area of theatre and society, and he has published books, articles and papers on the subjects of theatre and gender, Shakespeare and Renaissance theatre, the cultural history of popular performance, applied theatre and contemporary British theatre.

CHRIS MEGSON is Senior Lecturer in Drama and Theatre at Royal Holloway College, University of London. He has published recently on Howard Barker, David Hare and British theatre during the cold war. He is currently researching the ascendancy of 'verbatim' playwriting in the 1990s and the impact of the 1960s counterculture on British theatre practice.

BELLA MERLIN is an actor and writer. She has worked around the globe training performers in the fundamental processes of Stanislavsky's Active Analysis. *The Complete Stanislavsky Toolkit* (2007) is her most recent hands-on examination and implementation of his legacy. She also lectures in Drama at Exeter University.

STEVE NICHOLSON is Reader in Twentieth Century and Contemporary Drama at the University of Sheffield. He is currently completing the last of three books about the impact of censorship under the Lord Chamberlain on twentieth-century British theatre, and has also written a history of the stage portrayal of the Soviet Union and Communism. He has published widely on the history and aesthetics of political theatre in the first half of the twentieth century and on contemporary playwrights.

DAN REBELLATO is Professor of Contemporary Theatre in the Department of Drama and Theatre, Royal Holloway, University of London. His book on mid-century theatre, *1956 and All That*, was published by Routledge in 1999. He is currently completing *British Drama and Globalization: Ethics and Aesthetics in Contemporary Playwriting*, and has published on Sarah Kane, Mark Ravenhill, David Greig, Suspect Culture, Noël Coward and Terence Rattigan. He is also a playwright and translator.

JANELLE REINELT is Professor of Theatre and Performance at the University of Warwick. Formerly, she was Associate Dean of Graduate Studies at the University of California, Irvine, and President of the International Federation for Theatre Research, 2003–7. She is a former Editor of *Theatre Journal*, and serves on the advisory board of theatre journals in the United Kingdom and Canada. With Brian Singleton of Trinity College, Dublin, she edits a book series for Palgrave Macmillan entitled 'Studies in International Performance'. She has published widely on contemporary British theatre, feminist theatre and the politics of performance. Her current project is a book with Gerald Hewitt on the politics and dramaturgy of David Edgar.

LIB TAYLOR is Senior Lecturer in Theatre at the University of Reading. She has published widely on contemporary performance, theatre and gender and modern British drama. She is also a theatre director and some of her research takes the form of theatre practice, particularly in the area of multimedia performance and the theatre work of Marguerite Duras.

CATHY TURNER is lecturer in Performing Arts at the University of Winchester. Her current research includes *Dramaturgy and Performance*, written with Synne Behrndt and to be published by Palgrave Macmillan in 2007. She is a member of Wrights & Sites, a group of four site-specific artists who are authors of artists' publications, *A Mis-Guide to Exeter* and *A Mis-Guide to Anywhere*.

LES WADE is Associate Professor of Theatre at Louisiana State University, where he serves as Director of Graduate Studies and Co-Director of LSU in London. His book *Sam Shepard and the American Theatre* was published in 1997. He is also an award-winning playwright.

DUNCAN WU is Professor of English Language and Literature at the University of Oxford and a Tutorial Fellow in English at St Catherine's College, Oxford. He is the author of *Six Contemporary Dramatists* (1994) and was the interlocutor in *Making Plays: Interviews with Dramatists and Directors* (2000).

ACKNOWLEDGEMENTS

I am extremely grateful to the many people who have in different ways helped in the preparation of this volume; primarily to all my contributors (of course) and especially to David Hare himself, who has, as ever, been generous to a fault; to the ever-supportive Dr Victoria Cooper, Helen Waterhouse, Kevin Taylor and Rebecca Jones of Cambridge University Press; to my students and colleagues at the Universities of Leeds and Hull (especially Helen Gardner at the latter); and to Emeritus Professor Philip Roberts, whose wisdom, friendship and good humour have been a source of inspiration and strength well beyond the confines of this book.

CHRONOLOGY
THE PLAYS, TELEPLAYS AND SCREENPLAYS
OF DAVID HARE

By date of first professional production, broadcast or release; it has not been possible to establish precise dates for some of the work. All are original works of single authorship unless otherwise specified.

Inside Out
(with Tony Bicât; adaptation of Kafka's diaries)
29 October 1968, Arts Lab, London

Strindberg
(adaptation of Strindberg's diaries)
1969, Arts Lab, London

How Brophy Made Good
1969, Brighton Combination

Slag
6 April 1970, Hampstead Theatre Club, London

What Happened to Blake?
28 September 1970, Royal Court Theatre Upstairs, London

The Rules of the Game
(adaptation of Pirandello)
June 1971, National Theatre (at the New Theatre), London

Lay By
(with Howard Brenton, Brian Clark, Trevor Griffiths, Stephen Poliakoff, Hugh Stoddart and Snoo Wilson)
24 August 1971, Traverse Theatre Club, Edinburgh

Deathsheads
(one-act play)
December 1971, Traverse Theatre Club, Edinburgh

The Great Exhibition
28 February 1972, Hampstead Theatre Club, London

England's Ireland
(with Tony Bicât, Howard Brenton, Brian Clark, David Edgar, Francis Fuchs
and Snoo Wilson)
September 1972, Mickery Theatre, Amsterdam

Man Above Men
(TV play)
19 March 1973, BBC Television ('Play for Today')

Brassneck
(with Howard Brenton)
19 September 1973, Nottingham Playhouse; also televised 22 May 1975,
BBC Television ('Play for Today')

Knuckle
4 March 1974, Comedy Theatre, London
adaptation for BBC radio, Walter Hall, 1981;
also televised 7 May 1989, BBC Television ('Theatre Night')

Fanshen
(based on the book by William Hinton)
22 April 1975, ICA Terrace Theatre, London;
also televised 18 October 1975, BBC Television

Teeth 'n' Smiles
2 September 1975, Royal Court Theatre, London

Licking Hitler: A Film for Television
10 January 1978, BBC TV

Deeds
(with Howard Brenton, Trevor Griffiths and Ken Campbell)
8 March 1978, Nottingham Playhouse

Plenty
7 April 1978, National Theatre (Lyttelton), London
adapted for film by the author, 1985, TCF/RKO (Edward R. Pressman)

Dreams of Leaving: A Film for Television
17 January 1980, BBC TV

A Map of the World
March 1982, Adelaide Festival, Adelaide, 20 January 1983, National Theatre
  (Lyttelton), London

Saigon: Year of the Cat
(television film)
29 November 1983, Thames Television

The Madman Theory of Deterrence
(sketch, in *The Big One*)
1983, London

Wetherby
(film)
8 March 1985, Greenpoint/Film Four/Zenith (Simon Relph)

Pravda: A Fleet Street Comedy
(with Howard Brenton)
2 May 1985, National Theatre (Olivier), London
adapted for radio by the authors, 28 September 1990, BBC

Plenty
(film version of stage play)
1985, TCF/RKO/Edward R. Pressman

The Bay at Nice and *Wrecked Eggs*
4 September 1986, National Theatre (Cottesloe), London

The Knife
(libretto; lyrics by Tim Rose-Price, music by Nick Bicât)
1987, Public/Newman Theater, New York

Paris by Night
(film)
1988, Virgin/British Screen/Film Four International/Zenith

The Secret Rapture
4 October 1988, National Theatre (Lyttelton), London
adaptation for radio, Chris Venning, BBC World Service, 1991

Strapless
(film)
1988, Virgin/Granada/Film Four International (Rick McCallum)

Racing Demon
1 February 1990, National Theatre (Cottesloe), London

Heading Home
(teleplay)
13 January 1991, BBC TV ('Screen Two')

Murmuring Judges
10 October 1991, National Theatre (Olivier), London

Damage
(film, adapted from the novel by Josephine Hart)
1992, Entertainment/Skreba/NEF/Canal (Louis Malle)

The Rules of the Game
(adaptation of Pirandello)
12 May 1992, Almeida Theatre, London

The Secret Rapture
(adapted for film by the author)
1993, Oasis/Greenpoint/Channel 4 (Simon Relph, David Hare)

The Absence of War
2 October 1993, National Theatre (Olivier), London
(performed as third part of the trilogy; the first two parts, *Racing Demon*
and *Murmuring Judges*, were performed on the same day; also adapted
for TV, BBC, 1995)

The Life of Galileo
(adaptation of Brecht)
11 March 1994, Almeida Theatre, London

Skylight
4 May 1995, National Theatre (Cottesloe), London

Mother Courage and Her Children
(adaptation of Brecht)
14 November 1995, National Theatre (Olivier), London

Ivanov
(adaptation of Chekhov)
2 June 1997, Almeida Theatre, London

Amy's View
13 June 1997, National Theatre (Lyttelton), London

The Judas Kiss
19 March 1998, Almeida Theatre Company at the Playhouse Theatre,
London

Via Dolorosa
8 September 1998, Royal Court Theatre, London; also adapted for TV (BBC)
   by the author, 2000

The Blue Room
(adaptation of Schnitzler, *La Ronde*)
10 September 1998, Donmar Warehouse, London

My Zinc Bed
14 September 2000, Royal Court Theatre, London

Platonov
(adaptation of Chekhov)
11 September 2001, Almeida Theatre, London

The Hours
(film, adapted from the novel by Michael Cunningham)
February 2002, Paramount (Robert Fox, Scott Rudin)

The Breath of Life
4 October 2002, Theatre Royal, Haymarket, London

The Permanent Way
13 November 2003, Theatre Royal, York

Stuff Happens
1 September 2004, National Theatre (Olivier), London

The House of Bernarda Alba
(adaptation of Lorca)
5 March 2005, National Theatre (Lyttelton), London

Enemies
(adaptation of Gorky)
6 May 2006, Almeida Theatre, London

The Vertical Hour
9 November 2006, Music Box Theatre, Broadway, New York

DIRECTING WORK

A selective list. Where no author is indicated, the play is of Hare's own or shared authorship.

Christie in Love, by Howard Brenton, Portable Theatre, 1969
How Brophy Made Good, Portable Theatre (at Brighton Combination), March 1969 (co-directed with Tony Bicât)
Purity, by David Mowat, Portable Theatre, 1969
Fruit, by Howard Brenton, Portable Theatre, 1970
Blow Job, by Snoo Wilson, Portable Theatre, 1971
England's Ireland, Portable Theatre, 1972
The Pleasure Principle, by Snoo Wilson, London, 1973
Brassneck, Nottingham Playhouse, 1973
The Provoked Wife, by Sir John Vanbrugh, Palace Theatre, Watford, 1973
The Party, by Trevor Griffiths, National Theatre tour, 1974
Teeth 'n' Smiles, Royal Court Theatre, London, 1975
Weapons of Happiness, by Howard Brenton, National Theatre, London, 1976
Devil's Island, by Tony Bicât, Sherman Theatre, Cardiff, 1977
Licking Hitler: A Film for Television, BBC TV, 1978
Plenty, National Theatre, London, 1978
Dreams of Leaving: A Film for Television, BBC TV, 1980
Total Eclipse, by Christopher Hampton, Lyric Theatre, Hammersmith, 1981
A Map of the World, Opera Theatre, Adelaide, 1982
Plenty, Public/Newman Theater, New York, 1982
A Map of the World, National Theatre, London, 1983
Wetherby, 1985
Pravda: A Fleet Street Comedy, National Theatre, London, 1985
A Map of the World, Public Theater, New York, 1985
The Bay at Nice and *Wrecked Eggs*, National Theatre, London, 1986

King Lear, by William Shakespeare, National Theatre, London, 1986
The Knife, Public/Newman Theater, New York, 1987
Paris by Night, 1988
Strapless, 1989
Heading Home, BBC TV, 1991
The Designated Mourner, by Wallace Shawn, National Theatre, London, 1996
The Designated Mourner (film), 1996
Heartbreak House, by George Bernard Shaw, Almeida Theatre, London, 1997
The Judas Kiss (radio), BBC, 1998
Ivanov (radio), BBC, 1998
My Zinc Bed, Royal Court Theatre, London, 2000
The Year of Magical Thinking, by Joan Didion, Booth Theatre, New York, 2007

RICHARD BOON

Introduction

On 9 November 2006 previews of David Hare's new play, *The Vertical Hour*, began at the Music Box Theatre in New York.[1] Directed by Sam Mendes, it starred Julianne Moore, best known for her work as a Hollywood actress (which includes the 2002 film *The Hours*, for which Hare wrote the screenplay), and British actor Bill Nighy (whose association with Hare's work extends back over twenty-five years to the television film *Dreams of Leaving*). Although the show was the tenth of Hare's to play on Broadway (and at one point, in the late 1990s, he had three running concurrently), it was the first to première there and the only new play in the autumn season. Mendes, shortly before the first performance, recalled Neil Simon's remark that 'previewing in New York is like having a gynaecological examination in Times Square'; Hare himself admitted that 'Absolutely nobody opens a play cold on Broadway. Broadway's meant to be a place you reach, not a place you begin. It will be the most nerve-racking time of my life.'[2]

When the play officially opened on 30 November, the response of American critics was mixed. Whilst Nighy's performance met with unanimous acclaim, responses to Moore's were more equivocal. The influential Ben Brantley of the *New York Times* suggested that 'Much of *The Vertical Hour* feels like a musty throwback to the psychological puzzle plays of the 1950s',[3] whilst *Variety* described it as 'messy and unresolved'.[4] The *New York Post*, on the other hand, hailed it as 'one of the best plays Broadway has seen in years',[5] and John Heilpern of the *New York Observer* recognised it as 'a political play for a Broadway wasteland of boulevard comedies and Stephen Sondheim revivals'.[6] From a British perspective, Michael Billington of the *Guardian* took a line similar to Heilpern's – 'at a time when the bulk of Broadway theatre – and, to be honest, much of the West End too – is designed to offer sensation and escape, Hare's play engages the heart and mind' – and, placing Hare's play in the context of other recent British successes in New York such as Alan Bennett's *The History Boys* and Tom Stoppard's *The Coast of Utopia*, noted the 'delicious irony that Broadway, the ultimate temple of commerce, depends heavily on work subsidised by the British taxpayer'.[7] Hare himself (who some years before had famously fallen out with New York critics in the shape of Frank Rich, the so-called 'Butcher of Broadway', over a vicious review of the 1989 Broadway production of *The Secret Rapture*) professed himself generally satisfied: 'savaged in the *New York Times*, but otherwise rather well received, and playing to really intelligent audiences'.[8]

The play had originated in the playwright's fascination with the political position of liberal figures – especially academics – who, 'for sound idealistic reasons',[9] had supported the Iraq war. Its central figure is Nadia Bye, a former war correspondent with experience in Bosnia and Baghdad, now of the political science department at Yale, who accompanies her boyfriend on a visit to his estranged father, Oliver, a doctor living a secluded life in Shropshire. The form of the play is essentially a political and moral debate between the two. Pragmatic, frank and Right-leaning, she is 'pro' the West's intervention – though less, perhaps, from a position of cultural supremacism than from a more humane and moral American tradition of political 'can-do'. He, on the other hand, is fiercely opposed to the war. He is an idealistic liberal who hides the strength of his views behind a mask of cool ironic detachment, just as he hides from the world – and from the emotional wreckage of his private life – in his country retreat. As their confrontation develops, and notwithstanding the presence of the son, their relationship takes on increasingly erotic undertones as Nadia slowly falls in love with Oliver.

Hare sees *The Vertical Hour* as a companion piece to his earlier Iraq play, *Stuff Happens* (National Theatre, 2004). But it is very different in form and scale. Where *Stuff Happens* is a large-cast, epic play which imagines the lead-up to the attack on Iraq through both verbatim re-creations of real speeches, meetings and press conferences and fictionalised versions of private meetings between members of the American and British governments and other key international figures, *The Vertical Hour* is an intimate piece. Essentially, it is a love story, set after the key events with which it is concerned (the title of the play is a military term, referring to the amount of time available to bring viable medical help after a catastrophic event), and contemplative in tone. According to Gaby Wood, Mendes suggests that

> there are two strands to Hare's work – what might loosely be called the Brechtian strand, which are the public plays about the railways, the judicial system, the church; *Stuff Happens* would be among these. The other is the Chekhovian strand, which would include *Skylight*, *The Secret Rapture* and *The Vertical Hour*.[10]

This is by no means an inaccurate nor an unfair distinction, and one which Hare himself, as an adapter of both Brecht and Chekhov, would surely recognise:

> Whereas one's the public story of what actually happened, this one – for me – is about: in what way are our lives different than five years ago, and in what perspective do we need now to see our lives? Western life is like a painting: our colour has been changed by another colour being painted on the top – we're looking at ourselves very differently from the perspective of what our so-called enemies believe about us. It's led to a rich period of self-examination.[11]

It would be wrong, however, to see Hare as a playwright of two different and separate voices. *The Vertical Hour* is as much about the large questions of public life as is *Stuff Happens*: questions of the nature of patriotism and heroism, of the self's responsibility *to* the self and, crucially, of the rights and wrongs of intervention, be it the intervention of one sovereign state into the affairs of another, of a college professor into the lives of her students, or of a father into his son's romantic relationships. When Michael Billington applauds the play for 'the force of [its] central argument: that you cannot separate public actions from private lives and that flight from reality is ultimately a sin',[12] then he might equally be offering a summative statement of Hare's key concerns as a political dramatist fast approaching the fortieth year of his career. The public and the political, the private and the behavioural, exist on one continuum, and whether the critical lens of Hare's theatre is fixed on the grand scale or on the intimate, then its focus is the same: the scrutiny and analysis of the very values by which we live our lives.

The Vertical Hour – its particular nature as a political play, the apparent paradox of its staging on Broadway and the critical response it provoked – is paradigmatic of the body of Hare's work as a whole, but only to a limited extent. One of the most striking features of the Chronology of Hare's work produced for this book (see pxiii) is what it reveals about the sheer variety of output he has produced since he began writing in the late 1960s.

Of the fifty-five performed pieces, very nearly half are original stage plays of his sole authorship. Of the remainder, there are five theatrical collaborations (including two – *Brassneck* in 1973 and *Pravda* in 1985 – with Howard Brenton), ten stage adaptations from dramatic or non-dramatic sources (the former including English versions of plays by Brecht, Chekhov, Lorca, Pirandello – two versions of *The Rules of the Game*, in 1971 and 1992 – and Gorky), five television plays and seven feature films. Of these last, he wrote and directed three and provided screenplay adaptations for four more, of which two were of his own stage plays. There is also the libretto for one opera.

Even within the body of solo-authored, original stage work, there is a great diversity of scale, form and subject matter, ranging from a short, 'one-off' sketch such as *The Madman Theory of Deterrence* (1983) to the epic grandeur of the National Theatre Trilogy (*Racing Demon, Murmuring Judges* and *The Absence of War*, 1990–3) by way of smaller-scale, more intimate pieces such as *My Zinc Bed* (2000), *The Breath of Life* (2002) – and, of course, *The Vertical Hour* (2007) – and one monologue, *Via Dolorosa*, which he performed himself for the first time in 1998. The work has found homes on the subsidised and commercial stages, in village halls, arts labs, provincial repertories and the West End, as well as in the National Theatre and on Broadway. Moreover, within and beyond the Brechtian and Chekhovian strands to the work identified by Mendes, we may also see a wide diversity of experimentation with style and genre ranging from the violent Artaudian aggression of his earliest pieces to satire, documentary and verbatim theatre, pastiche, a (more-or-less) Shavian theatre of ideas and what Hare himself has identified as 'stage poetry'. I stress 'experimentation', because the writer himself has always been distrustful of notions of 'pure' genre or 'pure' style, and one consistent theme of his career has been the way in which the plays have, whatever their particular subject and intent, also interrogated their own nature and that of theatre generally. I think in particular of the self-consciously performative behaviour of characters in early plays such as *Slag* (1970) and *The Great Exhibition* (1972), and in later plays like *The Absence of War* (1993);[13] of the testing to its limits of genre in *Knuckle* (1974); of the epic, Brechtian theatricality of *Fanshen* (1975); of the amalgamation of detailed naturalism and live rock-gig in *Teeth 'n' Smiles* (1975); of the film-of-the-novel-within-a-play-Chinese-box structure of *A Map of the World* (1982); and of *Amy's View* (1997), another assault on the straitjacket of genre, where a 'country-house' light comedy is shockingly torpedoed by the tragic death of a central character. In *Amy's View*, as in Osborne's *The Entertainer*, the world of the theatre becomes a metaphor for wider social reality, and indeed we may see the totality of Hare's career-long experimentation with genre, style and form as representing nothing less than a continuing interrogation of the relationship between the performative and the real, whether it be inside or outside theatre buildings.

Running parallel to Hare's work as a stage and screen dramatist are what in effect are two secondary careers. It is worth remembering that his ambition as a young artist was not to write, but to direct, and indeed he has done so consistently throughout his career, and on both stage and screen. He has directed not only his own work (including the seminal *Plenty* in 1978), but also the work of other contemporary dramatists (including Howard Brenton's *Weapons of Happiness* in 1976) and work by Vanbrugh, Shaw and Shakespeare. As I write, his current project is the direction of Joan Didion's stage adaptation of her own book, *The Year of Magical Thinking*,[14] for a Broadway première at the Booth Theatre in March 2007.[15] And, in addition, he is a stimulating public speaker and lecturer, and has published three books and numerous articles related to his own work and to the theatre, politics, society and culture generally; indeed, what we may loosely define as Hare's journalism – his cultural criticism – is a small but respectable body of work in its own right.

This book sets out – as a 'Companion' should – to give as wide-ranging and diverse an account of the work of one of our most important modern playwrights as it can. But that does not (cannot) mean that it is either comprehensive or exhaustive. If only for reasons of space, there have to be omissions. The absence of focused treatments of Hare's work as an adapter, and of the reception of his plays overseas (especially in the United States) are a matter of particular regret to your editor: the interplay between Hare's own work and his versions of Chekhov, Brecht, Pirandello and the rest would be a fascinating site of critical interrogation, whilst analysis of responses to his work when it is displaced into different cultural contexts would raise equally fascinating questions about a dramatist frequently (and, to some extent at least, misleadingly) viewed as quintessentially 'English'. But the issue of 'coverage' is in any case a vexed one. 'Grand narratives', of whatever kind, are always problematic, and can offer only partial perspectives; indeed, the grander the narrative, the more partial the perspective.

On what should such narratives be based? On the life of their subject?[16] But that is surely a matter for the critical biographer, and of only limited relevance to a book such as this. Even if one restricts oneself to Hare's *professional* life – his career – it is difficult to produce an entirely and compellingly comprehensive account. The bare bones are clear enough: he emerged as a playwright in the late 1960s as one of a whole generation of radical, left-wing political dramatists who developed their craft in the hot-house of the revolutionary Fringe movement, and led that generation, and its political and stylistic concerns, on to the stages of mainstream theatrical culture in the 1970s, when the epic 'State of the Nation' play in many ways set the agenda of theatrical innovation. Like others of that generation, Hare found the 1980s a difficult time, as Thatcherism both stole the ideological ground from the Left and, more pragmatically, assaulted the culture of public subsidy which had done so much to enable and support its artistic expression. Unlike some of his fellow political dramatists, however, he adapted and survived, and went on from the 1990s onward to produce not only what is arguably the ultimate 'State of the Nation' project – the National Theatre trilogy – but the development of a new form of political drama; what he himself has termed 'stage poetry', a kind of smaller-scale, 'submerged epic'.

So far, so uncontentious. But the career of any creative artist is inevitably more complicated – even, more mysterious – than that. A closer analysis of the trajectory of Hare's career inevitably problematises so crude a narrative, and fails to do justice to its rich complexity. Nor is Hare himself always an entirely helpful guide. He delights in confounding expectation with his plays and films, and, as I have pointed out elsewhere, his publicly stated views about his work and career

> may sometimes seem contradictory and paradoxical: see, for example, how his mind changes, and changes back, about documentary theatre, or the value of making adaptations, or working in television. Similarly, he is often ambivalent about subjects where one might expect certainty, such as the important roles played in his career by the Royal Court and National Theatres. This apparent contrariness to some extent begs the question as to how possible it is to 'trace his evolution as a dramatist' . . . 'Evolution' may imply a kind of purposeful, linear progression, a clear and coherent sense of development. It may even suggest that later work must by definition be 'better' than earlier work. There is, of course, some truth in this: playwrights, like any other committed professional workers, have a sense of the direction of their own careers, and learn their craft, gain experience, and become more confident as they grow older: but there is a neatness to the idea that is misleading . . . It is part of the academic's job, and the critic's job, to find pattern and discern order, but it is not necessarily a pattern or an order intended or even felt by the playwright [himself].[17]

With that warning in mind, then, what kind of 'pattern or order' is to be found in this book?

The first point to make is that I have deliberately opted for an approach which combines the practical and professional with the academic and theoretical, and my choice of contributors reflects that. They fall roughly into three main categories: those who are themselves are or have been theatre practitioners and industry professionals (Tony Bicât, Peter Ansorge and Richard Eyre); academics (myself, Lib Taylor, Duncan Wu, John Bull, Cathy Turner, Steve Nicholson, Janelle Reinelt and Chris Megson) and what we may term 'academic-practitioners' (Les Wade, Michael Mangan and Dan Rebellato all have additional careers as playwrights, whilst Bella Merlin works as a professional actress and also lectures at Exeter University). Even these categories are oversimplified: both Ansorge and Eyre have published as theatre historians, whilst few theatre academics nowadays do not regard the practical investigation of theatre and performance inside and outside the classroom as anything other than a central element of their job descriptions. Some of my contributors have written, with great authority, about the playwright before; for others, this is their first foray into Hare studies. Four of them – Bicât, Eyre, Ansorge and Merlin – have worked closely with Hare in various professional roles, as co-writer, director, television producer or actor. Hare himself, though initially hesitant about appearing in a book of which he is the subject, discusses (in Chapter 11) his film career, in an interview which he feels offers the most comprehensive account he has yet given of his feelings about that work.

Aside from an insistence on the practical dimension, I hope my contributors feel I have imposed as little as possible upon them. There is no overarching theoretical approach (another 'grand narrative'): the reader will find here a variety of critical voices, ranging from the historiographical to the cultural materialist (my own approximate and maybe slightly old-fashioned stance) via, amongst others, the feminist (and gender studies) and the deconstructionist. Views may at times conflict, but also find unexpected and enlightening synergies – the better, I hope, to stimulate interest, and the desire to explore further, on the part of our readers.

The book is divided into four parts. (Even this proved not unproblematic: is *Fanshen* (1975) best placed as a collaboration or an adaptation? Is *Saigon: Year of the Cat* (1983) a television *play*, a television *film* or a cinematic film . . . ?) The first – 'Text and Context' – offers a chronological treatment of Hare's career to date, placing the work in the context of social, political and theatre history. It begins with Tony Bicât's memoir of the career of Portable Theatre, which he co-founded with Hare in 1968. It is, I believe, unique in offering so thorough a personal account of that enormously influential group, and succeeds admirably in giving an almost visceral sense of the spirit of the work and its time, as well as giving us keen insights into Hare at the very start of his career. Chapters then proceed on a (roughly) decade-by-decade basis. My own provides a more formal account of the Portable work before offering an analysis of how Hare's work developed through the 1970s, with particular regard to his negotiation of the move on to mainstream stages. Lib Taylor continues the story into the 1980s, discussing Hare's response to the onslaught of Thatcherism, and comparing his use of female protagonists – one of the key features of his writing throughout his career – with the contemporary explosion of theatre writing by women (one of the few positive theatrical developments of that benighted decade). Les Wade addresses what for many remains Hare's crowning achievement, the National Theatre trilogy of the early 1990s, and in doing so intellectually rescues Hare from that critical view which has portrayed him as a tired and compromised liberal, even a reactionary, who sold out to the establishment years ago. Duncan Wu tackles the textual and visual 'stage poetry' of the small-scale, more private plays of the decade, and does so on the level of close textual analysis, finding parallels with Shakespeare and raising the kinds of issues of spirituality and faith which have come increasingly to preoccupy the dramatist. The section concludes with a chapter by Peter Ansorge, who uses his discussion of *Stuff Happens* (2004) as an imaginative opportunity to look back over Hare's career as a political dramatist of a very particular kind.

Part II, 'Working with Hare', speaks to the importance of collaboration in the playwright's career. He has collaborated with other writers – most notably Howard Brenton – on a number of occasions, but Cathy Turner extends the discussion to ponder a wider sense of the collaborative, considering the kinds of dialogue into which Hare has entered not only with other writers, but with the 'real' people who have been the subjects of 'verbatim' pieces such as *The Permanent Way*, and with audiences, as well as with the other theatre makers who have shared in the production of his work. One issue raised by Turner is the ethical dimension to collaboration, and this is further addressed in the following chapter, Bella Merlin's 'Acting Hare', a tightly focused account and analysis from the 'inside' of the processes of the making of *The Permanent Way*. Merlin is both participant in and observer of the relationship between writer, director and actor (or in this case, 'actor-researcher') in one particular project; Richard Eyre, on the other hand, is uniquely placed to offer a career overview of working with Hare, having directed no fewer than six of his plays. In 'Directing Hare', his focus is in significant part on the relationship between writer, director and designer, reminding us that, however distinctive the voice of any particular writer might be (and he describes Hare as having 'the pen of a polemicist but the soul of a romantic'), theatre remains the most collaborative of all the arts.

'Hare on Screen', the third part of the book, comprises two chapters. In the first, John Bull unpicks the complex relationship between Hare's television and film work, wrestling with difficulties of definition and characterisation. His work on Hare's first play for television, *Man Above Men* (1973), recovers, through the courtesy of the BBC Records Office at Caversham, what had effectively become a 'lost' work. Just as my own account of Portable differs widely in approach and tone from Bicât's, so Bull's scholarly agonising over what was television and what was film stands in marked contrast to Hare's own attitude in my interview with him, which forms the following chapter. Taking the differences between the two media largely as read, Hare's comments slide unproblematically between the 'fabulous' nature of *Strapless* (1988; cinema) and *Dreams of Leaving* (1980; television). Nonetheless, his work in each medium is significant in its own right; it is to be hoped that the indication he gives that he regards his career as a film maker (rather than as a screenwriter) as over proves premature.

The fourth and final part of the book is 'Overviews of Hare'. Here, contributors were given a freer hand to offer particular perspectives on Hare's career, seen as a totality. Unsurprisingly – given that the writer himself has described it as his subject – two chose to write about history. Steve Nicholson offers a wide-ranging analysis, problematising the notion of playwright-as-historian by drawing attention to the complex relationships between reality and the processes of writing history (especially recent history) and fiction; in doing so, he also contributes to the debate initiated by Turner and Merlin with regard to documentary and verbatim forms. His key point, that Hare's fundamental interest in dramatising history resides in his passionate belief that we must learn from the past, not least in the sense of understanding that things *need not have been so*, is surely the right one. By contrast, Janelle Reinelt's treatment of the same subject attends in close detail to just two plays: *Plenty* (1978) and *A Map of the World* (1982). Noting that she was born in the same year as Hare, she charts her own intellectual and emotional journey in parallel to Hare's, judging the plays, as a good historiographer should, in terms of the contemporary cultural context of the time of their making – particularly, the emergent post-colonial and second wave feminist discourses of the decade. In doing so, like Wade she revitalises what was in danger of becoming a sterile debate concerning the politics of Hare's portrayal of women. As with history, gender questions sit near the heart of Hare's project, and Michael Mangan's chapter develops the debate by relocating it into the wider arena of gender politics generally. He writes about Hare's characterisations of *men*, and especially about the recurrence across a number of plays of the dominant 'alpha male', often perched on the top of a triangle of complex relationships involving sons, daughters and lovers – or figures occupying equivalent roles. It is a theme Hare returns to in *The Vertical Hour*, though Mangan did not know it at the time of writing. The final chapter of Part IV, and indeed of the book, is Chris Megson and Dan Rebellato's jointly written examination of the relationship between Hare's theatrical output and his other public utterances, including his journalism; this is a theme touched on variously by other contributors (see Ansorge, for example, and Nicholson). Their primary focus is on his lectures. In what is perhaps the most critically ambivalent piece in the volume, they argue that 'Hare's long-standing commitment to the pure, transparent and direct communication of subject matter in performance' has led to an increasing unease with theatre, pointing to his monologue *Via Dolorosa* (1998) as a site of competition between the instincts of a playwright and those of a lecturer.

Hare himself has said of *Via Dolorosa* that 'one of the effects of one-man shows is that you feel that at the end of the play you know the person on stage terribly well'.

> And there wasn't a night where there weren't lots of people waiting for me at the stage door.
>
> At first this alarmed me because I'm not used to that as a playwright. The playwright's an anonymous figure. But the reason they were waiting for me was they felt they knew me because they'd spent an hour and a half or more in my company.[18]

These well-intentioned 'stage-door johnnies' had been entertained, enlivened and politically engaged by Hare's play, but they did not, of course, know David Hare. They knew 'David Hare', the particular version of himself he had constructed in the writing and performance of his play. Likewise, this book can only be about *a* 'David Hare', the particular version of the dramatist which its contributors – including myself – have themselves constructed. Indeed, one of the advantages of a book such as this is that it allows – positively encourages – a multiplicity of perspectives to be opened, and a variety of voices to be heard. (For other versions of 'David Hare', I refer the reader to the Bibliography that appears towards the back of the volume.) Hare's voice, too, is multifarious, but it is nonetheless a single voice, and, as his long-time friend and collaborator Richard Eyre suggests, one which is both distinctive and historically significant:

> It's beyond argument that he's been one of [the British theatre's] leading voices: eloquent, passionate, forceful, romantic, politicised . . . it's something that is unique, and he has solidly pursued an often difficult furrow of writing about public life and ideas of how people should live, through a variety of distinctive milieux. And, of course, there is his constant proselytisation about the medium of theatre, and a demonstrated passion that it's worth caring about this medium. So it seems to me that there is no way of representing David's contribution as anything less than central.[19]

NOTES

1. David Hare, *The Vertical Hour: A Play* (London: Faber, 2007). At the time of writing, the play awaits its British première.
2. 'Can David Hare Take Manhattan?', *Observer*, 12 November 2006, http://arts. guardian.co.uk/features/story/0,,1945835,00.html (accessed 26 February 2007).

3. Ben Brantley, 'Battle Zones in Hare Country', *New York Times*, 1 December 2006, http://theater2.nytimes.com/2006/12/01/theater/reviews/01hour.html?ref=theater (accessed 3 December 2006).
4. Quoted in John Heilpern, 'About Our Special Relationship . . .', *Observer Review*, 3 December 2006, p15.
5. *Ibid.*
6. *Ibid.*
7. Michael Billington, '"A Five-Course Meal after a Diet of Candyfloss" – Hare Hits Manhattan', *Guardian*, 1 December 2006, p9.
8. Email to the present writer, 5 December 2006.
9. 'Can David Hare Take Manhattan?'
10. *Ibid.*
11. *Ibid.*
12. Billington, '"A Five-Course Meal . . ."'.
13. Indeed, one commentator has suggested that 'What chiefly preoccupies Hare is the analogy between public life and acting' (John Bull, *New British Political Dramatists* (London: Macmillan, 1984), p66).
14. Joan Didion, *The Year of Magical Thinking* (New York: Knopf, 2005).
15. A selective list of plays directed by Hare may be found on ppxviii–xix.
16. For those who are interested, Hare was born in 1947 at St Leonard's in Sussex; in 1952, his family moved the few miles to Bexhill-on-Sea, where he attended the local prep school; in 1960, he became a boarder at Lancing College, before going up to Jesus College, Cambridge to read English, where his career in theatre effectively began. He has been Resident Dramatist at the Royal Court Theatre in London (1970–71) and at the Nottingham Playhouse (1973); he co-founded Portable Theatre in 1968, the Joint Stock Theatre Group in 1975, and Greenpoint Films in 1982, and has been an Associate Director of the National Theatre since 1984. He was knighted in 1998 and is a Fellow of the Royal Society of Literature. He has been married twice, currently to the leading fashion designer, Nicole Farhi.
17. Richard Boon, *About Hare: The Playwright and the Work* (London: Faber, 2003), pp5–6.
18. Quoted in Boon, *About Hare*, p157.
19. *Ibid.*, p226.

I
Text and context

I

TONY BICÂT

Portable Theatre: 'fine detail, rough theatre'

A personal memoir

Portable Theatre was formed on a hot summer day in August 1968.

We were in the small kitchen of the flat in Earlham Street, Covent Garden, which David Hare shared with two other people from Cambridge. I'd dropped in for a cup of tea. David said, 'I'm thinking of starting a theatre company; would you be interested?' I didn't say yes immediately. He brought the tea across and I looked at the radio sitting on the shelf by the sink. I said, 'We could call it Portable Theatre. You know . . . pick it up, put it down.' Then we sat down and wrote a press release, the gist of which was that, after a certain modest reluctance, we had succumbed to the pleas of assorted theatrical luminaries and started an exciting new theatre company: Portable Theatre. We also wrote two letters asking for what would now be called sponsorship, for the two items we felt we'd need: a van and an electric typewriter. I knew from being in bands we'd need a van, and in those pre-photocopying days we needed an electric typewriter to cut the stencils to Roneo the scripts. What these scripts might be, we hadn't a clue. In one of the first of a series of lucky breaks, Olympia gave us a typewriter and Volkswagen gave us an extraordinarily generous discount on a camper van.

This wasn't, of course, really the beginning. It had taken both of us several years to get to this point. We had met at Cambridge. David came up in 1965, a year after me. I had spent my first year at the university playing jazz drums in a band with two American postgraduates and Daryl Runswick, who later went on to play bass with John Dankworth. At the end of my first year (1965), the Americans had gone back to the States and Daryl had decided to take his classical music studies more seriously. I had been largely unaware of Cambridge Theatre, which I suspected had all the vices of professional theatre and none of its virtues. In my second year I met Malcolm Griffiths, who was then President of the ADC (Amateur Dramatic Club); he was planning a production of Genet's *The Balcony*.[1] Malcolm was astonished to meet up with someone else at Cambridge who had read the play and possessed a copy of it in French, illustrated with photos of the original production by Roger Blin. He asked me to be his assistant. For students it was an extraordinarily ambitious production, and I found myself having to direct odd bits of the play. Malcolm would leave me in the room with a hastily blocked scene and go off to fire-fight elsewhere on the production. I then directed a Sunday-night production at the ADC of Adamov's *Ping Pong*, a fairly obscure minor absurdist work. This was under the patronage of Independent Theatre, which tended to do more challenging work. It seemed to go well and in Malcolm's last summer term (1966) we co-directed *Henry V* in Sidney Sussex Gardens during May Week. Malcolm gave me the bits of the play he wasn't interested in to do, which was how I found myself directing David, who was playing Mountjoy the Herald. We became friends.

We were totally different characters and came from vastly different backgrounds. My artist father had left home at 15 to paint scenery and eventually design for the Ballet Rambert and the Mercury Theatre. Though of French origin, he was born in Southend; I never met his English family until after his death, and so on that side I felt completely deracinated. My Russian mother was born in France. She was educated in England but only appeared English in the most superficial ways. My only living relative from that generation, as far as I knew, was my Russian grandmother and a coterie of so-called aunts and uncles who had a more secure grasp on their backstory than on the Britain of the 1950s. I was acutely conscious of the fact that I would not have been born at all had it not been for two great historical events: the Russian Revolution and the Second World War. I had, however, grown up in a highly cultured environment, being taken to plays, concerts and art galleries from an early age: seeing Laurence Olivier in *The Entertainer* at the age of 12 had a profound effect on me. This hot-house cultural atmosphere was coupled with daily exposure to the harsh, unglamorous realities of my father's life as a professional artist. David envied me my exotic bohemian background and I envied him the stability of his 'normal' background. However much he railed against his Englishness, his background gave him a secure sense of belonging that I knew I would never possess. Howard Brenton said that all Englishmen have a policeman in the head, and David was no exception. He would always learn the rules before breaking them and I would always try and invent some new ones. I was born to be an outsider and to a certain extent embraced that role, particularly as all my attempts to seem at ease in the culture failed to convince even me.

We both hated Cambridge; David, because he thought that was the way the world was (an extension of the hypocrisies of public school), and I because I knew the world wasn't like that. I had spent a formative 'gap year' largely in Paris. We both had an abiding love of English literature, which we had come at from different angles. David was very well educated. I, like my autodidact father, was very well (but precociously) read. I had been saved from educational failure by a couple of very good and determined teachers. To a large extent, we both felt betrayed by the English faculty, which seemed obsessed with petty squabbles and meaningless judgements (D. H. Lawrence – good, Laurence Sterne – bad) and totally out of touch with practical reality when talking about the theatre. David has written elsewhere about Raymond Williams,[2] whose reputation had brought us both to Jesus College. I think my year saw a bit more of him than David's and I had a couple of supervisions with him, where he told me, with a smile, 'You know you won't do well in the exams writing like this – but I can see it's very important for you to do so.' I went to all his lectures and it was impossible not to be moved by his passion for literature and his desire to relate it to people's lives; to give them the gift that had manifestly transformed his own. His acolytes, who actually taught us, seemed to be singing a hymn to which they knew only the words and not the music.

I inherited Independent Theatre and David and I ended up running it together. As the name suggests, it was in some sense an alternative to the Cambridge theatrical establishment represented by the ADC and the Marlowe Society. In my last year (1967), I directed Kafka's *The Trial* (in Jean-Louis Barrault's version) in the same week as the Marlowe Society's big annual production at the Arts Theatre. Traditionally nobody wanted that week at the ADC and the theatre was often dark. All eyes and most of the available student acting talent – including David, as it happened – were concentrated on the Marlowe Society. Despite this we got very good audiences and I remember standing after the theatre had emptied and watching the crippled *Sunday Times* critic Harold Hobson slowly leave the theatre, helped by his wife. I was amazed at his dedication in coming to review a student production. I was even more amazed when he gave it a good review and praised my direction. David continued to run Independent Theatre after I left, though he didn't direct anything for them. In this way he maintained a shrewd foot in both the establishment and the alternative camps. In the summer vacation of 1967 David found some money from the old Greater London Council, and Independent Theatre put on *The Hollow Crown* in Waterlow Park in Highgate. We had promised them *Richard II*, so they were justifiably annoyed, but it was a valuable experience in mounting a show with limited resources for the paying public.

I think what we brought to that initial meeting was frustration. If you had asked us what we wanted to do we would have both replied that we wanted to make films. We had lived in the Arts Cinema in Cambridge and saw the established theatre as an outmoded pastime of the privileged elite. David was assembling library footage for the inspirational Richard Dunn at

A. B. Pathé for a series of documentaries called *Sex and Society*. His episode was about the Duke of Windsor. I, after failing to get on either the BBC or the ATV training schemes, was 'gigging' and doing half a dozen other activities, ranging from selling antiques in the Portobello Road to writing a musical with my brother Nick, who was already establishing a career as a composer in the theatre. I was, in truth, 'spinning'. I knew I didn't want to spend the rest of my life behind a drum kit. Although I was writing quite a lot, I didn't want to be any kind of artist: I had seen at first hand that the life of an artist was too hard. I was drawn to television and had done work experience at Granada in 1964 before going to university, working on a TV play (*Big Fleas Have Little Fleas*) directed by Stuart Latham and written by Jack Rosenthal. Television was an exciting place to be and, unlike the theatre, it seemed a blank page, free of ghosts, though in those heavily unionised days it was very hard to get into. Oddly, neither of us thought we were writers; it was only clear once we'd started Portable that we'd have to write at least the first show ourselves. Not for the first time, Kafka came to our rescue. I gave David Kafka's diaries to read. We assembled *Inside Out* and put it on from 29 October for a week at the Arts Lab in Drury Lane. This was our next stroke of luck. Jim Haynes' Arts Lab was a unique institution.[3] It was part coffee bar, part arts centre, part flop house; morning rehearsals involved clearing the people who slept in the theatre out of the place. Jim's artistic policy was – 'Sure, go ahead.' So J. G. Ballard hung the walls with pictures of car crashes, people played free jazz and recited concrete poetry and Jim smiled benignly on it all. He was a genuine cultural hero. We put the text of *Inside Out* in for the Arts Council's new play scheme and of course heard nothing for weeks. We had almost given up hope when I ran into David Robbins, for whom I had written a review of a documentary about Jimi Hendrix for the *International Times*. He said a friend of his who read plays at the Arts Council was raving about a play he had read based on Kafka's diaries; the friend's name was Nicholas de Jongh, now drama critic of the *Evening Standard*. We got an Arts Council new play grant, which at the time provided two things: money for the author of the play and a guarantee against loss. David and I ploughed our money as authors back into the company; in its whole history we never took more than expenses from Portable. The scheme, in one form or another, financed Portable. We charged £20 a night for a performance. The only snag was that you had to wait until the Arts Council had read and approved the play, but in our second year we persuaded them to give us the equivalent of six grants for new, unread plays, so we could plan our season.

Our first company was Neil Johnston, Nicholas Nacht, Hilary Charlton, Maurice Colbourne and Bill Hoyland. David and I directed the play together.

The staging was cinematic, in the sense that it consisted of short scenes with blackouts; there was no set except for four chairs, and only a few simple sound and music cues. This black-and-white, simplified style, with its declamatory speeches and choral sections, initially became the house style. It was also the style that David adopted for his first play, *How Brophy Made Good*, which was about a self-publicist who said 'fuck' on television. The show was well received and we followed it again at the Arts Lab with a double bill of two monologues: John Grillo's *Gentleman I*, performed by John himself, and David's *Strindberg*, based on Strindberg's diaries, with Maurice Colbourne. *Gentleman I*, a play about schizophrenia, was an interesting experience for me. John was recovering from a near nervous breakdown after performing in Christopher Hampton's *Total Eclipse* with Victor Henry at the Royal Court. Not for the first time, art and life began to get muddled.

After this we lost our actors Neil and Maurice: they went off to start Freehold with Nancy Meckler and Café La Mama refugee Beth Porter.[4] Although they never said it, I suspect that one of the attractions of physical theatre was that you didn't have to work with intellectuals from Cambridge. I had, however, brought into the mix another unsung hero of Portable: Gus Hope. She became our unpaid administrator, and from her tiny flat off Charlotte Street she ran our office, housed the mighty Olympia typewriter (it was almost as big as the van) and kept our files under her bed. She sent off our press releases to schools, army camps, universities – anywhere – and amazingly, thanks to her industry, we got bookings, to the extent that David had to mount a revival of *Inside Out* with a different cast in January 1969.

Our first out-of-London booking was at the University of East Anglia. I had known Snoo Wilson, a school friend of my brother, most of his life. I had visited him at UEA while still at Cambridge. The new university, although only partly built and surrounded by a sea of mud, seemed a refreshing contrast to the old one. We took *Inside Out* there. Embarrassingly, Snoo, not having any publicity material, had used a photograph he had of me and plastered posters of my face all over the university and student haunts in Norwich with the legend, '*Kafka*'. Whenever we went back to UEA afterwards, I would be greeted by people saying, 'Kafka's back.' Later in the year we went up to see Snoo's play *Ella Day Bellefeses's Machine*, ably directed by Jonathan Powell. We asked Snoo to write a play for us, and when he left UEA in June 1969 he joined Portable.

Early on we discovered that, although you could ask people to write plays for you, and they swore they would, the plays frequently didn't turn up. By this time David was reading plays at the Royal Court where his old school friend Christopher Hampton was Literary Manager. David did this with his usual diligence and industry. He did not drive at the time and frequently sat in the van with his nose buried in a play. I remember him saying to me, after reading the umpteenth play, 'You know, I think I could do this.' The result was *How Brophy Made Good*, a one-act play which we premièred at the Oval House.[5] The Oval House was another very significant venue in Portable history: Peter Oliver and his staff provided us with free rehearsal space, the use of their Roneo machine to duplicate scripts and a place to perform. *Brophy's* birth was quite painful. David was in a spectacular state of nerves and the last few pages he actually wrote sitting in my flat trying lines out, with me urging him on – rather in the manner of a situation comedy writing team. I took the play into rehearsal and David and I would meet up every evening to discuss progress, but it was clear that he was itching to take over, so, once I'd got it on its feet, he did. In the end we shared the directing credit. One of the good things about our collaboration was that we were brave in different ways, so together we were a good team. David was terrified of making a fool of himself, whereas I regarded that as almost a precept of artistic activity. He was much better than I was at finishing and polishing the work. I was very good at the initial risk, but once that was taken I tended to get bored and look around for more risks. Over the years my role in Portable developed much more as a supporter of other people's work than as a propagator of my own. This was not from any high-minded altruism, but rather from the fact that I had no real theatrical ambitions. I became very ambitious for Portable, and so naturally ambitious for the Portable writers. *Brophy* was a reasonable success; even reading it today you get the authentic Hare voice, and many themes are touched on that David went on to explore in greater depth later. The performance gained David his first agent, Clive Goodwin. Margaret Matheson, who worked for Clive, was deputed to see the show and later she and David married.

One of the writers who did deliver was Howard Brenton. The legend is that David and Howard met at a Portable performance where Howard was the only member of the audience. Well, it's a good story and it might easily have happened, but actually I introduced them and suggested we commission Howard. At first, David was a little reluctant: 'Didn't he write that dreadful play at Cambridge?' Cambridge failure is probably worse than any other kind, and the knives had gone into *Ladder of Fools* (1965) in a spectacular way. It was true that *Ladder of Fools* was not a great play, but, not for the first time in my life, I found myself in total opposition to everybody else. The play seemed to me to be clearly the work of someone with a real theatrical voice. Its faults were the faults of ambition, of imagining more than you knew how to achieve. I sought Howard out after he left and told him that I liked many things in the play. *Christie in Love*[6] was commissioned and delivered in 1969, and David directed it superbly. When it was published

David wanted to put me down as producer, but I said I thought that sounded pretentious. I suggested instead that I was credited as 'set builder', as I had helped Snoo build the set. Years later I was to be lectured by Peggy Ramsay[7] about the importance of not being frivolous about billing.

For Portable, *Christie* was a massive leap forwards. It remains the best play we did. Its effect was – and still is – electric, even now when serial killers have become a tedious cliché of drama. The set, devised by Howard, was a simple wire netting pen filled with old newspapers. The beauty of this was that all the venue had to provide was some old newspapers. The pen was light, easily set up and dramatically very effective. *Christie* shocked people and disturbed them, and there was something satisfying about driving off in our van and leaving them with a pile of dirty newspapers and, since the venues were often wet, a nasty smell as of a decaying corpse. In Brighton, David and Snoo were stopped by the police while fly-posting. Our poster bore the words, 'John Reginald Halliday Christie killed women and then he fucked them'. We were fined for obscenity, a definite badge of honour in the world of fringe theatre.

In 1969, as well as the remount of *Inside Out*, Portable performed and toured the double bill of *Strindberg* and *Gentleman I*, along with Snoo Wilson's pram-based production of *Pericles*, *How Brophy Made Good*, *Christie in Love* and Snoo's play *Pignight*. *Pignight* was about a Lincolnshire pig farm taken over by gangsters and turned into a factory farm; it rings with its denunciation of the horrors of factory farming, a cause not to become fashionable for many years. As so often was the case in his career, Snoo embraced a subject that critics at the time found incomprehensible, largely because their world stopped at Watford.

The critics did, however, embrace the idea of Portable as a political theatre. History has largely labelled us as that; but we were a funny kind of political theatre. Portable was never agitprop, nor was it a didactic political theatre. We were never a 'Political Theatre' in the same way that, for example, 7:84 was.[8] What drove us, apart from the rampant egos of 'university wits'? We wanted our work to shock. Plays like *Brophy* and *Christie*, and later Howard's *Fruit* (1970) and Snoo's *Blow Job* (1971), were designed to shake the audience and therefore the establishment. They certainly did that to some audiences, while of course baffling others. (When Howard wrote his film *Skinflicker* in 1973, initially as a 'Play for Today' for the BBC, he said he wanted to create 'a black hole in the evening's TV'. Of course, TV wouldn't let you do that. Indeed, when I finally made it for the cinema, the BFI, who had financed it, came very close to destroying the negative. It has never been shown on TV, though it was shown at the Almost Free Theatre in London in February 1973.) We had a very strong sense of wanting the voice of our generation, brought up on rock music, the 'Nouvelle Vague' and demonstrating against the Vietnam War, to be heard in the theatre. We had ideas about Poor Theatre gleaned from, among other things, the experiments Peter Brook did at the Round House before he left for Paris. These fed into an ethic of a simple spectacle that would *change* something, even if it was only the mood people walked home in. It was anti-bourgeois, anti-Conservative and anti the conventional theatre, but it was slightly vaguer about what it was *for*. Like 'the angry young man' label on writers of an earlier generation, writers who were neither particularly young nor particularly angry, our 'political' label was a convenient way for critics to generalise about very different figures and (if they were on the Right) to dismiss us.

Left-wing, confrontational, aesthetically radical . . . foul-mouthed, certainly . . . Does that make a political theatre? There was no party line and we seldom discussed politics in terms of the actual plays. We were all Labour voters, but the plays expressed a very wide range of opinions and beliefs. David's socialism, leavened as always with his wit and humour, was born of a very genuine anger at an unjust society, but his most withering scorn was reserved for the fashionable and self-regarding Left. Howard was an avowed Marxist but his Marxism was coupled with a generous humanity that would have put him in the Gulags in any Communist state that has ever existed. Snoo was driven by a heady concern for the environment and a desire for a theatre of gods and monsters that would liberate the audience's imagination in the way his own was liberated. He could never believe that everybody didn't share his endless curiosity about the world. Howard always said that I was a right-wing anarchist, and I would often play that role. It was easier to be the joker in the pack, to keep the peace, to keep the show on the road and to hide my very real confusions. It was years before I could make sense of my European inheritance and understand why I felt like a Martian most of the time. Touring the plays, however, united us all. It was a shared belief that by taking new plays to new places we would in some way help the revolution, the revolution that surely, given the state of the country, could not be far off. The irony was that we would all of course have wanted different revolutions and, almost certainly, have been amongst the first to be shot.

In Portable's first year we covered more than 30,000 kilometres and played in an enormous variety of locations and before many very different audiences. As an education in theatre it was superb: stage managing, lighting, costumes – we did everything. It forced you to watch your mistakes every night. I found the constant changes of location and audience very stimulating, though David often found it a sort of torture. Despite the bone-cracking fatigue, it was also an opportunity to discover the United Kingdom. I was always deeply touched by the generosity of those who had invited us, and for the most part they were very receptive. It brought home to me how unlike London most of the country was, and convinced me that, wherever and whatever my audience was, it was in the wider country, not the metropolis.

In 1970, David remounted *Christie in Love* at the Royal Court's Theatre Upstairs.[9] It was the same production, but although Bill Hoyland reprised his fine performance as Christie, David was advised to recast the other two parts, I think by Bill Gaskill, the Artistic Director. At the time I remember thinking this was oddly disloyal; in retrospect I realise that it was sound advice from Gaskill and a good example of David's theatrical pragmatism. *Slag* was performed at Hampstead, and by almost apostolic succession David succeeded Christopher Hampton as Literary Manager at the Royal Court. The Arts Council increased our money and we were able to commission Howard Brenton to write *Fruit*, a confrontational political satire which ended with instructions on how to make a petrol bomb. David was due to direct my first play, *I Want To Be Like Sammy Davis Junior* – a sort of pantomime about sex and race – but at the last minute, feeling he couldn't handle the musical aspects of the play, backed out. I felt unable to tackle it on my own and so mounted a quick production of Strindberg's *The Creditors* to cover our commitments. I discovered how much I liked working in the round: a 360-degree viewpoint removed one of the big problems I had with theatre.

Later in the year I directed David's *What Happened to Blake?* As before, and with the help of Jenny Gaskin's design, we tried to burst out of the confines of small-scale touring to create some kind of grand spectacle from our little van. *Blake* often formed half of a double bill with *Fruit*, with which it shared a cast. James Warrior gives a flavour of what it was like touring the work:

> I remember arriving at a chapel just outside Aberdeen where we were expected to give a performance of *Blake* in their church hall. The audience turned out to be entirely composed of non-conformist Presbyterian ministers and their wives. There were about 50 of them in all. They had come to see what they expected to be a reverential presentation of the life of the great religious, visionary poet and painter, William Blake. David Hare, of course, was more interested in the fact that Blake used to shag his own sister . . . Worse was to come. This was quite close to the beginning of the tour and, at this stage, we had only fully rehearsed Howard's *Fruit* [directed by Hare]. *Blake* was not going to be ready for performance for another week. So David addressed the gathered audience, apologised for the incorrect advertising of the play and offered them a performance of the innocuous sounding *Fruit* instead . . . They watched the first half of the play in complete silence even though every other word was 'fuck' . . . However, when the interval came, not one single person came back. I have been in a number of plays where enraged people have left the auditorium muttering or even shouting about not wishing to be insulted by this rubbish,

but I have never before or since been in a play which has entirely emptied a theatre.[10]

Blake, which is about how society treats genius, was also performed as part of the Royal Court's 'Come Together' Festival.

David was not with us when, returning from playing *Fruit* in Wales, we had a serious crash: an idiot in a Mini drove out in front of us. The van (with me driving and five actors in the back) turned over and spun round. Miraculously, no one was hurt. We were in a brand-new VW van, hired because ours was so broken down. When I recovered I accused the long-suffering Arts Council of trying to kill us, pointing out that had we been in our crappy old van we would all be dead. When they still refused to give us more money I demanded a meeting with Lord Goodman, the legendary lawyer, fixer and then Chairman of the Arts Council. Gus Hope and I went to see him. We presented our case, and a Council official gave Goodman the facts and figures and explained how we had exceeded our budget and how, with the best will in the world, the Council had no more money to give us. Goodman listened in silence and then launched into a savage dressing-down of the official, the only purpose of which seemed to be to impress Gus and me. He ended his humiliating tirade with the words: 'Give these people what they want!' As we left the room, Goodman called me back: 'You should get a building; if you get a building, we'll give you lots more money.' Little did I know that I was hearing the raison d' être of UK theatre subsidy for the next thirty years. We got a new van and continued to be happily homeless; however, I began to see the crash as a sign that touring days were coming to an end. Sooner or later our luck would run out. David and I had often discussed the kind of theatre we would like: a flexible but well-equipped 'black box', seating no more than three hundred, with pleasant but unpretentious public spaces, a coffee bar and so on. In 1974 I was in Amsterdam at a film festival, and was shown round exactly the space we would have wanted in 1969. As Ritsaert ten Cate showed me round the new Mickery Theatre,[11] I realised with a shock that, even if this was given to me tomorrow, I would not want it. There was an earlier siren call in 1971 when we took *Amerika* to Dartington and they offered us a base. I remember looking out at the orchard drenched in white blossom, as beautiful women in Laura Ashley served us home-made muesli in hand-thrown bowls, and saying . . . no. Wherever theatre was to be made, it was not here.

David's integration with mainstream theatre continued: *Slag* was revived at the Royal Court in 1971 and he was commissioned to write another play for Hampstead: *The Great Exhibition*. Our grant was increased, and so were the number and quality of venues. As new arts centres sprang up and universities (where we had formerly played in refectories) acquired purpose-built studio theatres, we surfed a wave of interest in new drama.

In 1971 I directed Genet's *The Maids* and David directed *Purity* by David Mowat. This double bill of published plays was a deliberate attempt to try and move outside the core of Portable writers and also, at least for our opening run at the theatre at the University of Kent at Canterbury, to use proper sets and costumes. David was dissatisfied with *Purity* and we did not tour it. By the dress rehearsal he had grown to dislike both the play and his production of it. I think it marked for him a turning point, a realisation that he did not want merely to interpret a naturalistic play that had been previously performed, but to always use his directing energies either to stage his own work or to explore new work. We both hated to see a play done by Portable where people just got up from desks and put things in filing cabinets: the dull texture of TV naturalism. The production – in drag – of *The Maids* was interesting for me because the power struggle of the two maids, Solange and Clare, was mirrored by the professional experience of the two actors, Bill Hoyland, a battle-hardened Fringe star, and Pete Brenner, a student actor, whom we had plucked from UEA. The Madame was played by Sue Johnston, Neil Johnston's wife, who had heroically stepped in when I couldn't find a drag artist prepared to tour on Portable money! She did a superb job in very difficult conditions and brought enormous authority to the role – an intimation of her future career. Occasionally the psychodynamics of the cast created some electric performances. I also retranslated the end of the play, changing quite a lot of it. Nobody noticed. I then adapted and directed Kafka's *Amerika*. Here I was bolder, and wrote quite a few scenes that were not in the novel at all. Many people said how true I'd been to the novel: a useful lesson.

I was not involved in *Lay By* by Howard Brenton, David Hare, Snoo Wilson, Stephen Poliakoff, Brian Clark, Hugh Stoddart and Trevor Griffiths, so I will let two people who were there take up the story.[12] Snoo Wilson first:

> David Hare, who was running the script department at the Royal Court, had – as a challenge to the theatre – assembled all the seven writers of *Lay By*, and then passed it over. Directing *Lay By*, I favoured my own co-writing for inclusion in the scenes, though there is plenty from the rest of the writers. There was so much material it was like organising a newspaper. You just did it by instinct. In retrospect, the odd thing is that David wasn't at the helm, since the whole newspaper theatre thing was his idea (or rather Erwin Piscator's – there is nothing new under the sun), but when Michael Rudman at the Traverse came up with the money to do it in a late night slot, David . . . stood back

because he had elected to direct *Blowjob*, another Portable commission. I think I did an OK job, but it was more script-editing than directing.[13]

Now James Warrior, a stalwart member of the Portable company, on whom the play made a big impression:

> *Lay By* was an incredible play. If you subjected it to the sort of academic scrutiny it would get if it were being studied as part of a university literature course, it would come out very badly. A poorly structured, minor play, but somehow it captured the spirit of its time and I think it was as important as *Look Back In Anger* had been in the effect it had on British theatre.[14]

By 1971, we had a subsidy of £8,000; almost £80,000 in today's money. We had created – and could now afford to pay ourselves to run – the company we had always wanted. The trouble was that neither of us wanted the job. David now had a firm foothold in the established theatre and I was beginning to have some success in at least getting my TV scripts read. I was also anxious to spend more time songwriting and working with my brother's music. We discussed with the Arts Council the idea of using our money to mount four big shows a year to play in the Arts Council's new group of larger touring venues. We suggested large-cast, big political plays like *England's Ireland*. They would have none of it. It seemed to me we had merely helped to construct the walls of the ghetto. Fringe theatre in the four years we had been going was now a recognised genre, and the Arts Council gave the impression that the Fringe was where new drama should stay. We wanted to reinvent Portable and burst out on to bigger stages but without making the compromises with conventional theatre that seemed inevitable. It was not to be; perhaps, too, they sensed that our hearts weren't really in it. Theatres should be allowed to die, but we hated the idea of giving the money back. So we asked Malcolm Griffiths to take over and run what became The Portable Theatre Workshop Company (POTOWOCA).

At the Edinburgh Festival in 1971 we had three companies running. The plays were *Lay By*, directed by Snoo, *Blow Job*, written by Snoo and directed by David, and Malcolm's POTOWOCA production of Chris Wilkinson's *Plays for Rubber Go-Go Girls*. In 1972, Michael White, impressed by the group effort of *Lay By*, was persuaded by David to finance the writing of *England's Ireland*. Howard Brenton, David Hare, Snoo Wilson, David Edgar, Francis Fuchs, Brian Clark and I all went to a cottage in Wales. There we hammered out the play, working in groups of two. I worked mostly with Howard. When the play was finished, I wrote the songs with my brother Nick. In the spring of 1972, David's *The Great Exhibition* went on at Hampstead. In September that year we staged *England's Ireland*, calling ourselves 'Shoot' to distinguish us from Malcolm's POTOWOCA, which by now was touring our old venues. *England's Ireland* had a large cast and was performed successfully at the Round House, the Glasgow Citizens and the Mickery in Amsterdam. It was the kind of big political show we wanted to do, but it proved to be a one-off – though I think planted the seeds of *Brassneck* and *Pravda*.

David, despite the howls of right-wing critics, was very much part of the non-Fringe theatre. His growing confidence and naturally combative attitude played well with the press. He had famously terrified Michael Billington, then and now drama critic on the *Guardian*, into taking him seriously. Howard and Snoo were writing for other theatres and I had begun the process of getting the finance for *Skinflicker*. When we set up POTOWOCA, the Arts Council had insisted that we hire a professional theatre administrator. Gus Hope was long since gone and our one W. H. Smith-account-book-profit-and-loss methods were considered way too primitive, given the amounts of money we were getting. David and I remained sleeping directors of Portable. Malcolm did interesting work with the company, but the administrator failed to administrate. In eighteen months the company was bankrupt. Portable ended officially at a creditors' meeting at our accountants, Griffin Stone Moscrop, who waived their fees. Our lawyers did not. I paid them and David paid the outstanding National Insurance arrears. It was over.

Our future careers are largely a matter of public record. We don't have reunions, and when we meet we do not reminisce. The questions, particularly in the context of this volume, are: had Portable any significance other than being the nursery slopes for a group of writers? Did it achieve any more than to launch their careers? Our success was in showing that there was an audience around the country for new work and that it could be staged and toured comparatively cheaply. My feeling was that our failure was in never quite achieving a style that matched some of the innovation in the writing.

David continued directing his own work until the conventional theatre was able to understand it enough for Howard Davies to make the great leap with *The Secret Rapture*, which allowed David to finally have the success he so richly deserved. He has spectacularly achieved the ambition of big political plays on major stages. I remember sitting in the expensive stalls at the National Theatre at the first night of *The Secret Rapture* and watching the well-heeled audience around me laughing at a play that was basically about what a bunch of shits they were. How is this magic achieved? I wondered. If Howard and Snoo have been comparatively less successful, I think it is because there seems no equivalent in conventional theatre of what Portable at its best achieved. I can only describe this as 'fine detail co-existing with rough theatre'. To my mind, Howard's work often looks better in less polished productions and Snoo's plays suffer from directors trying to top an already volcanic imagination, when what is needed is highly disciplined underplaying.

There were several codas to Portable. Nick and I formed an ad hoc band to play the songs we wrote for Howard's *Scott of the Antarctic* at the Bradford Ice Rink. I directed Snoo's *A Greenish Man* on TV, and David directed my first play, *Devil's Island*, for Joint Stock at the Royal Court. We collaborated again on *Teeth 'n' Smiles*. In 1974, I wrote and directed my second film, *Dinosaur*, which was about a subsidised theatre company touring England during a general strike.[15] I put much of our experience and many of the dilemmas I felt about state-sponsored dissent into this. Also, insofar as one could in a 16-mm film, something of the magic of moving through Britain.

Portable taught me that I needed to work in 360 degrees, to physically change my viewpoint with the action. It also gave me a real love of working on location, which is in a sense finding your theatre where you can, not in a controlled environment peopled by the ghosts of others. I have noticed a fashion for some members of my generation to feel embarrassed and to apologise, even ridicule the heart-on-sleeve politics of their early work. I'm glad none of us does that. I remain a friend and not uncritical fan of David, Howard and Snoo, and try to see all their work. I enjoy their company and feel proud that I shouted their wares when nobody knew their names.

NOTES

The author would like to acknowledge the generous assistance given by Snoo Wilson, James Warrior and Will Knightley in the preparation of this chapter.

1. Malcolm Griffiths went on himself to become a director of alternative theatre (later taking over Portable), and founder of the Independent Theatre Council.
2. See, for example, David Hare, 'Raymond Williams: "I Can't Be a Father to Everyone"', in *Obedience, Struggle and Revolt* (London: Faber, 2005), pp145–71.
3. See Catherine Itzin, *Stages in the Revolution: Political Theatre in Britain since 1968* (London: Methuen, 1980), references passim:

In 1968, Jim Haynes – the expatriate American 'libertarian anarchist' who had started his counter-cultural activities in a bookshop-cum-theatre in Edinburgh in the mid-sixties – opened the Drury Lane Arts Lab, a warehouse at the top of Drury Lane converted into a variety of spaces for exhibitions, eating, drinking, theatre performances, music and cinema. In the one short year of its existence, it had an enormous impact, capturing the spirit of the counter-culture, presenting the first of a new generation of writers, actors and directors who were rejecting the structures of conventional theatre institutions. Portable Theatre, Freehold, Pip Simmons and the People Show either started [there] or played there regularly. . . . By the end of the seventies there were over 140

arts centres in England, Scotland and Wales which owed something to Jim
Haynes and his vision of an alternative culture.   (p9)

4. Freehold was one of the most influential of the early Fringe companies. Nancy
   Meckler went on to become Artistic Director of Shared Experience and the first
   woman to direct at the National Theatre. Café La Mama was one of a number
   of innovative American performance groups which had a considerable influence
   of the British Fringe. Hare himself acknowledges its influence on his own early
   play *What Happened to Blake?*
5. Originally a youth centre, the south London-based Oval House became an important venue for touring groups both to meet and to show work. In 1975 it hosted
   a conference of fifty theatre groups and thirty writers from the Fringe to protest
   against (leaked) proposals by the Arts Council to make arbitrary policy changes
   and funding cuts in the Fringe sector.
6. Howard Brenton, *Christie in Love*, in *Plays: One* (London: Methuen, 1986).
   The subject of the play is the appalling life of the serial killer John Christie, with
   whom the audience is forced to sympathise as a figure whose actions have a kind
   of integrity compared to the hypocrisy of the society around him.
7. The theatre agent who has achieved legendary status in the history of modern
   British theatre, in large part through her nurturing of successive generations of
   significant new dramatists.
8. The hugely influential 7:84 was founded by John McGrath in 1971 as a socialist
   theatre group aimed at working-class audiences in non-theatre venues. Its work,
   though seldom solemnly didactic, saw theatre essentially as a tool for political education: 'I believe that theatre can best achieve its independent artistic
   objectives by becoming part of the hugely complex movement towards a developed, sophisticated, but liberating form of socialism which is happening all over
   Europe' (John McGrath, *A Good Night Out* (London: Methuen, 1981), p98).
       The contrast between 7:84's brand of political theatre and Portable's was never
   clearer than at the 1971 Edinburgh Festival, when 7:84's first show, *Trees in the
   Wind*, performed alongside Portable's *Lay By*, *Blow Job* and *Plays for Rubber
   Go-Go Girls*.
9. The Theatre Upstairs was opened by the Royal Court in February 1969 as a
   laboratory theatre aimed primarily at those new young writers unable to get
   their work on the main stage. The 'Come Together' Festival in October 1970,
   organised by the theatre's Artistic Director William Gaskill, was a further attempt
   to bring together the new generation of Fringe theatre practitioners with the older
   tradition of the Court. Although the relationship was at times uneasy, Gaskill's
   initiative remains a significant moment in the history of modern British theatre.
10. Email to the author, 24 July 2005.
11. The Mickery Theatre was founded by its Artistic Director, Ritsaert ten Cate,
    in 1965 and was home for over twenty-five years to anarchic experimentation
    in avant-garde performance. It was of particular importance to British Fringe
    writers such as Brenton and groups such as the People Show and the Pip Simmons
    Group.
12. The collaboratively written *Lay By* was conceived as an exercise in 'public
    writing', with participating writers producing a continuous text scribbled with

children's crayons on wallpaper spread on the floor of a Royal Court rehearsal room. It took as its starting point a newspaper article about a rape case, and pushed the confrontational Portable style to the limit. Not only were genuine 'hard-core' pornographic pictures passed round the audience, but events on stage centred on a pornographer at work with his models and concluded with the characters being turned into 'human jam'. The intention was to challenge its audiences to confront the hypocrisy of its own response – disgust mixed with salacious fascination – to such events. Hare felt the play 'caught the authentic stink of pornography'. See Richard Boon, *Brenton the Playwright* (London: Methuen, 1991), pp58–60, 288–9.

13. Email to the author, 13 July 2005.
14. Email to the author, 24 July 2005.
15. The film featured Diz Willis, who ran the Norwich Arts Centre – a Portable venue – and who also performed in the Open Space run of *Lay By*.

2

RICHARD BOON

Keeping turning up

Hare's early career

A war. If only there were a war in England, not that endless – slow, sullen
defeat. Why don't the bastards take up arms against such a government?
Then we poets would be of some use, we'd do the songs, the banners, the
shouts . . .
Howard Brenton, *Bloody Poetry*, 1984

'British society needs not to abolish its institutions, but to refresh them.
For, if not through institutions, how do we express the common good?' So
wrote David Hare in conclusion to the Introduction of his 1993 book *Asking
Around*,[1] in which he provides an account of the mass of research out of
which he produced the trilogy of plays – *Racing Demon, Murmuring Judges*
and *The Absence of War*[2] – which was for some the signal theatrical event
of the 1990s. These were plays in which, through a forensic dissection of
the operations of the Church, the Law and the Labour Party respectively,
Hare offered a panoramic and fiercely critical view of the state of the nation
in the (as it turned out) final years of a period of Conservative government
that had begun in 1979 with the election of Margaret Thatcher as Prime
Minister of Great Britain. Taken as a whole, they present a picture of a
divided country run by an intellectual elite, inward-looking, self-regarding
and concerned only with the preservation of its own power and status; an
elite that has surrendered moral leadership and social responsibility to the
vagaries of market-force economics. The institutions over which it presides,
insofar as they function at all, do so only because of the continuing goodwill
and hard work of those isolated individuals, usually at or near the bottom
of the pile, who 'do the dirty work'. As a character in *Murmuring Judges*
puts it, 'Let's hear it for the guys who keep turning up' (p78).

The sheer scale of the trilogy – six years in the making and produced on the
Cottesloe and Olivier stages of the National Theatre – is in itself testament to
Hare's ambition as a leftist dramatist who believes that the theatre is a proper
place in which to tackle the major social and political issues of contemporary
society. Where else, other than at the heart of the theatrical establishment,
should one engage with such issues? Where better to analyse and denounce

the social and economic costs of Thatcherism whilst celebrating the courage and humanity of its victims? How more appropriate than to address the state of the nation – as represented by the health of three of its great institutions – through the critical lens of a fourth, the theatre?

Yet, even at the time, dissenting voices were raised, notably by that generation of 'In Yer Face' young dramatists who came to prominence in the 1990s, who heard in Hare a voice which belonged to the past (specifically the 1970s) and which no longer spoke to the present with the urgency it desperately required. This view played into larger narratives about the dramatist's career, narratives which suggested that, in common with others of his generation such as Howard Brenton, Trevor Griffiths, John McGrath and David Edgar, Hare had been robbed of his subject by the collapse of socialism and the rise of liberal capitalism in the 1980s, and that, if his career had subsequently prospered (unlike Griffiths's, for example), then that was no more than an indication of the degree to which he had abandoned or at best softened his radical politics. He had, in effect, 'sold out'. Ironically, this was a charge that had been levelled before, in the 1970s, when (with the exception of McGrath) all the playwrights mentioned above, including Hare, had to a greater or lesser extent moved away from their roots in the practices and politics of the radical Fringe to occupy mainstream stages. Critics have always seen in Hare the figure of a soft middle-class liberal, compromised by how he has chosen to position himself politically within the theatre, and indeed within public life generally (he is, after all, *Sir* David Hare, knighted for services to theatre in 1998, Lancing- and Cambridge-educated, Fellow of the Royal Society of Literature, occasional media commentator, husband to a leading fashion designer and sometime banquet guest at Buckingham Palace); from this point of view, 'Let's hear it for the guys who keep turning up' sounds at best the faintest of political rallying cries and at worst a wheedling justification of the status quo. And these are perhaps the dominant critical narratives of Hare's career: on the one hand, the familiar story (addressed directly by Edgar in his 1983 play *Maydays*) of the disillusioned leftist, betrayed by history and drifting inevitably into reaction and complicity; on the other, the image of the playwright as 'Le Carré's Honourable Schoolboy, forever trying to undermine England from within and enjoying every minute of it'.[3]

Neither narrative does justice to the particular trajectory of Hare's career, though the notion of the writer as a 'mole', burrowing into the fabric of official culture and exposing its workings, is neither wholly inaccurate nor unattractive. His fascination with institutions is one of the defining characteristics of his body of work, from the early experiments with Portable to the present. It is a fascination hedged around by ambivalence, an ambivalence which is present not only within the subjects of the plays themselves, but also in the ways in which the playwright has chosen to position himself in relation to the theatre itself as an institution. His early plays especially – and plays, too, are kinds of institution – reveal a conscious and experimental interrogation of the possibilities of form, structure and genre. It is from this perspective that I intend to examine the early, formative years of Hare's career up to his 1978 play *Plenty* ('the play I had been trying to write for a long time'),[4] regarded by many as one of the most important plays of the postwar years. In doing so, I shall to a limited extent map Hare's career alongside that of his long-time friend and collaborator, Howard Brenton, the more clearly to identify the trajectory on which Hare launched himself as a political dramatist of a particular kind.

Hare's key role in the creation and development of Portable Theatre at the University of Cambridge in the late 1960s has been reasonably well documented,[5] and Tony Bicât's contribution to this book only adds to our understanding of what has since come to be seen as one of the most important and influential of the many Fringe groups that emerged at the time. Portable's reputation rests on two key achievements: that it was a writers' theatre, helping launch the careers of a number of the most significant British playwrights of the latter part of the twentieth century (primarily Hare himself and Howard Brenton), and that it was a political theatre. The first point seems to me incontestable, but, as Bicât observes, if Portable was a political theatre, then it was 'a funny kind of political theatre'. It pursued no specific political agenda, it had no manifesto. Indeed, it is notable that Hare's own comments on the creation of Portable do no more than imply a political *dimension* to what was conceived of as a wider engagement with culture – including the theatre – and society generally:

> What we had in common was that we thought we were living through a period of extreme decadence, both socially and theatrically. We just couldn't believe that the official culture was incapable of seeing the extreme state of crisis that we thought the country was in.[6]

This is not to suggest that Hare was disengaged from contemporary politics: far from it. He shared with many of his generation anger at, and frustration with, the failure of the Wilsonian socialism of the 1960s to deliver on its promises. Equally, he saw little cause for optimism in the leftist alternatives proposed by revisionist thinkers such as his own (largely invisible) tutor at Cambridge, Raymond Williams.[7] And if the great wave of dissident and utopianist thought that swept the West in the late 1960s – *les événements* in France, civil rights movements in the USA and Northern Ireland, protests against the Vietnam War everywhere – was inspirational and energising, then the brutality with which it was suppressed, and its decay into defeat and disillusionment, only fed his political anger. But the specifically political was only one aspect of a wider disenchantment with 'official culture' generally, and one which Richard Eyre traces back to pre-Cambridge days, suggesting that, while Hare 'can sometimes seem to have emerged fully-formed at the age of nineteen, in Cambridge, as the "scourge of academia"', his early life in Bexhill-on-Sea, a 'world of petty bourgeois gentility and the quiet desperation of people's lives' was 'quite crucial'.[8] Eyre's comments point to what is perhaps the single most important focus of interest throughout Hare's career (and in doing so enables what seems otherwise an improbable leap between the Hare who contributed to some of the most scabrous and violent of the Portable plays and the Hare who wrote *The Secret Rapture* twenty years later): the disjuncture between private realities and public representations of those realities. His mission, and Portable's, was concerned, as one of its writers suggested, with forcing on newly found audiences 'a guilty awareness of a darker reality beneath our smooth façades'.[9]

The emergent Portable house style – volatile, nihilistic, confrontational – set out to challenge the complacencies of public life, addressing 'closely-knit social situations in a process of extreme decay'[10] and typically dealing with taboo subjects such as pornography and sex crime. But, as Howard Brenton, a key figure in the group, explains:

> If you set up an antagonistic theatre touring to people who have never seen the theatre before, it transforms itself into political theatre. It has a political effect. And the anarchic, antagonistic theatre becomes increasingly one of political content. This is what happened to us.[11]

It was Brenton whose understanding of the new French philosophy of situationism[12] – a revision of classic Marxist thought, rooted as much in broad cultural understandings as in economics, which perceived society as 'an obscene parade', a 'spectacle' by means of which the working classes were kept oppressed – gave structure to the largely instinctive, visceral hostility to official culture felt by the group's founders, Bicât and, particularly, Hare. Even then, the political aspect of Portable's work was to be located less in the content of the plays than in the aesthetics of their style of performance, and that was driven by the perception that, along with other manifestations of the official culture, 'the theatre of the day was rhetorical, over-produced, lavish, saying nothing – all those things'.[13] The situationists' own slogan – 'Disrupt the Spectacle! The Obscene Parade, Bring it to a Halt!' – was perhaps the nearest Portable came to a political manifesto.

Hare's own narrative of his career consistently stresses that at the time he thought of himself primarily as a director rather than a writer, and that he was effectively forced into writing when a promised script by Snoo Wilson failed to appear. His earliest plays, *Inside Out* (1968) and *Strindberg* (1969), were both adaptations of their subjects' diaries (Kafka's in the first case): not unobvious choices of subject for a writer fascinated by the dark underbelly of society, and indicative of where Portable's interests lay, though in both cases conventionally literary – even wordy – in approach. *How Brophy Made Good* (1969) had as its central character a man who said 'fuck' on television; a situationist gesture of a kind, and rather more of a taboo-breaker than might be apparent to modern eyes (when the theatre critic Kenneth Tynan made the same gesture on the BBC in 1965, one Conservative MP called for him to be hanged). *Brophy*, however, which Hare co-directed with Bicât, began to articulate a more developed sense of theatricality, and the emergence of a Portable house-style: simple, bare stagings, little 'dressing' and cinematic 'wipes' between short scenes. (Both Hare and Bicât admit the importance of film as an influence on their early stage work.) Speaking of his direction of Brenton's 1970 play *Fruit* – of all the Portable plays, the one most clearly influenced by situationism: it concludes with a petrol bomb being thrown on to the stage – Hare says:

> We worked on a deliberately and apparently shambolic style of presentation, where people simply lurched on to stage and lurched off again, and it was impossible to make patterns. That is to say, we worked on a theatrical principle of forbidding any aesthetic at all . . . It was impossible to make aesthetic patterns, and it was impossible to apportion moral praise or blame.[14]

His own *What Happened to Blake?*, produced in the same year, similarly worked in terms of a 'stripped-down', dislocative and implicitly confrontational stagecraft. What Hare was beginning to evolve here, in his own writing and in the direction of his own and others' work, was a set of stylistics and a craft of the stage which learned from the Portable experience of touring to non-theatre venues, was rooted in a practical and pragmatic understanding of the nature of theatrical space, and was capable of articulating Portable concerns in increasingly sophisticated and complex ways. Brenton explains:

> Portable plays weren't plays for stages – the space between the people defines the actual physical theatre, the space between the audience itself and the actors. And that space and relationship becomes an almost moral force in the writing and in the presentation – a sense of bodies and will and concentration, and laughter or abuse.[15]

What was being proposed was a new 'public' theatre, freed of the tyranny of the proscenium arch and other established forms, and profoundly (if uncomfortably) more democratic. This was the spirit that informed the creation of the two experiments in public writing undertaken by Portable, the multi-authored *Lay By* (1971) and *England's Ireland* (1972), the most ambitious of the Portable projects, the most confrontational, and the most overtly (at least in the case of the latter) politically engaged. They were also the shows which effectively bankrupted and killed the company.

In Brenton's view – and it is perhaps the view which has contributed most to the received wisdom of theatre historians – the failure of late 1960s counter-culturalism was mirrored by the failure of the Fringe to fulfil its mission to find new audiences outside the middle classes, becoming a 'cultural cul de sac':

> [Audiences] became theatrically literate and the discussions afterwards stopped being about the plays' content and began to be about their style. And also we began to know the circuit too well. Those two things made it not dangerous any more. And somehow it had to be risky, it had to be dangerous, it had to be a gut operation or else it was no good. And so we began to try and get big shows out.[16]

His own career trajectory from 1973 onwards, with *Magnificence* (Royal Court, 1973), *The Churchill Play* (Nottingham Playhouse, 1974) and *Weapons of Happiness* (National Theatre, 1976), provides the most straightforward example of a Fringe writer moving into the mainstream of theatrical culture. This was the moment perceived by their critics when the ''68 generation' 'sold out'. For Brenton, however, the move was both inevitable in purely pragmatic terms and an opportunity to bring into the mainstream content, and the means of expressing that content, that had been developed on the Fringe. The plays identified above, though highly individual, nonetheless show a progressive and coherent development towards a public form of drama which was capable of exposing oppositional, broadly socialist ideas to as large an audience as possible, and in doing so challenged the dominance of traditional humanist drama in its heartlands. Hare shared Brenton's ambition; when he directed *Weapons* at the National in 1976, both saw the event as a kind of military incursion. Despite that, Hare's own career path in the 1970s is less easily mapped.

By the time of Portable's collapse, Hare had written or co-written six of its shows and directed five. It was not particularly unusual that he should also have been active outside Portable; most of its members were. Neither *Slag* (1970) nor *The Great Exhibition* (1972) was a Portable play; *The Rules of the Game* (1971) was an adaptation of Pirandello made for the National, whilst *Man Above Men* (1973) was a first excursion into television. From 1968 to 1971, he was also first Literary Manager, then Resident Dramatist, at the Royal Court. This suggests a dramatist, still young, flexing his muscles in a variety of ways and places, but also not averse to working in what for others was 'enemy territory'. Tony Bicât notes that, even in pre-Portable days at Cambridge, Hare kept a 'shrewd foot' in both 'alternative' and 'official' student theatre camps. *Slag* was the first of Hare's plays for the commercial stage, being written (or at least rewritten: a one-act version had been produced for Portable) for the producer Michael Codron. Hare was unapologetic: 'I have . . . enjoyed writing for [Codron] . . . I think that if you can possibly survive in the commercial theatre you should, because otherwise you're just blocking up the subsidised theatre for new writers.'[17] *Slag* has achieved canonical status: it may be seen to some extent as the first of the writer's mature works, the play in which his distinctive voice begins to be heard, and it continues to be published in his *Plays: One*.[18] This is not entirely unreasonable, given that, among other things, it represents the first clear articulation of Hare's career-long fascination with the relationship of individuals to institutions. Drawn in part from his own experience of public school, the play is set in an exclusive but failing girls' school (Brackenhurst) where three women teachers try to create an alternative society. Their idealism founders on impracticality and self-indulgence, and degenerates into a dark fantasy of mutual manipulation and power-gaming which is redolent of Genet. The play essentially is a satire of the failed idealism of the 1960s counter-culture generally and what Hare saw as some of the wilder posturings of early feminism specifically.

> It's about every institution that I'd known – school, Cambridge, Pathé and so on. They are all the same. That is how institutions perpetuate themselves. With rituals that go on inside them – ever more baroque discussions about ever dwindling subjects . . .[19]

The crucial thing about Brackenhurst, the supposed 'battleground of the future', is that it is rooted in the past, and continues on its crumbling way irrespective of those who seek to change it. *The Great Exhibition*, like *Slag*, performed at the Hampstead Theatre Club, offers a similarly bleak picture, finding in the figure of a corrupted, self-dramatising Labour MP unable to leave his Hampstead home the embodiment of all that has been wasted in the Labour years. In both works, idealism confronts despair and loses, leading to a kind of madness which is expressed through increasingly bizarre conduct and in the form of self-consciously performative behaviour. This kind of knowing theatricality constantly reminds audiences that they are watching a play, not reality, so inviting critical judgement. If these are not Portable plays in fact, they are certainly Portable plays in ethos and spirit. Indeed, *Slag* was written precisely as an attempt to lodge the Portable aesthetic behind the proscenium arch of the conventional theatre.

Hare's own, retrospective view of *Slag* is that it is overly schematic, and he is also rather dismissive (more so than its director, Richard Eyre) of *The Great Exhibition*. Both stand, however, as early and inevitably experimental attempts at the kind of public writing he wished to put on mainstream stages. His next play took that project a step further. *Brassneck* was co-written with Howard Brenton and staged at the Nottingham Playhouse in 1973. The play charts the fortunes of the Bagley business empire from the idealism represented by the 1945 Labour general election victory to the corruption scandals of the 1960s. Set in the Midlands, the story is one of postwar decline, of social and political opportunity lost to a voraciously capitalist culture of self-serving greed, bribery and betrayal. The target is the self-serving con-spiracy of public life, in which both political parties are implicated; indeed, the play is most angry when dealing with its Left-leaning figures, whose treachery is seen to be the greater.

Although *Brassneck* is typical of neither Hare's nor Brenton's work gen-erally (they claim, only half-jokingly, that it was written by a third man, 'Howard Hare'), it nonetheless remains a play of great significance to both of them, for what begins to emerge from it is a more fully developed and theorised model of what their new public theatre might be. One key feature is simply the scale and scope of its ambition. This was to be a theatre – the creation of a theatrical form – which could deal with the great historical and political issues of public life as they were reflected in and mediated through the private and domestic lives of its characters. Slides projected at the back of the stage provide the historical context to domestic scenes (for example, images of the Coronation in 1953 form the backdrop to the vainglorious if shambolic Bagley family wedding), thereby enabling an ironic juxtaposition of public and private narratives. The episodic structure of the play rests on critical moments in the Bagley story, feeling no need to fill in gaps in nar-rative or individual character development. Articulating that structure is a stagecraft which works in terms of 'wipes' between scenes and largely bare settings (including a railway station, a golf course, the countryside and a strip club), which are indicated only by carefully chosen, essential detail. The overall effect, crudely, is to make audiences work; to require them to fill the gaps themselves, thereby engaging with the play with a profound and – crucially – *critical* concentration.

What Hare and Brenton were postulating was nothing less than a 'British epic theatre', with an inevitable debt to Brecht but a greater one to the lessons learned at Portable. It was Brenton who offered the clearest formulation: a 'British epic' is

1) a play that is many scened, the short scenes choosing precise 'windows' in a story
2) the 'windows' have to be authentic, to ring true and
3) at the same time they must be part of an argument, one illustrating the other, progressing to a conclusion that is believable, in the simple sense of 'men and women would do that' and also be clear in intent and
4) it is the message of a play that comes first.[20]

The slightly breathless style and distended grammar of the third point perhaps suggests that the theorising of 'British epic theatre' was an incomplete process (or that Brenton's interest in theorising it was limited), but the intent is clear. Although both Brenton and Hare were at this stage of their careers suspicious of the usefulness of Brecht as a model, their epic theatre shared with his the underpinning principle that this was a form of drama which was designed, as Althusser has it, 'to make the spectator into an actor who would complete the unfinished play'.[21] At that fundamental level, 'British epic' was a breakthrough for both writers, and hugely influential on the plays that were to follow. This is most apparent, though not unequivocally so, in Brenton's output; in Hare's case, it was not until *Plenty* that an obviously recognisable 'British epic' play emerges.

That *Brassneck* was produced at the Nottingham Playhouse is significant, for it was at that theatre, under Richard Eyre's stewardship, that some of the most iconic and influential plays of postwar British drama were produced: *Brassneck* was one, Brenton's *The Churchill Play* (1974) and Griffiths's *Comedians* (1975) notable amongst others. These were 'State of the Nation' plays, and all contributed significantly to the establishment of the ''68 generation' as, if not the dominant force of the mainstream theatre, then a considerable, and agenda-setting, power within it. Yet what is striking is that, *Brassneck* aside, and despite what was already a close personal association with Richard Eyre, Hare wrote nothing for the Nottingham theatre, bar the relatively minor *Deeds* (1978), a collaboration with Brenton, Griffiths and Ken Campbell designed as a 'farewell gift' to Eyre. The sequence of plays between *Brassneck* and *Plenty* (1978), which formed the mainstay of Hare's output for the decade and established him in the mainstream, was variously produced elsewhere: in the West End, on tour, at the Royal Court and, in the case of *Plenty* itself, at the National. This bears out Hare's contention that 'I've never had a "home", theatrically – never had a theatre that regularly did my work – since Portable. But I think most writers enjoy whoring around, actually, much as they pretend to need a home.'[22] According to Eyre,

> At Nottingham, [Hare] was smart enough to see that, if he was writing a new
> play – *Plenty*, which was an expensive play to stage – and he was being courted

by Peter Hall to go to the South Bank, it was much better not to offer it to the Playhouse, but to have it done in London in repertoire with the cast of his choice . . . Obviously I would have loved to do *Plenty*; I thought it was a wonderful play. But I think he made the right decision, and he was pretty (and I think he would admit this now) ruthless in his exploitation of Peter's support of him. So he took the opportunity.[23]

Eyre's comments might be seen to endorse the view of Hare as the ruthless, calculating careerist who abandoned his Fringe roots, but his wider point is somewhat different: 'David is a very smart impresario. He's got the instincts – though not the patience and the energy, because it would stop him writing – of a producer. He's really, really smart about the particular time to do a particular play, and at what sort of theatre.'[24] Indeed, much of Hare's subsequent reputation has developed on the perception that his plays, more than anyone else's, succeed in capturing the zeitgeist of their particular historical moment. Hare's own account of himself and his career is rather more relaxed, though by no means inconsistent with Eyre's, inasmuch as it values theatrical instinct above all: 'I don't think of it as having a career. I just think of it as following my nose, from one subject to another.'[25]

The plays leading up to and including *Brassneck* are all more or less straightforward satires, driven by anger and a withering scorn for 'official culture' that places them spiritually, if not always actually, within Portable. Those which follow it – *Knuckle* (1974, Comedy Theatre), *Fanshen* (1975, Joint Stock Theatre Group), *Teeth 'n' Smiles* (1975, Royal Court) and *Plenty* (1978, National) – each finds its own 'home' and, within the overarching ambition to continue to evolve a public theatre drawing on the newly established principles of 'British epic', a distinctive and increasingly positive voice. In many ways, the most distinctive of them is *Fanshen*; indeed, it remains unique in Hare's body of work. The play was written with and for the Joint Stock Theatre Company, a group which Hare co-founded 'among the ruins of Portable Theatre'[26] in 1974 with Fringe pioneers Max Stafford-Clark and David Aukin. Ironically, it was at the time an attempt to create a kind of 'home': a place to house the kind of work its creators found difficult to place elsewhere. The group was to become a very significant force in the evolution of modern British theatre, not only through the plays it produced, but – and perhaps as importantly – through the working method it pioneered.[27] Cathy Turner offers a detailed analysis of *Fanshen* and its working methods elsewhere in this book (see Chapter 7), but two points are worth making here.

First, and despite reservations expressed about Brecht in his earlier career, *Fanshen* is the most Brechtian of Hare's plays (and indeed of any British play of the last sixty years). To that extent it is quite untypical of the rest of his output. But it is an unavoidable speculation that the kind of immersion in Brechtian – or pseudo-Brechtian – aesthetics and working methods that the emergent Joint Stock method was evolving was of considerable signifi-cance to a writer actively engaged in the creation of his own epic-style public theatre, not least in developing an ability to handle large and complex sub-jects with discipline and subtlety through dramaturgies which demanded the active critical engagement of audiences. Second, it is notable that, for the second time in only six years, Hare had been instrumental in the creation of a theatre group that was to have a challenging and vitalising influence on British theatre culture. That alone makes him a significant figure in the history of modern British theatre.

By 1980, and following some of the most innovative and exciting theatre work of the decade, the momentum behind the Joint Stock group was begin-ning to fade, to the extent that its continuing existence was in doubt. Hare's advice to the company administrator tells us a lot about his attitude to the theatre and how it works:

> you have to have an outstandingly good reason for continuing a theatre group once its initial impetus has gone . . . you cannot just inherit a 'shape' and a 'structure' and pretend it's going to work, because it isn't . . . I'd say stop and start again, unless there is someone around with a strong *artistic* sense of exactly what work they want to do, and how they want to do it . . . I really think it better to pack it in.[28]

One is reminded here of Brenton's credo that, for any play or theatre project, the 'scaffolding' must be constantly set up, dismantled and set up anew,[29] advice which sits instructively next to Hare's instinctive views about 'home-lessness' and 'whoring around'. Nonetheless, it remains true that when, with *Knuckle*, Hare 'followed his nose' onto a commercial, West End stage with a play which attacked commerce, the results, at least in terms of audience reception, were unsurprisingly mixed.

Part of the attraction for Hare of *Fanshen* had been the sense of liberation the writing of it had given him: he was 'sick to death with writing about England . . . this decadent corner of the globe';[30] he may have been thinking specifically of *Knuckle*, the play which he had produced around the time of his initial involvement in the creation of Joint Stock. In many ways, *Knuckle* charts territory similar to that of *Slag* and the other early plays. Its setting is England, characterised as a 'shabby little island delighted with itself', and, within that, the Home Counties. The play rests on a central, ironic conceit: despite the setting, the form of the play is borrowed from the 'hard-boiled' school of classic American detective fiction, with Guildford and Eastbourne standing in for the mean streets of downtown LA. It is a pastiche. As with the heroes of Dashiell Hammett and Raymond Chandler, Hare's central figure, Curly Delafield, is a world-weary, wise-cracking, self-parodic character, though a gunrunner by trade, whose detective activities are confined to the search for his missing sister, Sarah. His investigation leads him into the dark world (sic) of the Surrey stockbroker belt, a world of outward civilisation and culture and inward corruption, as enshrined and personified by his hated father Patrick; a capitalist world every bit as corrupt and self-serving as that of *Brassneck*. Unlike *Brassneck*, however, *Knuckle* is not straightforwardly a satire. It has its satirical edge, but, by Hare's own account, this is the play which has 'the first stirrings of a slightly different voice, a voice which is in earnest. The play has a morality.'[31]

Again, some comparison with Brenton is instructive here. The play which took Brenton into the mainstream of British theatre was *Magnificence*, in which a hot-headed young radical, Jed, attempts the terrorist assassination of a corrupt (male) Cabinet minister known as 'Alice'. It is an act apparently driven by a situationist-inspired politics, designed to disrupt 'the obscene parade' of public life. In fact, it is shown to be misplaced, incompetent and counter-productive, motivated as much by personal revenge as by any clearly formulated political thought. For Brenton, the play represents a final rejection of political extremism in favour of a less glamorous but more realistic alternative: that of 'corny work', the position represented by Jed's friend Cliff. What is significant about Brenton's play compared to Hare's, and what helps us begin to identify the emerging nature of Hare's own political theatre, is that where Brenton's play overtly embraces a wide social reality, and delights in finding a violent clash of stylistic voices in which to do so, Hare's focus is more exclusively private, is fixed on one social class and is written throughout in one stylistic voice. Brenton's 'Alice' and Hare's Patrick are very similar figures, and recognisably inhabit the same world; but where Jed literally explodes into 'Alice's' world from what is in effect another social reality, Curly – who, like Jed, is a figure bent on revenge, and who, structurally at least, occupies a position in Hare's play analogous to Jed's in Brenton's – is always and forever part of his father's. That sense of morality to which Hare refers turns around the figure of the missing, mysterious Sarah, who may have been murdered, may have committed suicide, who never physically appears in the play but who is ever-present. Her character, as pieced together by Curly through his investigations and his own memory, emerges as one of a certain dangerous innocence: she is socially, morally and sexually 'wide open', destructive of herself and others, but she 'never lied' and whose opposition to her father and all he represents is unrelenting. It is she, not Curly, who has an equivalence with Brenton's Jed, but where

Jed's extremism is political, hers is moral – even spiritual – and where his death marks the death of a brand of political action, hers remains a mystery. Was she murdered? Did she commit suicide? Is she dead at all? Her absence stands as a constant admonition to all who knew her, most of whom (as Curly recognises) would prefer her to have been murdered, lest a suicide appear their responsibility. Her cause in the play is championed by her friend Jenny, who, according to Hare, was 'the most admirable person I've ever drawn . . . who is meant to be a good person',[32] and who for Curly represents the opposite end of the moral spectrum to his hated father, Patrick. It is a position unexpectedly endorsed and reinforced by Patrick's housekeeper, who asks a question that comes to assume ever-greater importance in Hare's career: 'I wonder why all the words my generation believed in – words like "honour" and "loyalty" – are now just a joke' (p248).

Knuckle remains one of Hare's most popular and frequently revived plays, and it stands as a key moment in his career as the play within which he begins to articulate clearly what his central concerns as a playwright were to be: 'I never until I wrote *Knuckle* felt I had anything uniquely valuable to say as a writer. I felt I was just plugging a hole.'[33] Yet it is not entirely satisfactory as a play. The problem is not that Curly fails to solve the puzzle of Sarah's fate, nor that he gives up trying, nor even that he fails to 'get the girl' in the shape of Jenny: those sour jokes are at the heart of the play's analysis of the all-pervasive, corrupting nature of capitalism, which argues that those who are complicit within a corrupt system *know* that they are complicit within it, *know* that they are playing a destructive and dehumanising game. To this extent, *Knuckle* succeeds admirably in exposing the limitations of genre. For all that the classic detective fiction of Chandler and Hammett is shot through with paradox, ambivalence and moral relativism, it is still inadequate for Hare's purposes: it is insufficient as a means of unlocking the world about which he wanted to write. Rather, the problem of the play resides in its craft, and in what is only a partial absorption of the newly found principles of an epic, public theatre. There is a certain fluidity to the stagecraft, with an insistence on rapid transitions between economically staged scenes, and an attempt to play with audience perspective through the use of what are effectively asides – 'windows' of insight, often in storytelling form – but overall the action is rather one-paced and lacking in dramatic rhythm, with too many scenes of similar location, duration and style. In Hare's own cinematic metaphor, too much of the action is 'in mid-shot'.[34]

These are issues which seem to me to be addressed more successfully in *Teeth 'n' Smiles*. If *Knuckle* made the world of institutional commerce its target, then *Teeth 'n' Smiles* returns to academia. Its setting is the writer's alma mater, Jesus College, Cambridge, on the night of the May Ball of 1969, and the action centres on the shambolic efforts of the rock group booked for the gig actually to perform its sets. Hare's experience at Cambridge seems to have stood for him as a metaphor – or, more accurately, a metonym – of all that was wrong with the British establishment generally (detached from reality, self-absorbed, endlessly self-perpetuating), but the focus of the play is very much on the band, and especially on its songwriter, Arthur, and lead singer, Maggie.

> [The play] is about the fag-end of idealism. It's about utopianism when it turned sour. It's about that stage people reach when they will do anything for an experience, and having originally enjoyed the vitality of the experience, they then become addicted to the experience.[35]

Like Brenton's *Magnificence*, then, *Teeth 'n' Smiles* is concerned with what happened to the defeated counter-culturalists of the 1960s, and as such it represents Hare's first treatment of what was in many ways to become the subject of his career: history.

Maggie, like Sarah in *Knuckle*, is a kind of spiritual extremist. Ranged against her are the forces not only of Cambridge and all that it stands for, but also the commercial cynicism of the music industry as embodied by the band's ageing agent, Saraffian. And again as in *Knuckle*, two kinds of capitalism are represented: a paternalistic old guard and (prophetically) a younger, harsher, more brutal version. Given, however, that much of Maggie's own behaviour is scarcely tolerable, it is not at all apparent for much of the time where the play's moral compass lies. Drowning in a sea of drugs and alcohol, she parades her personal 'pain' – the prerequisite of any serious rock star – for anyone who will listen. She is self-indulgent, self-dramatising and destructive of those around her – particularly Arthur, her former lover, who clings desperately to the shreds of his old idealism. For all the passion of his songs and – when she is sober enough to sing them – the passion of her performance, the band is achieving nothing bar mindless anarchy; any hope of changing things it once has aspired to has been accommodated by an endlessly flexible and still entirely secure Establishment. As John Bull puts it, 'They set out to smash the place up, but succeed only in smashing themselves.'[36]

The optimism of *Teeth 'n' Smiles* is, as it is in *Knuckle*, minimal, residing in Arthur's highly qualified idealism and in Maggie's gesture in embracing the prison sentence she is to incur for drug possession. But in both content and form it represents a step-change in the development of Hare's 'public writing'. At its most straightforward, it shows an increasing mastery of simple technique: witness the way in which the release of information within the play, particularly regarding the nuances of the relationship between Maggie and Arthur, is handled. More than that, the subtle interplay between the private, on–off love affair between the two on the one hand and the public and political debate between idealism and despair on the other represents one of the defining characteristics of the kind of 'British epic' to which Hare aspired. The same is true of the relationship between the band's sets and the rest of the play; the performance of the songs – the band's sets effectively work as a 'gig-within-a-play' – both sits easily within the overall naturalistic frame and also opens another, critical 'window' on to the action. The long, self-justifying story Saraffian tells of his wartime flirtation with death at the Café de Paris seems a clumsy way of bedding the play in a larger historical and economic perspective; but analogous moments in the private sphere of memory – the story of Arthur and Maggie meeting on a Hebridean island, Maggie's childhood recollection of a priest's act of kindness and inspiration – succeed in providing intense moments of psychological insight that counter-balance and qualify the grubby despair of the failing present. Moments such as these – moments of a kind of perfection – become increasingly important in Hare's work, in *Plenty* and beyond.

Plenty is the play in which Hare finally realises the 'British epic', in something very near the form laid out by Brenton. It is also the play in which he finds his subject: history. The episodic structure, covering the period from 1943 to 1962 – from the war years to the Festival of Britain to the Suez Crisis to the declining years of the Conservative government before Wilson's general election victory of 1964 – intertwines the public narrative of Britain's slide from idealism and optimism to disillusionment and betrayal with the private narrative of Susan Traherne, wartime secret agent and diplomat's wife, in a series of vividly realised and precisely chosen 'windows'. Susan stands as the fullest exploration to date of that line of 'spiritual extremists' – the women of Brackenhurst, Sarah, Maggie – who cannot live within their society yet struggle to live outside it. She tells the truth, irrespective of the cost to herself or to others, and her personal story is one of a descent into a kind of madness, interpreted in clinical terms by those around her, but differently by Hare:

> I take a figure who says, 'This is not right. This should not be so', and I try to write about the cost of that way of life. I suppose that what the plays conclude – certainly *Plenty* does – is that not to be able to give your consent to a society will drive you mad, but, on the other hand, to consent will mean acquiescence in the most appalling lassitude. The choice tends to be dramatised within the plays as isolation – sometimes madness – or the most ignominious absorption.[37]

Expressed in such terms, it may appear that the play allows only a stark and deeply pessimistic choice between hopeless idealism on the one hand and surrender to the disillusioned cynicism of the establishment on the other. From the point of view of the characters (especially Susan), that may well, ultimately, be so, though it is not a formulation that does justice to what one critic refers to as 'the complicated sense of involvement'[38] that the play demands of its audience. That involvement, enabled by and articulated through the principles of 'British epic', is fundamentally analytical in nature, and insists the audience think of recent British history not simply in terms of what happened, but also and equally importantly in terms of why it happened and what else might have happened. History, crucially, must be learned from.

In a not dissimilar way, the issue of Hare's own 'complicity' in mainstream culture is a more complicated one than his critics would allow. From his origins on the radical Fringe in the late 1960s, he had, within a decade, seen his work performed in the West End and at the National Theatre, and begun writing for television. But he had also played a significant role as writer or Literary Manager at the Royal Court, then as now the most important forum for the development of new writing in the country, and at the Nottingham Playhouse which, at least for a brief period, was as important as the Court in promoting young writers. Moreover, he had co-founded and helped develop, in Portable and Joint Stock, two of the most significant and influential theatre groups in the history of modern British theatre. Yet in none of these cases was Hare's attitude to what he was participating in – or, indeed, helping create – free from ambivalence, scepticism and doubt. His own choice of theatrical heroes – Joan Littlewood, John Osborne, George Devine and Peggy Ramsay – is significant in this regard: all may all be characterised not only by their passion, but by a certain bloody-minded iconoclasm, the impulse to shout 'no' when the world is quietly mouthing 'yes'. Hare's instinctive distrust of the institution manifested in his work is equally apparent within his own professional career; as a political dramatist he has had many homes, but what has driven his work is that sense of 'homelessness', allied to a ruthlessly pragmatic desire simply to 'keep turning up' – the better to 'express the common good'.

NOTES

1. David Hare, *Asking Around: Background to the David Hare Trilogy*, ed. Lyn Haill (London: Faber, 1993), p8.
2. David Hare, *Racing Demon* (London: Faber, 1990); *Murmuring Judges* (London: Faber, 1991); *The Absence of War* (London: Faber, 1993). All quotations are taken from these editions.
3. Quoted by Michael Coveney in 'Worlds Apart', *Time Out*, 21–7 January 1983, p12.

4. Quoted in Alison Summers, 'David Hare's Drama, 1970–1981: An Interview', *Centennial Review* 36 (1992), p579.
5. See Richard Boon, *About Hare: The Playwright and the Work* (London: Faber, 2003), pp18–23, 61ff.
6. Hare, quoted in Catherine Itzin and Simon Trussler, 'David Hare: From Portable Theatre to Joint Stock . . . via Shaftesbury Avenue', *New Theatre Quarterly* 5, 20 (1975–6), p113.
7. See Hare's essay, 'Raymond Williams: "I Can't Be a Father to Everyone"', in David Hare, *Obedience, Struggle and Revolt: Lectures on Theatre* (London: Faber, 2005).
8. Quoted in Boon, *About Hare*, p220.
9. John Grillo, in 'An Excess of Nightmare', *Gambit* 6, 23 (1973), p19.
10. Quoted in Peter Ansorge, 'Underground Explorations No. 1: Portable Playwrights', *Plays and Players*, February 1972, p20.
11. Quoted in Catherine Itzin, *Stages in the Revolution: Political Theatre in Britain since 1968* (London: Methuen, 1980), p189.
12. See Guy Debord, *The Society of the Spectacle* (Detroit, MI: Black and Red Printing Cooperative, 1970).
13. Itzin and Trussler, 'David Hare: From Portable Theatre to Joint Stock . . .', p109.
14. *Ibid.*, p112.
15. Quoted in Catherine Itzin and Simon Trussler, 'Petrol Bombs Through the Proscenium Arch', *Theatre Quarterly* 5, 17 (1975), p20.
16. Quoted in Jonathan Hammond, 'Messages First: An Interview with Howard Brenton', *Gambit* 6, 23 (1973), p27.
17. Itzin and Trussler, 'David Hare: From Portable Theatre to Joint Stock . . .', p111.
18. David Hare, *Plays: One: Slag, Teeth 'n' Smiles, Knuckle, Licking Hitler, Plenty* (London: Faber, 1996). Quotations are taken from this edition.
19. Quoted in Boon, *About Hare*, p65.
20. Quoted in Malcolm Hay and Philip Roberts, 'Interview: Howard Brenton', *Performing Arts Journal* 3, 3 (1979), p139.
21. Louis Althusser, *Lenin and Philosophy and Other Essays*, trans. B. Brewster (London: New Left Books, 1971), p204.
22. Quoted in Itzin and Trussler, 'David Hare: From Portable Theatre to Joint Stock . . .', p113.
23. Quoted in Boon, *About Hare*, pp221–2.
24. *Ibid.*
25. Quoted in Itzin and Trussler, 'David Hare: From Portable Theatre to Joint Stock . . .', p113.
26. Hare in Rob Ritchie (ed.), *The Joint Stock Book: The Making of a Theatre Collective* (London: Methuen, 1987), p106.
27. See Ritchie (ed.), *The Joint Stock Book*.
28. Letter to Graham Cowley and the Joint Stock Policy Committee, September 1980 (Modern British Theatre Archive, University of Leeds).
29. Letter to the present writer, 16 January 1984.
30. Itzin and Trussler, 'David Hare: From Portable Theatre to Joint Stock . . .', p114.
31. Introduction to the *Collected Plays*, pix.

32. Itzin and Trussler, 'David Hare: From Portable Theatre to Joint Stock . . .', p114.
33. Quoted in Georg Gaston, 'Interview: David Hare', *Theatre Journal* 45, 2 (May 1993), p218.
34. Introduction to Hare, *Plays: One*, pxi.
35. Gaston, 'Interview: David Hare', p221.
36. John Bull, *New British Political Dramatists* (London: Macmillan, 1984), p74.
37. Summers, 'David Hare's Drama, 1970–1981', pp583–4.
38. Bull, *New British Political Dramatists*, pp81–2.

3

LIB TAYLOR

In opposition

Hare's response to Thatcherism

The crisis in British theatre in the 1980s, precipitated by a withdrawal of state funding for and a lack of investment in the arts, a failure of the political Left, and a loss of confidence in theatre as a political arena, resulted not in conspicuous critical resistance to Prime Minister Margaret Thatcher's market economy by British playwrights but a nervous retreat from mainstream politics and the 'State of the Nation' play. The tradition of epic dramas which dissected the condition of Britain, so prevalent in the 1970s, was subdued in a theatre either too timid or too financially insecure to challenge the prevailing climate. At the same time, the political shift to the Right and the enterprise economy produced a theatre audience less interested in 'committed dramas' than in theatrical spectacle. As Michael Billington commented, 'What I missed in 1986 were plays that addressed themselves to the particular spirit of our times: most especially, the privatising greed . . . It is almost as if the present is too vile or daunting to be properly encompassed.'[1]

By the beginning of the 1980s David Hare had established himself as one of a group of political playwrights whose work critiqued contemporary Britain from the Left. In *Plenty*, his final major work for the theatre in the 1970s, Hare produced one of the sharpest dramatic critiques of postwar Britain. However, the fundamental shifts in attitudes to the arts triggered by radical political change, which left committed playwrights in a state of disconcerted confusion, equally affected Hare, and his lack of theatrical work in the early 1980s reflects reluctance or inability to engage with the debates which were shaping the emergent Britain and its theatre culture. The first half of the 1980s, when significant historical events such as the Falklands War and the miners' strikes occurred, saw Hare write only *A Map of the World* for theatre. It took until 1985 for him to respond theatrically to Britain's shift to the right, but with *Pravda*, written with Howard Brenton, he launched an excoriating attack on 1980s British society, followed by a stark examination of how political ideology infects personal morality in *The Secret Rapture* in 1988. These two plays, together with *Racing Demon*, Hare's sharp 1990 analysis of political institutions through his study of the Church of England, scrutinise the functioning and legacy of Thatcherism with an insight not apparent elsewhere in British theatre.

The election of Margaret Thatcher's Conservative government on 4 May 1979 opened a new era. What was later dubbed 'Thatcherism' called for a return to the 'traditional values' of Victorian family life. Thatcher's introduction of a free-market economy and promotion of private enterprise fostered individualistic self-interest and avarice, and a denial of societal responsibility. It produced private wealth and public squalor, widening the gap between rich and poor. Throughout the 1980s, the Left struggled to find a voice; amid the dismantling of the Soviet bloc and evident oppression in Communist China, the Labour Party's disunity and a growing confidence in right-wing ideologies conspired to present policies of the Left as outmoded and unworkable. Traditional left-wing discourses lost credibility and struggled to defend union representation, the public services and the Welfare State against the association of individual enterprise with efficiency and modernisation. The Left adopted the Right's agenda, consenting to the values of a market economy, depriving both Parliament and broader public debate of effective opposition. In tacitly accepting the Tory tenet 'There is no alternative', the Left in effect colluded in sustaining the Tory Party's claimed new consensus.

Plenty and *A Map of the World:* shifting ground

Ironically, given Margaret Thatcher's resistance to feminist ideas, the one area of political theatre that flourished in the early 1980s was women's theatre. The late 1970s and 1980s saw women growing in confidence as feminism was assimilated into mainstream attitudes: the endorsement of women's rights by legislation in the 1970s resulted in the recognition of women's contribution to society and the workforce. The 1970s Women's Movement produced a generation of women playwrights, including Pam Gems and Caryl Churchill, whose drama challenged narrow representations of women and promoted equal opportunities. Max Stafford-Clark stated in the mid-1980s, 'Feminism has, without doubt, been the most influential and powerful political movement of my time at the [Royal] Court.'[2] Political drama was displaced on to feminist theatre, challenging male preoccupations in two ways. First, by connecting the politics of gender to class, socialist feminist playwrights were able to analyse the ideologies of the 1980s through the lens of gender politics, which not only allowed them to dissect women's social and economic role but enabled a renewed critique of the broader political scene. Second, feminist playwrights developed more complex representations of women, challenging what they saw as circumscribed depictions of women.

No writer could claim to be unaware of the complexity of gender politics at this point and Hare was no exception. Hare's *Plenty* (1978) was produced just before the Thatcher 'revolution' and it marks a turning point in his theatre writing. It is an exemplary 'State of the Nation' play, but, as Finlay Donesky acknowledges, it 'is the last [Hare] play in which public consensual values define the common moral ground'[3] and, though it is not a play about women's politics, the influence of gender issues can undoubtedly be traced through the work.

As the Callaghan government struggled through the 1978–9 'Winter of Discontent', dogged by industrial disputes and high unemployment, *Plenty*, which opened at the National Theatre on 7 April 1978 in a production directed by Hare himself, looks back on the seventeen years following the Second World War as a decisive period of lost opportunity and the retrenchment of traditional values, which defined Britain until the end of the 1970s. In this context, *Plenty* is a paradigmatic epic drama which uses a historical lens to analyse dissatisfaction with contemporary Britain through the private despair of its central character. But this character is a woman, Susan Traherne, and her dysfunctionality and disaffection in the 1950s and 1960s, following her time during the war in the Special Operations Executive, is presented as both an internalisation of Britain's malaise and a personal response to her own feelings of displacement. For Hare, Susan's depression is representative of Britain in decline, but its expression through her personal sense of dislocation from society chimes with a central tenet of the women's movement: that the Personal is Political. Susan's state of mind echoes the depressive isolation, disjunction and loss defined by women writers in influential 1970s feminist literature like Marilyn French's *The Women's Room* (1978) and Hannah Gavron's *The Captive Wife* (1970).[4] The historical narrative of *Plenty* connects 1978 to the failures which shaped pre-Thatcher Britain, but its central character reflects the discontent which incited contemporary women to promote women's self-determination.

The cyclical construction of *Plenty* begins in 1962 before flashing back to occupied France in 1943. A series of scenes of personal and historical significance are set in the interim, bringing the play back to 1962 before returning again to wartime France in August 1944 for the final scene. This complex historical frame locates the decline of postwar Britain in an inability to build social change into 1950s reconstruction. Simultaneously, it traces the corrosion of Susan's optimism and her personal disintegration. The opening (1962) scene reveals a bare room, the skeleton of a prestigious diplomatic house in Knightsbridge. In these remnants of established grandeur and wealth, Susan, her naked sleeping husband and her friend Alice are an incongruous group, almost inert. In the second scene set in 1943 France, by contrast, Susan is energetic and decisive. The following scenes trace the relationship between these moments and Susan's refusal to assent to the (re)assertion of outmoded public institutions and narrow moral codes. Susan's statement in scene 2 – 'I'm not an agent, I am just a courier'[5] – establishes her role as someone who does not effect change but who is affected by the decisions of others. Susan's resistance does not take the form of public protest, but is expressed as a personal refusal to participate and as individual dissent, often fruitless, which ultimately drives her to debilitated disintegration. She goes from her insistence that she wants 'to move on' (p29) in 1947 to the penultimate scene in a dilapidated Blackpool bed and breakfast in 1962, where she slips into a drug-induced stupor. Finally, she is in a state of utter stasis, completely unable to function.

Hare and his fellow leftist playwrights located blame for failure to effect significant postwar change, not with the Right's status quo, but with the Left's broken promises and inability to sustain effective and radical government. However, in the year following *Plenty*, Margaret Thatcher's Conservative government came to power and introduced policies of fundamental social change which altered the face of Britain, driven not by egalitarianism but by right-wing challenges to traditions and institutions. Thatcher's defiance made the Left's bewildered establishment flounder, unable to confront the erosion of traditional distinctions between Left and Right. The new climate left Hare and his male contemporaries feeling dispossessed of their theatrical voice. By contrast, Caryl Churchill's *Top Girls* (1982), with the self-interested Thatcherite Marlene as its central character, and *Fen* (1983), make links between women and a social underclass to explore exploitation enabled by early 1980s economic policies. It was not until five years after *Plenty* that Hare presented his next play on the London stage, *A Map of the World* (1982), and even this does not confront political change in Britain directly.[6]

A Map of the World focuses on global politics and Third World poverty, critiquing the West's failures in the developing world, and thus Britain's imperial role. Apparently set in Bombay at a UNESCO Conference on International Aid, the play sets up a debate between the right-wing Indian-born novelist Victor Mehta and a young left-wing journalist Stephen Andrews on the West's role in Third World aid. While Mehta asserts the right of Third World states to aspire to the civilisations and values of the old world, Stephen argues passionately for the continuation of aid to further the autonomy of Third World countries. The play comprises rhetorical argument rather than persuasive action and, although Stephen is ultimately killed while demonstrating his commitment to his viewpoint, his active engagement never dispels a suspicion of hypocrisy. Gradually the audience realise that what they are watching is a film within a play, indeed the layers unpeel to reveal that the

film is of a novel, in turn based on a 'real' incident (the incident drama-
tised by *A Map of the World*). This formal metafictionality enables Hare
to engage in abstract debates on truth and fiction and on art and reality,
reinforcing the play's interest in rhetoric rather than the politics of aid. Even
as a theatrical device, the double frame is not convincing, since the formal
interest of the 'film' scenes is vitiated by the play's reliance upon declamatory
speeches rather than 'filmic' action. *A Map of the World* places Hare in new
territory but his concern is primarily with notions of idealism, signalled in
a prefatory quotation from Oscar Wilde, 'A map of the world that does not
include Utopia is not worth glancing at.'[7] Hare's shift in thematic emphasis
matches some of his writing for film and television at this time. *Saigon: Year
of the Cat* (1983), like *A Map of the World*, focuses on post-colonial politics
and it seems that Hare's theatrical critique in the early 1980s was displaced
on to global issues, while his preferred medium became film.

Pravda: politics as grotesque satire

In 1984, Hare was invited to become an Associate Director of the National
Theatre with 'the aim of presenting plays on public subjects',[8] and this
prompted his production of *Pravda: A Fleet Street Comedy*, written with
Howard Brenton, first performed on 2 May 1985 at the National's Olivier
Theatre. This was Hare's first direct critique of 'the greed, cynicism, sloth and
moral gutlessness'[9] that characterised Thatcher's 1980s, addressing questions of freedom of speech, political integrity and corruption, and the self-
serving elite of Britain's class system. The play's theme is the radical changes
in the British press implemented by Rupert Murdoch's News Corporation
in its takeover of the *Sun* and *The Times* newspapers. It analyses the displacement of traditional newspaper personnel by aggressive market-driven
entrepreneurs as a metaphor for the replacement of a reactionary political
order by a new, equally corrupt, unbridled capitalism. It charts the rise of
the South African entrepreneur Lambert Le Roux, a thinly veiled Murdoch,
who acquires newspapers including *The Daily Victory*, the foremost British
broadsheet, an equally thinly veiled version of *The Times*. Placing him at
the centre of the British political milieu, the play reveals the hypocrisy and
bigotry endemic to the press and to the whole ruling class. Simultaneously,
it tracks the career of the hapless Andrew May, a journalist caught up in
a kind of Faustian pact, 'selling his soul' in order to become part of the
Le Roux empire.

Brenton and Hare create a theatrical lampoon similar to their previous
collaboration, *Brassneck* (1973), and the title '*Pravda*', meaning 'truth', is
a sardonic reference to the main Soviet newspaper of the time. Challenging

the prevailing economically driven trend for small-scale new work, the play is a 'comedy of excess', with a cast of over thirty and an inflated theatrical style adopted to satirise the excesses of 1980s capitalism. Similar to Caryl Churchill's *Serious Money* (1987), a satire on the selfishness and greed of stockbrokers in a deregulated market, *Pravda* is indebted to historical theatrical forms, specifically Ben Jonson's grotesque City Comedies. Likewise, Timberlake Wertenbaker, another successful woman playwright in the 1980s, realised her class-based analysis of contemporary capitalism via historical transposition, an eighteenth-century picaresque narrative, in *The Grace of Mary Traverse* (1985). In each play, for Hare and his female playwrighting contemporaries, historical borrowings make possible a critique of contemporary Britain and, with Le Roux, Brenton and Hare create a monster akin to Marlowe's Machiavellian Jew of Malta – brutal, manipulative and audacious. Caricatured figures such as Elliott Fruit-Norton, Leander Scroop and Cliveden Whicker-Baskett ridicule the idiotic and incompetent conformity of the 'fourth estate'. Inter-scenes comprising journalists' questions, newspaper vendors' cries and the direct address of individual characters provide information and seamless shifts from one scene to the next, which emphasise the play's fast pace, the urgency of the issues and the speed of change.

Initially, *Pravda* appears to have similar ambitions to its political theatre predecessors: a desire to expose 'England' as a myth and challenge its entrenched class and imperialist attitudes. It begins at the 'last party of summer'[10] in an idyllic English garden, near the village church and cricket ground, which it exposes as a comfortable, civilised facade for an outmoded, bigoted and ineffective set of governing institutions. However, rather than loading the message with presentiments of dystopian futures or failure to effect political change, Hare and Brenton go on to portray an all-too-successful transformation, but not the utopian revolution envisaged by the Left. Le Roux's brutish and amoral values are as abhorrent as those of the establishment he displaces. His systematic infiltration of Britain's ruling class is achieved with the complicity of his enemies, whose greed, disloyalty and ambition coerce them into Le Roux's web. Every stratum of British tradition – the aristocracy, the Church, a London club, Parliament, royalty, even English cricket – is penetrated by his corruption. But Hare's and Brenton's attack is not only on the odious Le Roux but on the archaic institution he dislodges and on the obsolete Left, whose confused, liberal views make it complicit in its own downfall. Like Thatcher's Conservative government, Le Roux is allowed free rein to implement his policies, which consist of opportunistically feathering his own nest and empowering others to do the same. However, although Le Roux is grotesque and morally inexcusable, he is attractive in comparison to his weak opposition. Rebecca Foley is the only character to stand up to him and, although she is the moral conscience of the play, she is sidelined and powerless. The unprincipled Andrew, championed by Le Roux, who sees him as easy prey, rises quickly to become editor of *The Daily Victory* – but only as long as he is useful. The 'Golden Finger' award for 'Editor of the Year', awarded to Andrew, is the supreme expression of Le Roux's 'two-fingers' attitude to them all and to his adopted country.

In the mid-1980s *Pravda* acted as a kind of prophecy for the newspaper industry, strengthening the interpretation of the play as a commentary on its time. By 1986, when the National Theatre revived the first production, Murdoch was trying to break restrictive union practices in Fleet Street by moving the production of his newspapers to Wapping. A 2006 revival of the play, directed by Jonathan Church for the Chichester Festival, however, begged the question of whether it could stand the test of time, given the fundamental changes in technology and employment that make aspects of the industry as represented in *Pravda* unrecognisable to a twenty-first-century audience.[11] Reviews of the play were as mixed in 2006 as they were for the original performance, with journalists caught between enjoying the satire and feeling threatened by its critical portrayal of the newspaper industry. In 1985, Michael Ratcliffe commented that 'Brenton and Hare are more interested in Lambert's destructive energy than in any sort of debate to match',[12] and critics unanimously praised Anthony Hopkins' chilling 'bull-like'[13] performance as Le Roux. The critics of 2006 were split in their assessment of whether *Pravda* is dated, with Michael Billington commenting on its 'prophetic accuracy about a world in which newspapers have become instruments of corporate business',[14] while Charles Spencer sees it as 'antiquated as a linotype machine',[15] but most acknowledge the enduring fascination of Le Roux even though political contexts have changed. Despite professional journalists' scepticism about the play, both productions were hugely enjoyable, commercial successes. The National revived the first production a year after its première and the Chichester performance contributed significantly to the revival of the Chichester Festival in 2006.[16]

Wrecked Eggs/Bay at Nice: politics and the personal

Pravda was a scathing direct attack on 1980s British politics, but the play does not conform to most of Hare's individual output in either form or subject matter, nor does it provide a model for his future work. Before it, Hare's writing had been largely concerned with how political positions are negotiated in relation to personal morality, and he returned to this preoccupation with the plays written in the latter half of Thatcher's premiership.

On 4 September 1986, the double bill *Bay at Nice* and *Wrecked Eggs* was presented at the National's Cottesloe Theatre, directed by Hare himself. The performances were not as well received as *Pravda* and seem slight in comparison with his other 1980s work. But, although neither play is set in Britain, and there is no overt connection to the British political system, Hare's examination of two contrasting cultures and historical periods is concerned with human relationships shaped by their cultural and political contexts.

The action of *The Bay at Nice*, the more substantial of the two plays, is set in a 1956 Leningrad art gallery to which Valentina Nrovka has been called to authenticate a picture by Matisse – *The Bay at Nice* – willed to the nation by a Russian émigré. Valentina's authority lies in her having been taught by Matisse in France as a young woman. The debates within the play are structured around notions of personal authenticity and moral responsibility. Both Valentina and her daughter Sophia seek to make principled choices in their family life. Sophia wants her mother's approval and financial support to divorce her respected schoolteacher husband, who is an influential member of the Communist Party, in order to marry an unambitious and unattractive elderly sanitation officer. Valentina sacrificed freedom and her artistic career to return to the Soviet Union in the 1920s after the birth of her daughter. For both of them, these difficult decisions enable them to live less comfortable but more committed, decent lives. In contrast, *Wrecked Eggs* is set in contemporary up-state New York, and focuses upon Loelia and Robbie, an affluent couple who are holding a party to commemorate their divorce. Only Grace, a publicity agent they hardly know, turns up. The play has little action, but reflects some of the issues of *The Bay at Nice*. It shows an American society scarcely different from the Soviet Union in its circumscription of personal decisions, but the American dream, in which all the characters are caught, replaces personal authenticity with self-determination. Robbie has changed his name and rejects his father, who was a cold-war spy; Grace is recovering from the latest in a series of abortions and Loelia lacks a sense of obligation to any long-term relationship. Their identity comes from the American work ethic but their lives are rootless and hollow. In both plays, it is the corrosive effect of ideology that defines the shape and scope of personal relationships. In *The Bay at Nice* divorce represents an attempt to retreat into a private life not delineated by the stifling and corrupting demands of public life; in *Wrecked Eggs* the deferral of the couple's divorce for just one day at the end of the play represents an attempt to cultivate qualities of 'Loyalty. Courage. Perseverance' in order to find 'something *more*'[17] in the relationship.

The double bill prefigures *The Secret Rapture*, not only in its concern with how political ideologies infuse personal and familial relationships but also in the profound sense of loss, apparent in *Plenty*, that re-emerges in much of Hare's 1980s theatre work, including *Pravda*. In *The Bay at Nice* Valentina is caught in the émigrée's plight, haunted both by her vibrant past in Paris and by a homeland which no longer even displays her art, while Sophia is disturbed by the impending loss of her children's love and the bleak existence determined by her decisions. In *Wrecked Eggs* the party is a celebration of loss, of the shattered marriage and of the aborted children, the 'wrecked eggs' of the title. All the characters experience feelings of loss endemic to an American dream of self-definition: Robbie denies his father and his past, Grace mourns her unborn children and Loelia regrets her incapacity to sustain a relationship.

The Secret Rapture: public confidence and private despair

Loss and bereavement also permeate *The Secret Rapture*. Rather than adopting the epic style of *Pravda*, the play is a chamber piece which returns Hare to exploring how ideologies of self-interest and greed infect familial relationships and personal morality. The play begins and ends with death, but the loss is not only for Robert and Isobel Glass themselves but for the kinder and more tolerant values they represent and the world they inhabited. This is not nostalgia for a class-ridden and bigoted England of *Pravda*, nor for an idyllic England of cricket and cream teas; it does not call for a return to 1960s and 1970s liberalism, but it does mourn the passing of a gentler, more caring society. Written in 1988, a year after Thatcher's Conservative Party was returned to power for a third term, *The Secret Rapture* is Hare's most direct theatrical response to Thatcherism to date. It looks back to *Pravda* in its concern with a disappearing England but it also looks forward to *Racing Demon* in its consideration of the efficacy of goodness.

The Secret Rapture was first performed on 4 October 1988 in the National Theatre's Lyttelton auditorium, directed by Howard Davies, and received almost unanimous critical acclaim. The critics, though sometimes perplexed by the play's ending, welcomed its complex engagement with contemporary debates. It received a less enthusiastic reception in New York in a new production directed by Hare in 1989, resulting in a very short run on Broadway. Though the play is concerned with the private and personal world, it is not straightforwardly naturalistic. The audience is asked to read the characters not only through their psychologies but also through their allegorical significance. Opposing reactions to 1980s ideologies structure the play, embodied in the responses of Marion French, a Conservative MP, and her younger sister, Isobel Glass, a graphic designer, to the death of their liberal-minded, antiquarian bookseller father, Robert Glass. The play begins at Robert's deathbed. Isobel, who helped nurse her father through his final illness, watches quietly while Marion searches for a valuable ring she gave her father as a mark of her love, and which she wants to retrieve before Robert's second wife seizes it. This encounter exemplifies the difference between the two sisters: while Isobel's reaction to Robert's illness was to care for him, Marion only knew how to express her love by presenting him with the expensive (and useless) ring. Through the relationship between the sisters, Hare scrutinises the impact of Thatcherism's ideological precepts upon private and personal interactions.

Isobel and Marion have quite distinct approaches to their daily lives and social responsibilities: Isobel's self-effacing kindness and altruism contrast with Marion's brisk self-interest. Their differences are exposed primarily in their attitude towards Robert's second wife, Katherine, a parasitic alcoholic incapable of sustaining her own life or taking responsibility for her actions. Katherine was the indulged companion of Robert's old age, and on his death she becomes dependent upon his daughters emotionally and materially. A product of the times and the legacy of the liberalism of the 1960s and 1970s, her damaged and destructive presence challenges both Isobel's compassion and Marion's espousal of self-reliance. Attempts to meet Katherine's needs ultimately destroy Isobel's business, which she runs with her partner Irwin Posner, under stress from a 'benign' takeover by Tom, Marion's Christian husband, whose promised support for unwanted expansion becomes an asset-stripping exercise.

Isobel's decency is her father's legacy and reflects a Britain before Thatcherism licensed aggressive self-interest. Marion, by contrast, is fully convinced that 'There's money to be made' and that it is irresponsible not to 'grab some dough for yourself'. She is helping 'drive the gravy train'[18] of a government founded on individualism and the market – or self-interest and greed. Yet Hare's critique eschews easy binary oppositions of good and evil. Undoubtedly Isobel is a more empathetic character than Marion, but she is destroyed by the very people she seeks to support – Irwin and Katherine. Marion's embrace of Thatcherite ideals gives her the power to act and to effect change, but it leaves her bruised, confused and bereft. The mood of loss which pervades the play is sharpened at the end, as Marion mourns not only her dead sister, but her own desperate isolation that not even Tom's Christianity can compensate for: 'I can't interpret what people feel . . . I've stood at the side. Just watching. It's made me angry' (p82). Ineffective and flawed as Isobel's and her father's ideals might have been, they were compassionate and sensitive to human feeling. Their vitality and warmth is far more engaging than Marion's desolate detachment, despite her political success. Marion ends the play restoring her father's house to 'an English sitting *room'*, but without Isobel and Robert it is no more than 'a perfect imitation of life' (p83).

Above all, *The Secret Rapture* debates the place of goodness in a secular society impelled more by characters like Le Roux, grotesque and contemptible, than Isobel's loyalty and integrity. Isobel represents the opposite of *Pravda*'s monster; her strong moral code and sense of personal responsibility are devoid of self-interest, guile or ideology. They spring from neither religious nor political dogma, but rather from her humanity and dependability. Beside Isobel's decency and integrity, Tom's Christianity and Marion's public service look devious and unprincipled. Isobel's convictions and codes of behaviour become politicised by their encounter with Marion's Tory rhetoric, delineating Marion's actions as calculatingly expedient. But, while they might disarm Marion, they never derail her and even at the end of the play the redemptive potential of Isobel's sacrifice remains uncertain.

Redemptive women

Isobel continues a line of female characters in Hare's work, including Susan from *Plenty*, Peggy from *A Map of the World* and Rebecca from *Pravda*, who, while invested with moral authority, lack agency. The critical effect of Isobel's goodness has been a matter of disagreement among critics. Michael Billington asks: 'Does she embody a supine English tolerance that allows itself to be exploited? Is she a shining example of integrity? Or is she a martyr half in love with easeful death?'[19] The title '*The Secret Rapture*' refers to a nun's desired union with Christ at the point of death and Anne Northof extends the notion of Christian allegory by suggesting that Isobel evokes the Virgin Mary as she dons a large blue raincoat in the final scene before leaving the room in bare feet.[20] For Northof, Isobel is the archetypal Christian martyr: 'she takes a vow to commit herself to caring for Katherine; she is betrayed by those closest to her; and she is finally murdered when she will not recant.'[21] Hare defined the play as a tragedy, with Isobel's goodness as the 'fatal flaw'.[22] Her refusal to be dishonest in her relationship with Irwin or compromise in her relationship to Katherine results in her death. There is no space for Isobel's anachronistic moral decency in a world that correlates genuine feeling with weakness and abnegates responsibilities of care. Isobel's goodness only causes resentment from Marion – 'You make me feel as if I'm always in the wrong . . . Oh, yes, well, we can't all be perfect. We do try' (p6) – and Katherine accuses her of hypocrisy: 'The others don't pretend. But you – it's all this kindness and tolerance and decency' (pp15–16).

The sacrifice of Susan Traherne can look equally futile. In postwar Britain, women, empowered by their essential employment during the Second World

War, were frustrated by a peace which reinstated traditional female roles. Although Susan is in no way a dependent woman, the sense of purpose the war gave her cannot be sustained once it is over. Susan challenges the 1950s single-woman stereotype: she is sexually active, she desires parenthood independent of an involved father, she can work independently in responsible jobs, but in a conservative postwar Britain she cannot sustain a career and her personal life is unfulfilling. Critics tend to characterise her behaviour as 'mad' and indeed Mick, her lover, states, 'She is actually mad' (p48) just before she shoots at him. Susan's 'insanity' can be connected to a history of women's dissent in which resistance and refusal are defined as 'madness', and in 1978 women in the audience were becoming familiar with these debates.[23] Nevertheless, Susan is not a positive role model and she ends up surrendering to her fantasies. *A Map of the World*'s view of women is no more positive, with Peggy Whitton doing little more than offering herself as the prize to whoever wins the debate. Rebecca, in *Pravda*, might resist Thatcherite self-interest and embody the voice of Hare's and Brenton's conscience but this does not endow her with power, and ultimately she is helplessly marginalised.

Hare has been criticised for idealising women as ciphers for his moral position, and in 2004 he wrote that some 1970s feminists were 'dismayed that at a moment when it was important to hear from a batch of talented women playwrights, a conspicuous line of roles for women was, inconveniently, being written by a man and performed with relish by a series of great feminist actors'.[24] Hare's theatre has provided some rare chances of substantial roles for female performers, generated in part by his abiding interest in the relationship of the personal to broader cultural and political landscapes. But, despite Isobel's and Susan's centrality to Hare's work, neither they nor Rebecca offer a positive role model for 1980s women seeking representations that dispelled outmoded stereotypes. Unlike Wertenbaker and Churchill, Hare never fully succeeds in integrating a gender critique into his analysis of 1980s Thatcherism.

Racing Demon: the politics of institutions

No examination of Hare's response to Thatcherism would be complete without some consideration of *Racing Demon*, which opened on 1 February 1990, in the National's Cottesloe Theatre, directed by Richard Eyre. A fuller analysis of the play is to be found elsewhere in this book, but it is worth noting here that, in *Racing Demon*, written close to the time when Margaret Thatcher was unseated as Conservative leader, Hare developed a direct and sharply analytical response to her politics, examining Thatcherism via the metaphor of the Anglican Church. The play marks the beginning of a major new project for Hare, the trilogy examining the British institutions of the Church, the Law and Politics, but *Racing Demon* was produced nine months before Thatcher's resignation and is therefore also Hare's final portrayal of Thatcher's Britain. Though the play is a model for the trilogy in its exploration of the private and personal ethics governing public institutions, it is also a device for analysing Thatcher's legacy in the light of her decline through Poll Tax riots, social unrest, high inflation and party disunity.

Ostensibly about Anglicanism, *Racing Demon* explores the conflict between liberalism and right-wing fundamentalism within the Church as metonymic of the broader British landscape. Bound to the State constitutionally, the Church of England is not only circumscribed by the State but functions as its instrument, imbricated in its hierarchies, ideologies and aspirations. Tensions within that relationship, as the Church struggles to find its role in a modern secular society, exacerbated by anxiety over declining church attendance and divisions over women priests and homosexuality, form the background to *Racing Demon*. Throughout her premiership, discord between Thatcher's government and Archbishop Robert Runcie's Church of England was palpable, provoked by the Church's failure to endorse Britain's invasion of the Falkland Islands in 1982 and fuelled by the Church effectively taking on the job of opposition to government at a time when the Labour Party was too embattled to fulfil the role. The Church's concern with social welfare, evident in the controversial *Faith in the City* report on urban poverty,[25] led to criticism of Thatcher's government and provoked irritation in both government and Church traditionalists. In this context, the Church was fertile material for Hare's examination of the 'State of the Nation'.

The play revolves around conflict between the evangelical Reverend Tony Ferris and the tolerant Reverend Lionel Espy, curate and vicar respectively of a socially deprived south London parish. Tony represents the new Right, a new broom sweeping away inefficiency and ushering in accountability whilst seeing the future of the Church as a high-street commodity to be advertised on a hoarding. Lionel represents the old Left, decent but ineffective. Hare uses the Church to analyse political structures through an institution which, though allied to government, is dependent on its own traditions, legislation, alignments and constitution. While Hare's sympathies lie more with Lionel's humility than Tony's brazen confidence, he does not create in Tony an amoral figure like Le Roux, or a self-interested character like Marion. In *Racing Demon*, Hare revisits a key issue explored in *The Secret Rapture* – the efficacy and viability of goodness. Like Isobel, Lionel is politically naive and he refuses to compromise or defend himself against his detractors until ultimately he is made a scapegoat by the Church for its failures. But he is impotent and cold, and his corner is fought by Frances Parnell, another woman in whom Hare invests moral authority but who is a more positive role model than either Isobel or Rebecca and occupies Hare's apparent position as an agnostic outsider. She asks the questions, and she is the final character on stage at the end of the play when her evocation of soaring skywards in an aeroplane strikes the only optimistic note.

In a very inauspicious time for Britain, Hare's plays of the latter half of the 1980s reconnect with the tradition of the 'State of the Nation' play, while continuing to emphasise the linkage of the personal with the political. But across his work of this period a strong critique of British life in the 1980s is articulated as much through the feelings of loss that are present in the plays as through the sharp political analysis of institutions and events.

NOTES

1. Michael Billington, *Guardian*, 1 December 1989, cited in Vera Gottlieb, 'Thatcher's Theatre – or, After *Equus*', *New Theatre Quarterly* 6, 14 (May 1988), p101.
2. Max Stafford-Clark (interviewed by Tony Dunn), '"A Programme for the Progressive Conscience": The Royal Court in the "Eighties"', *New Theatre Quarterly* 1, 2 (May 1985), p138.
3. Finlay Donesky, *David Hare: Moral and Historical Perspectives* (Westport, CT: Greenwood Press, 1996), p64.
4. Marilyn French, *The Women's Room* (London: André Deutsch, 1978); Hannah Gavron, *The Captive Wife* (Harmondsworth: Penguin, 1970).
5. David Hare, *Plenty* (London: Faber, 1978), p19; all subsequent quotations are taken from this edition.
6. *A Map of the World* was first presented in 1982 at the Adelaide Theatre Festival, Australia; it did not open at the National Theatre in London until 20 January 1983.
7. David Hare, *A Map of the World* (London: Faber, 1982), Preface.
8. Richard Boon, 'Hare on Hare', in *About Hare: The Playwright and the Work* (London: Faber, 2003), p106.
9. Benedict Nightingale, *New Statesman*, 10 May 1985, in *London Theatre Record* 5, 9 (1985), p420.
10. Howard Brenton and David Hare, *Pravda* (London: Methuen, 1985), Act 1, scene 1, p. 9.
11. A co-production between Chichester Festival and Birmingham Repertory Theatre Company, which opened on 13 September 2006.
12. Michael Ratcliffe, *Observer*, 5 May 1985, in *Theatre Record* 5, 9 (1985), p415.
13. Michael Billington, *Guardian*, 3 May 1985, in *Theatre Record* 5, 9 (1985), p418.
14. Michael Billington, *Guardian*, 14 September 2006, in *Theatre Record*, 26, 19 (2006), p1040.
15. Charles Spencer, *Daily Telegraph*, 14 September 2006, in *Theatre Record* 26, 19 (2006), p1041.
16. Audience figures at Chichester rose by more than a third in 2006.

17. David Hare, *The Bay at Nice/Wrecked Eggs* (London: Faber, 1986), p93.
18. David Hare, *The Secret Rapture* (London: Faber, 1988), p41. All subsequent quotations are taken from this edition.
19. Michael Billington, *Guardian*, 5 October 1988, in *Theatre Record* 8, 20 (1988), p1388.
20. See Anne Northof, 'Virtuous Women', in Hersh Zeifman (ed.), *David Hare: A Casebook* (New York: Garland, 1994), p188.
21. *Ibid.*
22. Kathleen Tynan, 'Interview', quoted in Donesky, *David Hare*, p113.
23. See Sandra M. Gilbert and Susan Gubar, *The Madwoman in the Attic: The Woman Writer and the Nineteenth-Century Literary Imagination* (New Haven: Yale University Press, 1979).
24. David Hare, 'Obedience, Struggle and Revolt', in *Obedience, Struggle and Revolt: Lectures on Theatre* (London: Faber, 2005), p26.
25. In 1985, the report *Faith in the City: A Call to Action by Church and Nation* was published by the Archbishop of Canterbury's Commission on Urban Priority Areas.

4

LES WADE

Hare's trilogy at the National
Private moralities and the common good

David Hare's trilogy of plays – *Racing Demon* (1990), *Murmuring Judges* (1991) and *The Absence of War* (1993)[1] – comprise a mid-career capstone, the culminating expression of the writer's abiding interest in private conduct and the public weal. Sweeping in scope, dialectical in tone, these works confirm Hare as one of Britain's most accomplished playwrights. If one, however, considers the drama that would soon follow on the English stage – the volatile, terse and often obscene theatre of Ravenhill, Kane, Crimp, Penhall et al. – Hare can appear rather conventional, the established writer of what Martin McDonough would describe as a 'dull and political and lecture-y' kind of drama.[2] While comparison between Hare's work and that of the 'in-yer-face' writers reveals vast differences in style, Hare's trilogy ventures into a moral space that a dramatist such as Ravenhill might recognise and affirm. Hare's trilogy exposes a collapse in Britain's national life in the last decade of the millennium. And, like the writers of Ravenhill's generation, he interrogates the nature (and possibility) of ethical action in this world adrift.

An effort that spanned over five years in research, writing and production, Hare's trilogy premièred at the Royal National Theatre between 1990 and 1993. Hare had early in his career explored the intersection of individuals and institutions, in works such as *Slag*, *The Great Exhibition* and *Teeth 'n' Smiles*. With the trilogy he returned to an examination of British institutions; these plays offer complex depictions of three principal arenas of English social life: the Church, Law and Politics. Christopher Innes credits Hare's trilogy for helping the National Theatre finally realise its intended mission, as a 'platform for national debate'.[3] Hare's plays, however, offer less reason for celebration than concern, for they reveal a nation in troubled health, with institutions mired in entropy and empty ceremony.

According to Ravenhill, 'Hare and the rest knew in the Seventies what they were against. Now nobody knows and nobody cares.'[4] Ravenhill's comment indicates not just a shift in British theatre; it recognises the profound changes that the 1980s and 1990s brought to British culture. Described as a post-ideological age, this time witnessed the ascendance of liberal democracy, the rise of global capitalism and the collapse of socialist vision. Ravenhill's often-cited passage in *Shopping and Fucking* underscores the demise of 'big stories' that once governed modern life, including 'The Journey to Enlightenment. The March of Socialism'.[5] The cultural situation Ravenhill identifies presented a dilemma for Britain's political playwrights. Demoralised by years of Conservative rule, many writers argued for political change but had come to question the viability of socialist critique. Rather than exhibiting any certitude, Hare's plays at this time demonstrate a political agnosticism. The trilogy confronted a considerable challenge – how to decry the corrosive effects of a Conservative hegemony (and the failings of British institutions) without appeal to ideology or political programme; how to secure the common good?

Richard Eyre has observed that writers such as Trevor Griffiths and Howard Brenton were 'robbed of their subject by the collapse of Socialism'.[6] Hare, conversely, has continued to find voice and audience, by exploring different aspects of the post-ideology dilemma. As most scholars attest, Hare has never operated as a didactic dramatist, and his works have never been 'political' in a pedagogical or programmatic manner. His memorable speech at Cambridge University signalled a break with strident political drama and its 'demeaning repetition of slogans'.[7] What Hare's career demonstrates is a turn from the broad critique of British culture to a more studied investigation of private moralities. In the plays preceding the trilogy (*The Bay at Nice*, *Wrecked Eggs* and *The Secret Rapture*), and in the trilogy itself, Hare's focus less concerns any structural overhaul than individual lives and actions; his theme is not revolution but responsibility.

Many critics have viewed this shift in Hare's writing as reactionary and regard Hare as a middle-class liberal, disillusioned by the demise of the postwar Welfare State. For such critics Hare – unlike Brenton, McGrath and Griffiths – has turned his back on collectivist politics and has retreated to interior emotion and a vague universalist humanism. That his plays would find such success at the National Theatre only corroborates Howard Barker's view of the theatre as the home of the 'liberal humanist propaganda ministry'.[8]

While I agree that Hare is no revolutionary, his work may indicate more than a mournful, backward-looking orientation. I suggest that Hare's focus in the 1980s, and consequently his outlook in the trilogy, may exhibit a progressive aspect, an outlook that recognises the failings of ideology and the need for new models of interpersonal relations. It may be that Hare's hope for political change involves a radical rethinking of the self and its moral imperatives.

Instead of highlighting Hare's writing as the expression of a failed post-war idealism, I wish to explore his work as a participant in a contemporary current of thought – the ethical turn – which emerged in philosophical writing in the 1980s and gained stature in the 1990s. This conceptualisation of ethics received attention through the works of many critical thinkers – such as Lyotard, Levinas, Derrida and Nancy. I obviously do not contend that Hare has been a student of continental philosophy; I rather suggest that his dramatic imagination and this conception of ethical understanding exhibit illuminating parallels, as both emerged as reactions to dominant political discourses and totalising world-views. In short, both explore the moral dimensions of subjects with no ontological safeguard, with no recourse to ideological assurance. Situating Hare's work in this context allows one to view him less as a reactionary than as a critical seeker, in sympathy with the ethical imagination of the times.

The ethical turn stands on the belief that the Western intellectual tradition has reached a limit point, that it must confront its inability to deliver any kind of full knowledge or ultimate teleology. According to Madison and Fairbairn, ethical investigation has 'clearly displaced earlier, more traditional concerns over epistemological issues' and has shifted focus to 'the realm of human *praxis*'.[9] This trend is of particular relevance to Hare, who has declared his interest in 'the intractability of goodness',[10] for it asserts, as Madison and Fairbairn argue, that 'the question of the *good* has pre-empted that of the *true*'.

Zygmunt Bauman's *Postmodern Ethics* stands as one of the earliest scholarly explications of this critical movement, and the work's publication in 1993 interestingly coincides with the staging of Hare's trilogy.[11] Bauman's discussion advances several key critical points concerning moral activity in a post-ideological age. Bauman stresses that rationalist attempts to universalise ethical experience must be discontinued (modernist investment in reason has led to oppression and genocide). Bauman also asserts that morality can no longer appeal to any transcendent or foundational authority. Drawing upon the thinking of Emmanuel Levinas, Bauman contends that the individual's only recourse is to commit to a moral orientation that appears in the subject's very becoming; that is, the moral impulse must be recognised as a kind of structural disposition (between self and other) that precedes any particular identity trait or communal affiliation. Bauman writes: 'one must assume that moral responsibility – being *for* the Other before one can be *with* the Other – is the first reality of the self, a starting point rather than a product of society'.[12] Moral action thus has nothing to do with external codes, political platforms, or systems of ethical conduct; it cannot be compelled from the outside. It is a rudimentary relation between self and other. This conception of the moral self offers no clear path to 'just' behaviour, and decision-making therefore cannot escape ambiguity. The kind of moral activity here advocated admits the messiness of human relations and the never-ending effort to re-administer acts of moral responsibility, in every new moment and every new encounter.

In assessing the importance of Hare's trilogy, Duncan Wu writes: 'No other work pinpoints Hare's concerns as a dramatist more accurately than the trilogy of plays composed between 1987 and 1993. By any standard it is a remarkable achievement.'[13] While his preceding plays had been smaller in scope, *Racing Demon, Murmuring Judges* and *The Absence of War* return Hare to the more expansive frames of his earlier writing. The plays reveal larger casts, an intricate and cinematic scenic structure, inventive devices of direct address. Nonetheless, despite the broader institutional contexts, these plays continue Hare's fascination with individual lives and moral decisions. The strategy parallels what Peter Buse discerns in the dramaturgy of Raven-hill, a concern with 'micro-politics' that centres on face-to-face encounters.[14]

Racing Demon sets the tone for the trilogy and establishes the ethical questioning that would thread throughout these plays. In *Asking Around*, Hare recounts driving in the summer of 1987 to the General Synod of the Church of England 'with no other motive but curiosity' and the 'vague suspicion that priests pretending to be politicians might present . . . an entertaining spectacle'.[15] Hare admits to finding much to satirise, but he dismisses any suggestion that his intent was parody. He writes: 'I wanted to put [the priests] before the public as examples of people whose way of life was genuinely valuable. Anyone who comes at the modern world from a different angle has my vote.'[16]

What provoked Hare's interest in the Church was its ability to assert an alternative or dissenting voice, in face of the Thatcher hegemony and the demoralised Left. During the 1980s the Church of England had in at least two highly public incidents set itself at odds with the Conservative government – in refusing to sanction British aggression in the Falkland Islands, and in publishing the report *Faith in the City*, which documented the plight of the inner-city poor (and by extension criticised Tory social policy). However, it was perhaps the performance of individual priests in the inner-city churches that most affected Hare's investigation of goodness. The playwright found himself astonished at the care and compassion these individuals bestowed upon their churches. In that many of these clerics did not put great emphasis on theology – some were, in fact, quite at ease in working in a post-Christian context[17] – such individuals modelled a kind of postmodern ethics that resisted system in favour of personal outreach and responsibility. Hare writes: 'their primary interest was not in ideology, nor, even less, in allocating blame. They just wanted to bandage wounds. Into the vacuum created by society's indifference, they were pouring as much love and practical help as they could.'[18]

Although Hare has at times expressed salutary opinions about the Church of England, *Racing Demon* offers little evidence of the Church's social efficacy. Beset with flagging attendance, stifling bureaucracy, and an increasingly secular (and multicultural) general population, the Church appears as an institution approaching a point of irrelevancy. The Bishop of Southwark serves as the embodiment of ecclesiastical authority, an individual concerned chiefly with power and the maintenance of tradition. He is often shown in High Church attire, inhabiting a kind of regal realm. He acts as the principal dramatic impetus in the play and seeks to remove Lionel, a priest experiencing spiritual doubt and emotional withdrawal, from his clerical charge.

Hare explores the difficult nature of ethical outreach through his depiction of inner-city clerics, who attempt to do good in a climate of government cutbacks, closed social programmes and prevailing conservative rule. The ministry team includes a trio of established friends: Lionel Espy, a middle-aged priest who favours social work over sacrament; Harry Henderson, a musically gifted priest who closets his gay identity; and Donald 'Streaky' Bacon, an egregious individual who espouses a free-spirited theology. The young priest Tony Ferris joins this group and incites a rift in the ranks, as he espouses a fundamentalist, belief-centred outlook.

An early scene inaugurates a pivotal debate between Lionel and Tony, as Lionel seeks to counsel Stella, a Jamaican immigrant who has suffered spousal abuse. Lionel patiently listens to Stella's story, then he offers a short and simple prayer. When Stella asks if that will help, Lionel responds: 'I don't know if God'll help you. But now you do have a friend. You have me' (p13). Tony overhears this exchange, and when Stella departs he asks Lionel why he did not tell her about Christ. Lionel chafes under Tony's interrogation and declares that 'Stella's not a case. She's a person' (p14). When Tony then asks what they, as priests, have in common, Lionel does not emphasise doctrine but responds, 'A desire to help people' (p21).

These opposing models of pastoral care embody differing attitudes toward moral authority. In a conversation with Southwark, Lionel relates: 'Our job is mainly to learn. From ordinary, working people. We should try to understand and serve them' (p3). Lionel understands that his primary duty involves care and compassion, and, in the terms of postmodern ethics, he subordinates himself before the other. He dismisses the evangelical element of his role, likening it to the tactics of salesmen. Tony, contrarily, premises his ministry on foundational authority. He points to the spiritual vacuum in contemporary society and advocates a commitment to commandment and transcendent, supernatural power. This stance inclines Tony to adversarial postures, as when he confronts Stella's abusive husband and assumes an imperative stand: 'Come here. I am speaking to you. Listen!' (p27). Tony summarily physically attacks Stella's husband, acting out his belief that Christ didn't bring peace but a sword.

Hare is clearly suspicious of Tony's ideological certitude, along with his willingness to embrace a market ethos in church administration. Yet he does not give any character an uncomplicated depiction. He reveals 'Streaky' Bacon as a rather innocuous free spirit, whose theology involves flowers and sunshine. Empathy may go to Lionel, who ultimately does lose his position (though he threatens to bring the clerical union to his defence). Yet none of the play's characters could be considered wholly positive models. Lionel visits shut-ins, runs programmes and so on, but he is estranged from his daughter. His marriage has lost all intimacy. Some critics have regarded Frances, a young woman who befriends Lionel, as the moral conscience of the play. She warns Lionel of the Bishop's designs and comforts him when his wife experiences a stroke. Coming from a church family, she has renounced her faith, though she retains a commitment to charitable outreach. The play concludes with her ascent on a plane, leaving for the Third World as a non-believing missionary. Her departure, however, seems more like an escape than a purposeful expression of social compassion.

Carol Homden has noted that *Racing Demon* exhibits an interrogative tone;[19] the play opens with a questioning prayer. The play indeed conveys a sense of frustration and yearning. Southwark relates that the Church admits 'a thousand different views' (p3) and contends that a priest's central duty is to administer the sacrament, 'to put on a show' (p4). Lionel nevertheless expresses the conviction that the Church can still do good. He recognises the intense need for something to countervail the materialist individualism of a secular and non-ideological world. Innumerable factors interfere with personal ethical outreach – pride, doubt, overwork, fatigue – nonetheless, such is the difficult, ambiguous labour of ethical relations, to act without assurance, without a fully explanatory world-view.

If Hare 'found his politics' in the writing of *Racing Demon*, his views come very close to a religious outlook. Hare has often acknowledged the spiritual themes in his work; he notes he 'wasn't remotely surprised' when *Wetherby* won religious awards.[20] Hare has, moreover, expressed interest in matters of the soul, being 'drawn more and more to feeling that there's something which isn't just what we're conditioned by'.[21]

This aspect of Hare's work aligns him with contemporary ethical theorists, many of whom have introduced religious aspects into their writing: Levinas and Derrida (Judaism); Lyotard, Eagleton, Badiou and Zisek (Christianity).

Such thinkers do not profess faith in any religious institution, nor do they appeal to the revelation or metaphysics of a supreme being. They employ religious images and conceptions to construct new models of ethical relations, models that demonstrate non-exploitative encounter. Any reference to the soul, therefore, need not introduce any unearthly realm; the term instead signifies an aspect of human experience, an agency that cannot be fully explained or determined by contextual forces. Bauman exhibits such religious tropes in his postmodern interpretation of a saint as one who does good beyond the injunction of doctrine or command; saints are thus '*unique* people, people who do things other people shirk – being too afraid, or too weak, or too selfish to do them' (p52).

As in the work of Badiou and Zisek,[22] who appeal to the writings of St Paul and express hope for a transforming historical moment (similar to the world-changing event of early Christianity), Hare reveals fascination with religious structures and outlooks that challenge political orthodoxy. In a lecture at Westminster Cathedral in 1996, he observed that the Church's 'determining values are in fact radically different from those of the rest of society'.[23] He identifies the transformational aspects of the Christian narrative: 'Christ was incontestably a man who preached the idea that one day everything will be reversed.'[24] Hare admits to being drawn in by the social message of the gospel – Christ's 'platform of redistributive justice' – but he distances himself from Christianity whenever believers start talking about a heavenly world to come. What Hare seems to desire is a daily practice of egalitarian saints, of other-directed individuals who perform acts of goodness without creed or catechism.

Informing the trilogy is Hare's animus towards the 'ideological prima donnas . . . dancing on the top of society' who remain insulated from the effects of their entrepreneurial policies; Hare wishes to focus attention on those beneath them, 'the people who do the dirty work', who 'mop up'.[25] In the second play of the trilogy, *Murmuring Judges*, Hare turns his attention to the English legal system. The work demonstrates the operation of the judicial system on three different institutional levels: the Bar, the police force and the penal system. What the play reveals is a sense of institutional disconnection, of systematic injustice that often leads to the 'mashing' of those caught in the cogs. As in *Racing Demon*, Hare investigates how individuals working within a dysfunctional apparatus envision goodness and maintain ethical sensitivity.

In many respects the order of lawyers and judges in the play corresponds to the figures of ecclesiastical authority in *Racing Demon*. The play shows lawyers, judges and politicians maintaining a kind of antiquated fraternity, a professional filiation undergirded by class privilege, Oxbridge education and shared aesthetic taste. The play's principal character is Irina Platt, an aspiring young lawyer from Antigua, who joins the firm of Sir Peter Edgecombe and immediately finds herself challenged by the profession's unspoken patriarchal conventions. Early in the play Sir Peter jokes about Irina's callowness, how she wore a green dress her first day in court and distempered a senior judge (p6). As this instance attests, *Murmuring Judges* reveals the legal world as an archaic system of paternal privilege and protocol, whose ceremonial wigs and robes mask a fundamental want of social awareness and concern.

Irina's race and gender mark her as an outsider, and she empathises with a young Irish labourer, Gerard McKinnon, who receives a sentence of five years in prison for assisting in a robbery. As Irina learns more of the case, she is moved by Gerard's plight – he's the father of two young children – and understands that Gerard is the victim of an anti-Irish bias on the part of the judiciary. She moreover suspects that his conviction involved some kind of illicit collusion between the arresting officer and the other individuals who participated in the crime.

The key question of *Murmuring Judges* involves issues of moral responsibility, the difficult and clouded situation of acting in an ethical manner. Amid the confusion of the police station, justice is seen as a kind of abstraction, far from the insufferable, day-to-day activities of the officers. Within this context Hare establishes a tension between Barry Hopper, Gerard's arresting officer, who receives a promotion for the arrest, and Sandra Bingham, a young, studious woman who, like her father, has chosen law enforcement as a career. Sandra becomes convinced that Barry planted evidence in the case and manipulated Gerard's accomplices (who had served Barry before as informants). A revealing debate ensues when these characters voice their differing opinions on the proper proportion of idealism and pragmatics. Barry defends a hard-knuckled attitude that allows for the compromise of rights and procedures. Sandra voices her opposition. She aligns with Irina in the play; the two women function in twin fashion, as individuals of conscience, who come to the call of responsibility over expediency.

The fundamental theme of *Murmuring Judges* – the role of law in the administration of justice – draws Hare into one of the primary concerns of postmodern ethics; that is, the relation between social law and individual singularity. For thinkers such as Levinas and Derrida, the individual should always be prized above the law, honoured as other – in his or her particularity.[26] While conventional legal and moral thinking has sought rational, universalist principles that can apply impartially in all cases, these thinkers see such an application as a kind of violence, a stripping of the other's alterity. For Derrida, justice cannot issue from a fixed system but should be recalculated in every moment of decision. These thinkers admit the insoluble dilemma of this view, given that resources are finite and that obligation cannot be directed to all individuals at all times. However, they assert the face-to-face obligation toward the other as the touchstone of any ethical relation (and the rudiment for any legal codification). Recognition of the singularity of the other should thus precede and inform any assertion of law.

Murmuring Judges demonstrates that administering the law is nothing if not a difficult and ambiguous undertaking. While Hare references no religious matter in the play, Irina functions as one of Hare's secular saints; she works to assure that the legal system has not failed in its ruling and tries to enlist Sandra in her prosecution of police malfeasance. Yet, her commitment to Gerard is a moral one. She visits him in his prison cell; she comes to him finally, not as a lawyer, but as a friend. And her actions do produce change. We learn that Gerard has begun reading about Irish history and may be radicalised in the process. And at the end, Irina's importuning leads Sandra to her own moral decision; the play concludes with Sandra asking to speak to the Chief Superintendent, suggesting that she will give testimony on Gerard's behalf.

Were one to order the plays of the trilogy on the basis of thematic development, an argument could be made for viewing *The Absence of War* first, as this piece establishes in clear terms the demise of socialist politics. In some sense, *The Absence of War* sets forth the problematic context that the other two plays seek to redress. The play draws its inspiration from the actual 1992 campaign of Labour leader Neil Kinnock, who allowed the playwright insider access to the campaign's planning sessions. Though the play gives a fictionalised account, it incisively chronicles Labour's inability to mobilise public sentiment, to enunciate its vision and values in any compelling manner.

The Absence of War begins with the public memorial service for the war dead staged before the Cenotaph. The event summons a memory of the nation bound by common sacrifice and mutual purpose. Many commentators have indicated the strong nostalgia Hare holds for the Second World War. Hare himself acknowledges this sentiment in *Writing Left-Handed*: 'it makes me sad to think that mine may be the last generation to care about this extraordinary time in English history'.[27] While Hare looks back fondly to this transformational time in English history, when the Labour Party rose to reorder government policy and British social life, the play's opening reveals the present-day party in an impoverished light, in a state of fracture and fatigue, a ghost of its former self.

The Absence of War depicts the Labour Party in a state of ideological confusion and lost vitality. The problems of the party symbolically coalesce in the person of George Jones, the Labour Party leader, who can be 'dynamite' in person yet fails on the public stage 'to come across' (p4). George's team of advisors brings in a new publicity advisor, Lindsay Fontaine, who comes from the world of advertisement and 'packaging experts' (p7). Her hiring serves as a tacit acknowledgement that the party needs an updating of image and message. She reports that seventy per cent of the populace believes that 'the Labour Party no longer stands for anything distinctive' (p28). The campaign team understands in a somewhat desperate way that something must be done to turn the tide of Tory dominance.

The title of the play brings with it an implicit question – in that wartime conditions can draw the nation together in common purpose, what might hold individuals together in 'the absence of war'? This question applies as well to the Labour Party in this time of ideological fracture. George remarks that the Tories experience strong cohesion, united by greed: 'money's a simple master' (p18). George views his own divided party with regret. He laments the decline of the unions, the old times he experienced growing up in the working-class politics of south London. He and his colleagues find themselves unable to relate to the general public and their own party members.

The sudden call for an election by the Conservative Prime Minister stirs long-restrained hope that Labour might rebound and see a new day. Lindsay challenges Oliver, George's principal advisor, who practises a micro-management style that keeps George in a 'corset', carefully controlled and scripted. She argues that passion might provide the jolt the campaign needs and, when George prepares for a major speech in Manchester, Lindsay suggests that he speak without notes, that he speak from the heart.

When George takes the stage and speaks simply and directly about his 'reason for being a socialist' (p95), one may view the moment as an opportunity to vindicate the socialist vision, to restore faith. George elicits approval from the crowd in his opening attack on the wealthy. He draws applause and incites hope that his might rediscover his voice and passion. He continues: 'My socialism is . . . it is concrete. It is real. It is to do with helping people' (p95). George here, however, begins to waver. His audience withdraws. Just at the moment that he might have inflamed his listeners, he resorts to the prepared speech he has carried in his jacket, taking refuge in his pre-packaged cautious and uninspiring rhetoric. The importance of this moment in the play is considerable, as George is granted one last chance to summon socialist inspiration; however, his stammering, along with the drift of the audience, indicates that the old language will not work. It suggests that there is no going back but only forward into a future, where new ideas and language must be fashioned.

George's subsequent defeat casts the campaign team into despondency. Oliver turns on George and mocks his love of the theatre. As he had mentioned earlier, 'tragedy's just a posh word for losing' (p20). What the election brought to harsh light was the party's deep-rooted defeatist self-regard. This is the message Malcolm delivers to George in his disclosure: 'They smell that you don't believe in yourself' (p86). At the end, George serves as the personification of the Labour Party and all its troubles – its disjointed message, its squabbling and back-biting, its lack of confidence and conviction. George's defeat is more than a personal disappointment; it signifies a historical marking point – the death of a viable socialist alternative.

A good deal of criticism has challenged Hare on the direction of his writing leading up to and including the trilogy. Homden argues that Hare's tragic treatment of individuals lost in inoperative systems, with no foundational assurance, may in fact contribute to 'the ideology of stasis'.[28] Fraser admonishes Hare for 'privileging the martyrdom' over any rationalist critique of institutional structure.[29] Finlay Donesky perhaps forwards the most compelling critique, arguing that the playwright responded to the defeat of socialism by seeking comfort in tepid, reactionary postures: '[Hare] is a liberal with a tender heart who wants British institutions to be more caring and just.'[30] Rather than arguing for new forms of activist collectivism, Hare retreats inward, appealing to a private sense of probity, one that Donesky views as universalist and essentialist – in short, we all really know what is good and right deep inside.[31] In sum, Donesky views Hare's inward turn as an expression of sentimentality, embracing a powerlessness that is finally complicit with the institutions he indicts.

In Hare's defence, Nicole Boireau has argued that Hare has retained his political passion and has pursued a 'special brand of revised radicalism'.[32] Though I am not in full agreement with Boireau's analysis, I do share the view that Hare's work – especially in the trilogy – possesses a complex political and ethical outlook, one that cannot easily be dismissed as reactionary or romantic. There is certainly nostalgia in Hare's plays, but his shift to questions of goodness and matters of individual decision align the playwright with strong currents of contemporary ethical thinking. One can view Hare as a questioning artist who has distanced himself from earlier positions in order honestly to confront the political and ideological realities of the present. In this regard, Hare has not retreated but moved forward.

Matt Wolf has written about how Hare's position in *Via Dolorosa* manifests a kind of ethical anguish, how the Middle Eastern situation presents no easy answers or unassailable moral verdict.[33] It is this unsettling position that, I believe, permeates the world of the trilogy. Hare exposes himself as a dramatist bereft of certainties and easy assurances. In keeping with an anti-foundationalism, he exhibits suspicion of any belief system that claims full explanation – whether Christian or Marxist. Hare explains: 'This kind of certainty . . . is not just deeply offensive, it is perceived . . . as being profoundly anti-humane.'[34] For Hare, such systematisation aims to totalise the many complexities of human experience (which results in a kind of effacement). While guidance is certainly desired, no authority can be fully trusted. In some measure, Hare's critique of British institutions conveys the sense that institutional 'knowledge' holds no special province or insight.

If there is a touchstone in ethical decision-making, it is not any political programme or utilitarian calculus, but the responsibility owed by the self to the other. John Bull has observed that Hare's plays are 'intensely interested in the particular individuality of the individual';[35] this orientation in Hare's work accords with one of the most basic tenets of postmodern ethics – the respect for singularity, for the protection of the individual against law or rule or group. This precept countervails the common view of the postmodern outlook, that it promotes an 'anything-goes' sensibility and thus engenders an ethical void. In his comment that 'character is more important to me than ideology',[36] Hare echoes Levinas's valuation of the individual – outside of whatever the character may espouse, represent or signify. In a post-ideological world, honouring the inviolability of the other, with no clear path or directive, comprises the core of ethical decision-making. One must summon the courage to act, in the face of contingency and uncertainty, with no assurance that there is any one best choice.

Hare's simple declaration, 'people live their lives together',[37] may offer the best insight into the world of the trilogy and the timeliness of its outlook. This emphasis on the profoundly social nature of human existence challenges those critics who characterise Hare's 'saintly' characters as mystically oriented individualists who 'find themselves' in their personal experience of goodness. Characters in the trilogy contest such a view. Lionel, Frances and Irina all labour with doubt; their experience is no self-absorbed celebration of inward goodness. Indeed, the ethical actions depicted in the trilogy focus less on isolated individuals than on the movement between self and other. Goodness is not a state of being; it is found in action directed toward another. Hare's characters are not modernist egos, autonomous and insular; rather, his characters exist 'in relation', in sociality, which for postmodern ethics is the very grounding of the ethical self. It is here that one may find a path to the wider recharging or 'refreshing' of institutional or cultural life, the way to the common good. As Bauman notes, 'It is the primal and primary "brute fact" of moral impulse, moral responsibility, moral intimacy that supplies the stuff from which the morality of human cohabitation is made.'[38]

When Hare speaks of appealing to a 'sense of justice' or a 'sense of humanity',[39] one need not rush to essentialist conclusions. Rather than invoking some Enlightenment conception of universality, Hare may be indicating, in a manner suggested by Levinas, a kind of basic ethical relation, a relation between contingent selves – a singularity of being that demands honour and respect. In his speculation on a progressive theatre, Baz Kershaw asserts that activist performance should focus on 'questions of ethical, social, and political value' that contribute to 'a sense of the human'.[40] Kershaw's use of 'human' does not invoke any transcendence or any 'liberal humanist notions of political or ethical global commonalities founded on logocentric laws'.[41] Rather, his 'sense of the human' gestures toward a redeeming construct, a positive assertion of value in a post-ideological world. In many respects Hare's plays seek a similar valuation; the trilogy particularly seeks to affirm a positive and enriching sense of the human, of human ethical regard, without appeal to foundation, to religion or ideology.

To conclude, I wish to return to the comparison of Hare and Ravenhill. It is a small but telling detail that Hare mentions *Shopping and Fucking* as one of the British pieces playing in Israel during his visit to the Middle East. While Hare cites the play as an example of sensationalist pop culture of the West, one may discern an ironic kinship between the two writers. *Shopping and Fucking* was first produced by the Out of Joint group, a later incarnation of the Joint Stock Company Hare co-founded in the 1970s with Max Stafford-Clark; Stafford-Clark in fact served as the director for Ravenhill's show. In recent years Ravenhill has followed in Hare's path and has taken residency in the National Theatre. And, in *Some Explicit Polaroids*, Ravenhill forwards an older character, inculcated in socialist politics, who must reorient himself to the present. Despite the aggression of his dramaturgy and its hip posturings, Ravenhill, like Hare, has been credited with a 'moralist impulse',[42] and what brings the writers together, I suggest, is that both have confronted the post-ideological world, both recognise its vacuity and ambivalence; yet both have responded with an affirmation of the ethical. Near the conclusion of *Shopping and Fucking*, when Mark deliberates over whether he should oblige Gary's plea, whether he should use the fork to relieve the teenager of his emotional torment, Ravenhill offers an exemplary instance of postmodern morality: in a moment of anguish and ambiguity, Mark decides to act, guided by no code or religion, without return or guarantee.

NOTES

1. David Hare, *Racing Demon* (London: Faber, 1990); *Murmuring Judges* (London: Faber, 1991); *The Absence of War* (London: Faber, 1993). All quotations from the plays are taken from these editions.

2. See Mimi Kramer, 'Three for the Show', *Time*, 4 August 1997, p70.
3. Christopher Innes, *Modern British Drama: The Twentieth Century* (Cambridge: Cambridge University Press, 2002), p225.
4. Quoted in Peter Buse, 'Mark Ravenhill', British Council, www.contemporarywriters.com, p1 (accessed 19 April 2006).
5. Mark Ravenhill, *Shopping and Fucking*, in *Plays: One* (London: Methuen, 2002), p63.
6. Quoted in Richard Boon, *About Hare: The Playwright and the Work* (London: Faber, 2003), p224.
7. David Hare, *Obedience, Struggle and Revolt: Lectures on Theatre* (London: Faber, 2005), p117.
8. Quoted in Finlay Donesky, *David Hare: Moral and Historical Perspectives* (Westport, CT: Greenwood Press, 1996), p12.
9. Gary B. Madison and Marty Fairbairn, *The Ethics of Postmodernity: Current Trends in Continental Thought* (Evanston, IL: University of Northwestern Press, 1999), p1.
10. Quoted in Judy Lee Oliva, *David Hare: Theatricalizing Politics* (Ann Arbor, MI: UMI Research Press, 1990), p181.
11. Zygmunt Bauman, *Postmodern Ethics* (Oxford: Blackwell, 1993).
12. *Ibid.*, p13.
13. Duncan Wu, *Six Contemporary Dramatists: Bennett, Potter, Gray, Brenton, Hare, Ayckbourn* (New York: St Martin's Press, 1995), p109.
14. Buse, 'Mark Ravenhill', p3.
15. David Hare, *Asking Around: Background to the David Hare Trilogy*, ed. Lyn Haill (London: Faber, 1993), p2.
16. Hare, *Obedience*, p228.
17. *Ibid.*, p218.
18. Hare, *Asking Around*, p6.
19. Carol Homden, *The Plays of David Hare* (Cambridge: Cambridge University Press, 1995), p204.
20. Quoted in Oliva, *David Hare: Theatricalizing Politics*, p174.
21. Malcolm Page (comp.), *File on Hare* (London: Methuen, 1990), p83.
22. See Paul J. Griffiths, 'Christ and Critical Theory', *First Things* 145 (August/September 2004), pp53-5.
23. Hare, *Obedience*, p223.
24. *Ibid.*, p236.
25. Hersh Zeifman, 'An Interview with David Hare', in Hersh Zeifman (ed.), *David Hare: A Casebook* (New York: Garland, 1994), p4.
26. See Jens Zimmerman, '*Quo Vadis?* Literary Theory beyond Postmodernism', *Christianity and Literature* 53, 4 (2004), p503.
27. David Hare, *Writing Left-Handed* (London: Faber, 1991), p77.
28. Homden, *The Plays of David Hare*, p238.
29. Scott Fraser, *A Politic Theatre: The Drama of David Hare* (Amsterdam: Rodopi, 1996), p196.
30. Donesky, *David Hare*, p10.
31. *Ibid.*
32. Nicole Boireau, 'Re-routing Radicalism with David Hare', *European Journal of English Studies* 7, 1 (2003), p26.

33. Matt Wolf, 'The Prime of David Hare', *American Theatre* 16, 1 (January 1999), pp64–6.
34. Hare, *Obedience*, p231.
35. Quoted in Zeifman (ed.), *David Hare: A Casebook*, p143.
36. Quoted in Liorah Anne Golumb, 'Saint Isobel: David Hare's *The Secret Rapture* as Christian Allegory', *Modern Drama* 33, 4 (1990), p565.
37. Quoted in Janelle Reinelt, *After Brecht: British Epic Theater* (Ann Arbor, MI: University of Michigan Press, 1994), p111.
38. Bauman, *Postmodern Ethics*, p35.
39. Quoted in Oliva, *David Hare: Theatricalizing Politics*, p181.
40. Baz Kershaw, 'Curiosity or Contempt: On Spectacle, the Human, and Activism', *Theatre Journal* 55 (2003), p594.
41. *Ibid.*
42. Caridad Svich, 'Commerce and Morality in the Theatre of Mark Ravenhill', *Contemporary Theatre Review*, 13, 1 (2003), p81.

5

DUNCAN WU

Hare's 'stage poetry', 1995–2002

'It is only now . . . that I realise, almost without noticing, that for some time my subject as a playwright has been faith', Hare has written.[1] This has never been more true than for *Skylight* (1995), *Amy's View* (1997), *My Zinc Bed* (2000) and *The Breath of Life* (2002) – works that, as Richard Boon has observed, 'show a steady progress towards increasingly "private" plays'.[2] Issues of faith are notoriously difficult to deal with on stage, and as a means of approaching them Hare began experimenting with what he himself has called 'stage poetry', a form that enables him to take his audiences to the heart of his characters' spiritual lives without sermonising – in fact, without necessarily using language at all. Besides explaining the themes of these important plays, this essay will unravel the mechanics of Hare's 'stage poetry'.

Faith is an explicit concern of *My Zinc Bed* from the outset. The most attractive of its characters, the successful businessman Victor Quinn, is a former communist who, in conversation with the alcoholic Paul Peplow, traces the course of his life from faith to disillusionment:

> VICTOR: I had faith. But then it was stolen from me. I was the victim of a robbery. Like millions of others. History came along and clobbered us on the head. No victim support scheme for us.
> PAUL: No.
> VICTOR: Just thrown out into the world and told to get on with it. Given a sharp lesson and told we could have no effect. Do I seem ridiculous to you?
> PAUL: Not at all.
> VICTOR: I have felt ridiculous. (*Victor shrugs slightly.*) What does it mean to say that I was angry? For years. 'I was angry.' Why? Because the world was not as I wished it to be. Yes.[3]

Victor's 'faith' rested in the Welfare State, the great achievement of postwar Britain; the 'robbery' was its curtailment at the hands of Mrs Thatcher and her government. That 'theft' had a devastating effect not just on society as a whole but on those who, like Victor, believed in socialism; the difficulty of adjusting to it brought home to Hare the importance of faith to his writing. 'I think you can see quite plainly that all socialist writers of the 1970s were thrown for a loop by Thatcherism', he has admitted, 'I was one of many socialist writers who wanted society to change in a particular direction. It changed in the opposite direction.'[4] The result was the end of hope: as Victor tells Paul, 'God is dead, so there's nobody upstairs' (p57).

If Victor is the representative of people like Hare, he might also be regarded as the exemplar of Blair's Britain. An erstwhile socialist, he has adapted to the world of the late 1990s in which faith has ceased to have meaning, where the businessman is king. But his habits of mind date from an earlier period: one of the first things he does during the course of the play is to give a job to Paul – an alcoholic poet with no experience or aptitude for the business in which Victor has made his fortune. 'I've fucked up every significant relationship in my life', Paul admits. 'I have a physio-fucking-what's-it-chemical relationship to alcohol. I'm sick as a fucking dog. I'm an alchie' (p79). This makes Paul a representative of the faithless – the massive constituency of people without the aspirations and beliefs that enabled Victor to survive the post-Thatcher era. Instead, Paul is the plaything of his addiction, the victim of a spiritual emptiness that prevents him from seeing the world as it is. And this, as the play suggests, is the situation in which most people in modern Britain find themselves. As such, they are directionless, without a secure footing in any value system, and endlessly susceptible to less benign forces. Hare uses alcoholism as a metaphor for any kind of compulsive behaviour, whether dictated by money, physical gratification, or the cheap thrills of the visual media; as he has suggested, *My Zinc Bed*

> asks if we are doomed to act out patterns from which we can't escape and if we are simply running around like rats along a course which our addictions commit us to. Or is there such a thing as a free act of will any more in a consumerist, capitalist society? Is there such a thing as an authentic action any more? Can you escape your own addictions?[5]

The point is that belief guarantees the ability to act freely – to perceive what is going on in the world and to take an 'authentic action'; indeed, throughout the plays discussed in this chapter, that ability is the essential hallmark of the undeceived. It is a kind of enlightenment. Take, for instance, Kyra Hollis and Tom Sergeant in *Skylight*. Several years before it begins, she managed his restaurants and became his mistress, but one day she walked out, leaving behind the comfortable life he gave her. Now, seeking her out after his wife's death, Tom attempts to lure her back to his world. But everything has changed – most obviously her perception of him. 'You've lost all sense of reality', she tells him.[6] And she's right: he has no sense of 'how everyone lives' (p72). Like Paul Peplow in *My Zinc Bed*, Tom has nothing to anchor him to the world. His life is a kind of lie, an untruth forged out of a desire to cocoon himself with material comforts; indeed, he cannot help lying to Kyra when he talks to her about his wife's death. 'Do you think, please, Tom, do you think I've believed the lies you've been telling me?' Kyra asks (p51). Tom's principal difficulty is that he is so alienated from life he can no longer perceive it, either in a political or personal sense. Kyra has chosen a harder path, one that has committed her to absolute fidelity to her convictions. Her departure from his life was something he failed to understand, and he now returns to her, in search of an explanation. 'You simply walked out!' he barks reproachfully.

> TOM: And what's more, you did not consult me. You made a decision which I never approved.
> KYRA: Approved? You mean, you signed no consent form . . .?
> TOM: (*At once catching her tone*) All right . . .
> KYRA: You took no executive decision? You mean you never 'discounted' me, was that your phrase? I was never filed next to Alice. Diminishing assets! . . . You did not downsize me, delayer me, you did not have a drains-up meeting to discuss the strategic impact of letting me go? You mean I just went and there was no management buy-out?   (p84)

This is not just a satire on business-speak (of which Hare is a sharp observer); Kyra rejects the assumption that human beings can be traded and trafficked like objects. Not only was Tom guilty of treating those around him like possessions, but he failed to understand her love for him. 'I always felt profoundly at peace', she tells him.

> KYRA: I don't know why, it still seems true to me: if you have a love, which for any reason you can't talk about, your heart is with someone you can't admit – not to a single soul except for the person involved – then for me, well, I have to say, that's love at its purest. For as long as it lasts, it's this astonishing achievement. Because it's always a relationship founded in trust.
> TOM: It seems mad to me.   (p38)

This is the most important exchange in the play, because it establishes the grounds of their incompatibility. Above all, Kyra values a relationship founded in trust, something Tom regards as madness. Her description of the love she sought from him sounds spiritual – 'love at its purest', and in leaving him she remained true to it. By contrast, he has a commodified, materialistic view of things. And yet there is nothing unworldly about Kyra: she is not a dreamer or a romantic. She possesses a clarity of vision denied to others.

Her work has taken her into the depths of the hardship experienced every day by ordinary people, from which Tom has insulated himself (p64). In fact, in his view the task of changing society for the better is futile, but it is one to which Kyra has given herself with the same spiritual intensity with which she once loved him. It begins with that most pragmatic of acts – that of perceiving the state of things before acting on the inner knowledge that she has the power to change the world for the better. 'Why do you think I'm working where I am?' she asks Tom. 'I'm sick of this denial of everyone's potential. Whole groups of people just written off!' (p75). But Tom fails to understand; to him, she is throwing her life away.

As Hare explains, Kyra belongs to a class of character discovered while researching his trilogy (*Racing Demon*, *Murmuring Judges* and *The Absence of War*) during the late 1980s and early 1990s:[7]

> I suddenly found myself in the company of a whole lot of well-intentioned people – sometimes ridiculous people, people who believed things I didn't believe, but who were more or less saying, 'The mess has been made and we're the poor sods who are going to have to clear it up'. And since they became my subjects I've been a very, very happy writer. They *are* my subject, these people: obviously, Kyra in *Skylight* is a prime example.[8]

It would be easy to write off Kyra as an idealist, but, as Richard Boon points out, she is 'not entirely the idealistic saint the audience might wish her to be'.[9] Perhaps it is idealistic to believe that it is possible to change the world, but her attitude is eminently practical and begins with an apprehension of the causes by which people may be damaged by poverty. Tom is trapped in a series of illusions, symptomatic of which is the compulsion to romanticise her. He returns to her because he is unable to forget her as she had been on the day she first entered his restaurant. 'A girl of eighteen walks down the King's Road . . . And in that girl, there's infinite potential. I suppose I just wanted some of that back' (p96). Far from releasing him, that memory imprisons him within a construct defined by the second-order emotion of nostalgia, light years from the 'real world' Kyra now inhabits – which, as she assures him, is 'not at all like the world which you know' (p71). Tom's longing for the girl she once was underlines his failure to appreciate the woman she has become; indeed, his tragedy is the failure to see that the girl in his memory no longer exists.

Such 'mirages' (if we may call them that) distinguish flaws in characters elsewhere in Hare's work. Sitting with Victor and his alcoholic wife Elsa on a warm summer evening, Paul in *My Zinc Bed* succumbs to the temptation to drink after an abstinence of sixty-eight days, as he recounts:

The liquid swelled out in my bloodstream, filling it with longing, as if what I were drinking were not tequila, not fermented grain, but life, the sensation of life, filling me with feeling till I overflowed. I stood in the garden, fear held for a moment at bay, beginning to feel I could help, beginning to feel I could live.

(p76)

This is, as Hare has noted, one of the great moments of Paul's life,[10] evoked with all the lyrical power of a religious ecstasy; like Tom's first glimpse of Kyra on the King's Road, it possesses an undeniable appeal. But it also suggests an insecure grip on reality: Paul's first alcoholic drink in months enhances his vision in a manner that is unsustainable and false. 'People say, "You drink to escape your problems." "Oh yes?" I mean, you could say that given that I can't solve my problems, escaping them isn't maybe such a bad idea' (p83). Intoxication may feel like an escape, but it cannot bring his problems any closer to resolution.

The alcoholic Elsa is a more extreme case. She tells Paul that only thanks to Victor does she exist, only thanks to him does she feel real (p88). The point is not to establish Victor in a position of power, but to reveal that as someone whose life has failed in the past, she is now completely dependent on him for any sense of reality – 'I was human trash', she tells Paul. 'My knickers ripped in half, my breath stinking of vomit and waiting to be thrown out with the empties' (p95). What's more, her redemption is conditional on her continuing partnership with Victor; without him, she would revert to what she once was. As Paul tells her, 'you have a husband, who's real, who's solid, who radiates solidness – computers! opinions! suits!' (p93). And that is why Paul too becomes obsessed with him: Victor gives them what they lack – a handle on the world, something they have lost, which Paul cannot replace, either through his involvement with Elsa or through drink. As he remembers making love to her, he turns to the audience and comments: 'The alcohol drained out of me and her warmth filled me. I vanished into her warmth and was consumed. The hour that followed was the happiest of my life' (p98). The allure of such things – sex and drink – is not denied. The point is that in Paul's case they're the only available means to achieve what Hare has called 'that lyric sense that human beings can suddenly have when they feel fifty feet high. It's so important to remind people that that's part of living.'[11] All the same, they cannot endow Paul with Victor's solidity, nor the ability to see the world as it is. 'I still believe in history', Victor tells Paul, 'A way of looking at things historically. You never lose that. The computer comes along. It's the next thing' (p15). If Victor has learned anything from Thatcherism, it is an understanding of human development that assumes the advent of 'the next thing', whether in technological or political terms. By contrast, Paul and Elsa have no security beyond what Victor provides for them. They are prisoners of their addiction.

Faith in these plays is fundamental to the ability first to see and then to act. This is the subject also of *Amy's View*, in which Esme Allen, a successful West End actress, is told by her grown-up daughter Amy, 'You've pretended it's funny to live in a dream.'[12] Amy is right: Esme's constructions of reality are as flimsy as the plays in which she stars. And yet there are ironies. Esme is sufficiently clear-sighted to recognise that her village fête is a kind of illusion, a sort of fantasy theme park (p45), and that the boardroom at Lloyds in London is sheer theatre (p99). But she is an actress, susceptible to the magic of illusion, and that compromises her ability to understand the world. She surrenders control of her finances to her next-door neighbour, Frank, with disastrous results: by the end of the play her affairs are being run by a 'hardship committee' that pays her a small allowance but takes everything she owns and earns (p117).

The mess into which her life descends is part of a larger critique of the British during the postwar period, for she is the representative of a tendency to live in the past. All the important decisions she makes during the sixteen years covered by the play (1979 to 1995) lead back to an unfulfilled yearning for one thing – her dead husband: 'Life with Bernard wasn't actually spectacular. It wasn't as if we were always in each other's arms. It was just calm. And we laughed at everything. That's all. Nothing crazy. But always with him, I felt whole' (p125). There's nothing inherently wrong with this, but, as its context indicates, her continuing dependence on a man who stopped existing many years before prevents her from engaging with the here-and-now. It is similar to Tom's dependence on the 18-year-old Kyra or Paul Peplow's on alcohol. As Hare comments: 'The story is of a woman who doesn't know how to live because her husband died when she was thirty-five and what does she do with the rest of her life?'[13] As a result, Esme makes a crucial error in rejecting her daughter's boyfriend Dominic on the grounds that he is not Bernard – a bad moral decision that leads ultimately to estrangement from Amy herself. The loss of her daughter is Esme's tragedy, as it is of King Lear – another parent who loses that which is most precious to him. In both cases the loss is self-inflicted.

Amy's view is that 'love conquers all' (p71).[14] Its most eloquent spokesman is Dominic: 'you have to love people. You just have to love them. You have to give love without any conditions at all. Just give it. And one day you will be rewarded. One day you will get it back' (p121). On the surface this makes Amy sound like a spiritual extremist, but her philosophy is grounded in an undeceived faith in human nature, as well as in pragmatism. We know that Amy is a shrewd and perceptive observer of the world because *Amy's View* is also the title of the newspaper she wrote and published as an 'Infant journalist' (p5). As an occasional journalist himself, Hare has a healthy respect for those who can write, without misconception, about the world around them – the highest form of journalism there is, and one he practises in his playwrighting. Accordingly, Amy is a better judge of her mother's situation than Esme herself, urging her to sue Frank for the losses she sustains with the collapse of Lloyd's: 'We are what we do, for Christ's sake. Have you never grasped that? . . . You have to take control of your life' (p102). This could equally well have come from the mouth of Kyra Hollis or Victor Quinn. For Hare, faith does not confine us to the cloisters; on the contrary, it is a guarantee of authentic action, empowering us to fight dragons as mighty as the insurers at Lloyd's.

We recognise from Shakespeare our desire, even at the height of tragedy, for the reassertion of fundamental stabilities, often as moments of transcendent clarity. So it is that Othello kills himself at the moment he kisses Desdemona: 'I kiss'd thee ere I kill'd thee. No way but this, / Killing myself, to die upon a kiss' (*Othello* 5.2.358–9). Aware, for the first time, of what has happened, he argues by this deed for the indestructibility of their love – and, for a moment, affirms it. Lear comes to his senses on a battlefield just in time to retrieve the relationship that is most precious to him – that with his daughter Cordelia:

> we'll wear out,
> In a wall'd prison, packs and sects of great ones,
> That ebb and flow by the moon.
>
> (*King Lear* 5.3.17–19)

The experiences he has suffered have brought him an insight he did not previously have – that politicians ('packs and sects of great ones') come and go. They wield power, but only for a finite period, where the love between him and his daughter is for all time. So strong is that conviction that, even at the moment of his death, Lear believes his love has returned the hanged Cordelia to life: 'Look on her! Look her lips, / Look there, look there!' (*King Lear*, 5.3.311–12). Love is the means by which Lear and Othello reconnect themselves to an ultimate truth from which they were once disastrously alienated. And that process, enacted on stage, works both as philosophical statement and emotional release. The word 'tragedy' evokes thoughts of unrelieved misery, but in a Shakespearean context it works because what is most important in life is validated. An acute reader of Shakespeare, Hare has long absorbed this into his work.

The 'miracles' in his plays speak eloquently of our deepest and most basic need – that for redemption. At the end of *Skylight*, it seems as if all is lost. Tom and Kyra have said goodbye for the last time. Then, unexpectedly,

Tom's son Edward visits Kyra with a hamper. He opens a linen tablecloth, lays the table with silver cutlery and takes out some napkins. 'Just smell the napkins', he tells Kyra. 'Oh Edward', she says, 'Thank you so much' (p100). The dialogue is finely understated. We are moving towards an epiphany, one hinted at in the final stage direction of the printed text. They sit down at the table, opposite each other. He pours coffee while she reaches for some scrambled eggs and toast. They begin to eat breakfast, smiling occasionally at each other, but at ease, neither speaking. The table, we are told, '*looks incongruously perfect in its strange setting*' (p102). 'Incongruously perfect'. Whatever else *Skylight* has to say, it reminds us that life is all too often a mess. In stark contrast, Hare offers a poetic vision of harmony that retains its meaning well beyond the few seconds it occupies on stage, appealing to our need for a love that transcends the imperfections in human relationships. None of this needs to be stated verbally: in Richard Eyre's original production at the Cottesloe Theatre, it was conveyed through an image that burned itself into the memories of those who saw it, and which had a powerful emotional impact. This is a way of thinking and writing that appeals strongly to Hare, and he perfected it during the close association he enjoyed with Eyre at the National Theatre during the 1990s.

Their next collaboration was *Amy's View*, the conclusion of which at first seems designed to offer a vision of unrelieved sadness. Everything has been taken from Esme – her daughter, her family, even her friends. 'My life is when the curtain goes up', she tells Dominic, 'My work is my life. I understand nothing else' (p123). Then, in the play's final moments, she prepares to go on stage. She and Toby, her co-actor, play characters who have emerged from a shipwreck. He pours a jug of water over her, soaking her head and the top half of her body. The stage directions say that Toby '*looks pitiful*', wearing no more than a strip of cloth round his middle, barely covering him, like poor Tom in *King Lear* (p127). Esme pours the rest of the water from the jug over him, so that he shivers. After a moment in the darkness, they turn to the curtains, concentrated on the task ahead, waiting for the play to begin. There is, say the stage directions, a '*curious innocence*' about them. 'So we're alone', Esme says. And then, in Richard Eyre's production at the Lyttelton Theatre, the curtain began to lift. It comprised layers upon layers of silk that rippled out before them, billowing up like some enormous, endless sail, opening finally to reveal darkness beyond. As this dream-like image filled the stage, the players stepped into the void.

It is very difficult to do justice to its visual impact in words, and impossible to evoke its effect on the audience. It was unbearably moving, and Eyre has rightly described its component parts as 'contributing to a cumulative poetic force' – all of which serves to underline the recognition that this kind of theatre is not about the construction of what we might call 'realism'. 'Part of the reason I love the end of *Amy's View* is that it's a pure piece of theatre', Eyre has said.

> There is nothing there on the stage; there's a completely bare stage and two pieces of white silk. All it is is two pieces of white silk, lighting and sound, and you're creating a storm and waves! And it somehow has an enormous emotional force, because it follows all the action of the play and comprises a cumulative encompassing emotional event that ties into the whole use of the theatre in the play as a metaphor for human relationships.[15]

As a critic, one addresses the text of the play as published; Eyre's remarks are a crucial reminder that theatre is much more than that. It speaks directly to our emotions using resources which the playwright may do no more than suggest. Though no longer part of the stage action, Amy's spirit suffuses the drama in the final moments of the play: it is as if her essential character is somehow abstracted from what has come before, so as to shape its denouement. This is what Hare has described as 'stage poetry'.[16]

It is a no less potent ingredient in the most recent of his plays to be discussed in this chapter, *The Breath of Life*, which concerns the first and last meeting of Frances and Madeleine, two women who were in love with the same man – Frances's husband, Martin. Madeleine now lives on the Isle of Wight – 'A part of England that's still England'.[17] As we know from *Amy's View*, references to 'England' reveal more about a character's state of mind than their geographical location. In this case it hints at the possibility that Madeleine is stranded in a past of her own making – what she calls 'The wreck of memory' (p50). She thinks she has the solution: 'We're free', she tells Frances. 'You learn the trick. To let go of time' (p52). But neither woman seems able to do this. In fact, Madeleine is inextricably trapped by the memory of the man she once loved but could not marry. She remembers her first meeting with Martin in Alabama in the 1960s, and the cheap hotel room in which they made love. She remembers the pale beige carpet, the pictures on the wall, the bed to one side, the window, brown curtains and a wardrobe. 'Everything in my life leading to that moment . . . And then – sure as fuck – everything would then lead away' (p38). Rather than submit to this, she walked out on him the next morning. If that had been the end of it, her life would have turned out differently, but fifteen years later she met him again, by chance, in the middle of London. 'Why did you leave me?' he asks. She tells him that she was frightened: 'Wanting everything and fearing I'd only get something. That was the reason' (p90). The irony is that Madeleine's original fear came true, for she would spend the next twenty-five years as

Martin's mistress – and remembers thinking: 'This is what it feels like. I've settled for less. He won't be my life. He'll be the commentary' (p91).

Whether she realises it or not, the affair has damaged her. We witness this from the outset: when Frances arrives, she finds Madeleine defensive about her age, resentful of her success as a novelist, and happy at the thought that Martin now lives in a place where tidal waves and earthquakes abound. Even Madeleine's choice of profession and location of her retirement home seem to be symptomatic of a trauma she has yet to confront. All of which is evidence, not of the ability to free herself from the past, but of her enslavement to it.

Frances too was damaged by the affair, but at least she knows it. She also identifies Madeleine's principal failing:

MADELEINE: My God, you think I live in the past!
FRANCES: I think you do.
MADELEINE: If it's living in the past: if that's the crime, if that's the accusation . . .
FRANCES: There's no crime. There's no accusation.   (p67)

Reluctant to acknowledge it, Madeleine tries to turn Frances's observation into part of an argument, feeling it to be an affront, perhaps a humiliation, that Frances understands more clearly than she does the tragedy of her life. The phrase 'living in the past' is a typical Hare understatement: Madeleine is frozen within the psychological, cultural and political constructs of her prime. Her flat is in 'a huge Victorian stone terrace' (p3), which makes it sound like some sort of memorial, while her frames of reference exclude contemporary culture, the only television programme she can cite being *Kojak*, a detective drama of the 1970s. 'My field is provenance. I seek the origin of things', she tells Frances, 'I discover. Then I describe' (p81). Intellectual activity is often symptomatic of neglect of other aspects of one's character, and this is so with Madeleine. Her academic mission, the analysis of remote history, sets her apart from the world, and has enabled her to deny the lessons of her own past. At the beginning of the play she says that she has not 'said his name in a while' (p6), and in the final scene she specifically requests that 'we not talk about him', declaring that 'it's boring living in the past' (p79). She can see neither that the past is where she now resides, nor that her failure adequately to acknowledge it has compounded the trauma of the affair. She tells Frances not to keep thinking about what happened because the past is always the same.

MADELEINE: He always leaves you. He never doesn't. There it is. He runs off with a milk-fed American with a magnificent figure and finds God.
FRANCES: How do you know?

MADELEINE: Because – just guessing – but that's generally the form God takes when He presents himself to middle-aged lawyers. And middle-aged is putting it kindly. Aren't I right? Forget it. Forget him.　　(pp79–80)

'Aren't I right?' There is arrogance in this, and an irony. Frances came to the Isle of Wight seeking 'Some sort of end to the pain' (p73), a healthier objective than merely numbing it with endless study – the solution Madeleine prefers, designed to help her forget. But forgetting is not the solution, for the crowning irony in this most ironic of plays is that the expert in provenance needs to be taught how to trace the source of her own suffering by a woman she regards as her inferior – Martin's former wife – who has no difficulty remembering.

FRANCES: What happened was: he saw me in a garden. He walked into a garden and saw me one day. Some birds flew over and the sky was bright blue. I was seventeen . . . The garden's full of people. There's a man, and he's heading towards you with a smile on his face, as if he already knows you. When we married I'd never known anyone else. That's why it's now so hard to escape.

MADELEINE: I think you will.　　(pp90–3)

This is the gift Frances can offer Madeleine, for (as Madeleine recognises) Frances has already found a path out of the confining effect of the original experience. Intense, intoxicating experiences can often spell disaster for those of Hare's characters who have them, as we have seen, and it is necessary for the individual to find some way of neutralising their effects before they can move on from them. In this respect Frances is one of the lucky ones: unlike Tom as he describes the 18-year-old Kyra, or Esme as she recalls Bernard, she is not declaring moral blindness. On the contrary, she is more self-aware than they were. She recognises both the seductiveness of the past and its tendency to detach us from the world as it is. In that understanding lies the promise of her liberation. Tom and Esme had not even been aware of their separation from reality; Frances sees it all too clearly. That is why Madeleine confidently assures her that she *will* escape, suggesting in turn that she may follow suit, as the play's final moments suggest:

MADELEINE: I'll come with you to the ferry. Then I'm going to walk on the esplanade. Feel the breath of life on my face. (*Madeleine looks round for a moment.*) Go down. I'll follow.

FRANCES: Thank you.　　(p93)

Frances leaves; she can be heard going down the stairs. Madeleine goes to her computer, but is distracted by the framed photo Frances has left on the desk. She picks it up: it shows herself and Martin, 'absurdly young' (p83).

Instead of leaving it where she found it, she puts it into a drawer. It is no more than a gesture, but carries a weight of symbolic meaning. It looks forward to a time when, having recovered from the pain of an affair that has long ended, she can safely discard it, ready to feel the 'breath of life' on her face. The play is, finally, about hope.

Changes in Hare's two protagonists are signalled by the lightest of touches, but in performance the effect is powerfully emotional. Their essential characters undergo turbulent alteration before our eyes, though all we see are outwardly mundane actions matched by Hare's characteristically understated dialogue. The drama is internalised, and yet by a kind of magic we follow Madeleine and Frances into the play's emotional resolution – a further example of 'stage poetry'. *The Breath of Life* takes its power from the seriousness with which it treats sexual betrayal – not as fantasy or intrigue, but as emotional reality. Indeed, the entire drama depends on the ability of Frances and Madeleine to perceive it clearly, and to take authentic action to extricate themselves from the traps constructed for them by the past. Where they find enlightenment, Tom Sergeant, Paul Peplow and Elsa Quinn remain ensnared.

Hare's 'stage poetry' is a crucial element of a larger evolution in his writing since 1995, in which his characters are shown entering new phases in their lives, often using few words, but drawing on the total resources of the theatre. I will not forget the experience of turning round at the end of an early performance of *Amy's View* at the Lyttelton Theatre to see many of the audience still seated, clutching handkerchiefs to their faces, unable to move. Such a powerfully articulated vision guarantees the quality of Hare's mature work.

NOTES

1. David Hare, *Via Dolorosa; & When Shall We Live?* (London: Faber, 1998), p6.
2. Richard Boon, *About Hare: The Playwright and the Work* (London: Faber, 2003), p51.
3. David Hare, *My Zinc Bed* (London: Faber, 2000), p106. All subsequent quotations from the play are taken from this edition.
4. Duncan Wu, *Making Plays: Interviews with Contemporary British Dramatists and Directors* (London: Macmillan, 2000), p172.
5. Boon, *About Hare*, pp163–4.
6. David Hare, *Skylight* (London: Faber, 1995), p72. All subsequent quotations from the play are taken from this edition.
7. Hare's research is documented in *Asking Around: Background to the David Hare Trilogy*, ed. Lyn Haill (London: Faber, 1993).
8. Wu, *Making Plays*, p173.
9. Boon, *About Hare*, p52.
10. *Ibid.*, p174.

11. *Ibid.*
12. David Hare, *Amy's View* (London: Faber, 1997), p103. All subsequent quotations from the play are taken from this edition.
13. Wu, *Making Plays*, p197.
14. Amy echoes a similar character, Isobel Glass in *The Secret Rapture*, who says, 'The great thing is to love. If you're loved back then it's a bonus.' See David Hare, *The Secret Rapture* (London: Faber, 1988), p5. For more on Isobel Glass, see my *Six Contemporary Dramatists: Bennett, Potter, Gray, Brenton, Hare, Ayckbourn* (New York: St Martin's Press, 1995).
15. Wu, *Making Plays*, p203.
16. See Boon, *About Hare*, pp53, 153.
17. David Hare, *The Breath of Life* (London: Faber, 2002), p4. All subsequent quotations from the play are taken from this edition.

6

'Stopping for lunch'

The political theatre of David Hare

Stuff Happens, David Hare's 2004 play about the Iraq war, begins with a parade of the Republicans. Colin Powell, Donald Rumsfeld, Dick Cheney and Condoleezza Rice all take the stage in turn.

Colin Powell tells us what he learned about the nature of war while fighting in Vietnam: 'After Vietnam many in my generation vowed that when our turn came to call the shots, we would not quietly acquiesce in half-hearted warfare for half-baked reasons . . . War should be the politics of last resort.'

Donald Rumsfeld comes on next as 'one-time champion wrestler, University of Chicago' and ex-assistant to Richard Nixon. Other actors discuss his reputation:

> RUMSFELD'S FIRST FRIEND: When you play squash with him, you are
> lucky not to have your head taken off with his racquet.
> RUMSFELD'S SECOND FRIEND: In locker-room terms, Don is a towel-
> snapper.

Then Vice-President Dick Cheney steps forward: 'I had other priorities in the sixties than military service.' An actor reads from a memo:

> Memo from Dick Cheney, October 12th 1974. We will be unable in the short
> term to fix the drainage problem in the sink in the first-floor bathroom.
> The White House plumbing is very old and we have had the General Ser-
> vices Administration working for some time to figure out how to improve the
> problem.

Cheney is followed by Condoleezza Rice who, among other concerns, tells us that her favourite composer is Brahms: 'He's passionate without being sentimental.' Then the actor playing Paul Wolfowitz steps forward. 'The word "hawk" doesn't do Wolfowitz justice', a colleague tells us. 'What about velociraptor?'[1]

It is not untypical for David Hare's plays to begin with a group of actors stepping forward and addressing the audience on a particular political issue.

But the actors, or rather their characters, frequently address politics in unpredictable ways. Audiences at the National's Lyttelton Theatre in September 2004 may well have come to *Stuff Happens* expecting a usefully partisan and possibly predictable anti-war play. It is arguable that the actual play overturns those expectations. Hare's Republicans do not conform to the stereotypes presented in the majority of our newspaper and television debates. In the first instance, the stars of the younger Bush's administration are sharply contrasted with each other. They come alive, brightly and wittily, as rounded dramatic characters. There is humour but not of the kind normally presented by television satirists. Hare's Cheney evokes a politician whose rise to power depends on knowing the trivial aspects of his job as well as the terrifying. Rumsfeld, snapping a towel in the locker room, evokes a competitiveness that comes from the campus rather than Capitol Hill. Rice's remarks about Brahms provide her character with an unexpected sense of mystery and therefore an intriguing isolation from her peers.

There is no hypocrisy on display, nor indeed any noticeable conflict between the characters' private and public selves. These Republicans tell us precisely who they are and what they believe. And they believe different things. Powell displays a conscience about the morality of war that is clearly absent from the thinking of Rumsfeld and Wolfowitz. Rice is non-committal on any of the big issues. The audience is drawn into a dramatic situation which is rich in conflict and promise. In his 'Author's Note' to *Stuff Happens* Hare writes, 'This is surely a play, not a documentary, and driven, I hope, by its themes as much as by its characters and story'.

Hare's treatment of George Bush is a case in point. This is not the caricature often presented in newspapers and on current affairs programmes. From the moment that George Bush strolls on to the stage we are never looking at a man who is lost for words. Hare's President carries authority, often playing the homespun Texan for effect, in order to keep his real cards close to his chest:

> I am the commander – see, I don't need to explain. I don't need to explain
> why I say things. That's the interesting thing about being the President. Maybe
> somebody needs to explain to me why they say something. I don't feel like I
> owe anybody an explanation.   (p10)

Hare's Bush explains very little about the decisions he takes during the course of the play. Rather, he listens. Presiding over a meeting of his National Security Council at Camp David, at which our main Republicans are present, he gives nothing away. Yet it is clear that the centre of power lies with him. And it becomes even clearer that a main part of his agenda is to make a simple example out of Iraq. Hare is careful in this scene not to provide the usual explanations for the 2003 invasion of Iraq. There is no discussion, for instance, of taking over the oilfields or of completing the unfinished work of Bush senior in the Middle East. In *Stuff Happens*, the main argument about ridding the world of a bloody dictator is left to Tony Blair. Rather, Iraq is chosen by Bush as an example in the war on terror because it is 'do-able'. Watching, listening to his colleagues with only the occasional interjection of a 'Huh', Bush finally nods in agreement at the argument put forward by Wolfowitz in the scene (p25). Unlike Afghanistan, Iraq is indeed do-able.

At this point an actor steps forward and announces: 'They stopped for lunch.' Bush whets everyone's appetite by telling them, 'There's chicken noodle soup.' Everyone is pleased. 'Smells good.' 'We bake our own bread here', Bush tells them with some pride. Then he adds: 'It's good to be eating this kind of food. It's comfort food. It's good to be eating it now' (pp22–3).

Later in the day, after having given the official nod to planning a unilateral invasion of Iraq, Bush invites everyone to stay for supper. There's 'fried chicken, corn bread, mashed potatoes and gravy' (p25). After eating supper, Hare tells us that 'nobody wanted to leave' (p25). Bush proceeds to complete a jigsaw puzzle of the White House in the company of his wife, Laura. Condoleezza Rice leads everyone in a chorus of 'Amazing Grace'.

Lunch and supper are, of course, breaks from the main political business of the play. A grave, fateful course of action has been decided upon, one which will go on to fuel the main action of the play. Stuff is about to happen. But first Hare invites us to contemplate his characters in a moment of domestic calm from which they draw unexpected strength. For these Republicans aren't just looking for 'comfort food'; they are also seeking unity among themselves. And they seem to have found it in the decision to invade Iraq.

The protagonists in David Hare's plays often stop for meals. Breakfast, lunch and supper in *Racing Demon* (1990), *The Absence of War* (1993) and *Skylight* (1995) are key moments of insight into the development of the characters and story. We first meet the Reverend Lionel Espy, the unlikely anti-hero of Hare's play about the Church of England, *Racing Demon*, on his knees praying to God. Lionel questions whether the idea of the silence of God, his perpetual absence from the world, is any longer a useful tool for the work needed to be done in his run-down working-class parish:

> God ... The joke wears thin. You must see that. You never say anything ... It's this perpetual absence – yes? – this not being here – it's that – I mean, let's be honest – it's just beginning to get some of us down. Is that unreasonable? ... God. Do you understand? (p1)

Espy's doubts are not those of an angry theologian. He presents his case with typical English hesitancy (' – yes?' –), wit ('The joke wears thin') and even courtesy ('Is that unreasonable?'), qualities which of course immediately endear him to the audience. In scene 2 he is invited to lunch by the Bishop of Southwark. Before sitting down to the 'fishcakes in duck fat' (p1), the Bishop tells Lionel he has no time for self-doubt or questioning of the Church. Like many characters at the top of the professions in Hare's plays, the Bishop has only a minor interest in people's actual belief or lack of belief in a job. 'After all, what are we? Lionel? What is the Anglican Communion? It's a very loose church. I don't have to tell you, we all agree on very little. Almost nothing. Start talking to our members and you'll find we hold a thousand different views' (p3).

This is more or less what George Jones MP, Leader of the Opposition, tells us about the Labour Party in *The Absence of War*:

> we always have this dilemma . . . [the Party] has no organisations . . . It has no schools. It did have once. They were called unions. But the communities that produced them have gone. The industries have gone. So now . . . [we] recruit from the great deracinated masses. The people from nowhere. Who have nothing in common. Except what they say they believe in. And that doesn't always end up being enough.   (p18)

This is a thread running through the treatment of English institutions in Hare's plays. It is as true of his portrait of the Foreign Office in *Plenty* (1978) as of the Church of England in *Racing Demon* or the Labour Party in *The Absence of War*. As the actual authority of these institutions declines, so a ruthless attempt to hold on to power begins on the part of those still in control. This is most brutally summed up by the philosophy of Sir Ian Charleson, Head of Personnel at the Foreign Office in *Plenty*. When Susan Traherne comes to plead for husband's promotion, Sir Ian agrees that her husband, although a clever man, is only making 'haste slowly' (p457). 'Certain qualities are valued here above a simple gift of being right or wrong,' he tells Susan: 'Qualities sometimes hard to define . . .' (p458). Susan asks whether her husband is working in a profession where 'nobody may speak their mind' (p458).

Sir Ian replies to this criticism with a crucial speech:

> That is the nature of the service, Mrs Brock. It is called diplomacy. And in its practice the English lead the world. The irony is this: we had an empire to administer, there were six hundred of us in this place. Now it's to be dismantled and there are six thousand. As our power declines, the fight among us for access to that power becomes a little more urgent, a little uglier perhaps. As our influence wanes, as our empire collapses, there is little to believe in. Behaviour is all. This is a lesson which you both must learn.   (p458–9)

This is precisely the lesson that the Bishop of Southwark attempts to teach Lionel Espy in *Racing Demon* before they enter his palace in order to sample his wife's fishcakes: 'Only one thing unites us', the Bishop tells Lionel. 'The administration of the sacrament. Finally that's what you're there for. As a priest you have only one duty. That's to put on a show' (pp3–4). It has to be said that, as dramatic characters, Sir Ian Charleson and the Bishop of Southwark put on a very good show. As horrified as we may be by their underlying cynicism and lack of idealism, their lack of candour and sheer showmanship delight audiences. 'It's funny', says the Bishop. 'Yesterday, you know, we had the salmon. And there's no denying poached salmon's very nice. But all the time I was thinking, when do we get to the fishcakes?' (p1).

The Bishop, of course, has decided to destroy Lionel Espy. That is why he has invited him to lunch. Similarly in *Stuff Happens* George Bush's hospitality relates directly to his intent to invade Iraq. Fishcakes and chicken soup provide a warm respite from the ice-cold task ahead of both men. An invitation to lunch or supper, however, doesn't always imply a dark or sinister purpose in Hare's work. After a general election is called at the start of *The Absence of War*, George Jones summons his colleagues to his London flat to discuss his strategy, the 'war book' for a Labour victory. 'How do you like them?' is the first line of the scene. 'I like them scrambled', replies George (p38). His new Head of Marketing, Lindsay, is cooking in George's flat as they await the arrival of his 'war' cabinet: 'Ah, yes!' exclaims George,

> Scrambled eggs! When I go to a diplomatic banquet, I don't even eat, I sit and think, I'll be home in an hour. And I'll be eating scrambled eggs. I like them with chilli peppers and cream. (p38)

Then the rest of his campaign team arrives with more 'comfort' food. Unpacking big supermarket bags, the team enjoys a simple meal and a camaraderie that instinctively lead an audience to believe they are the more worthwhile political party. George's spirits rise for the first time in the play. His strategic mastermind Oliver starts to speak with a drink in his hand. According to Oliver, beliefs count for little in life, and at first sight he appears to be another spokesman for naked establishment duplicity:

> Elections, you see, people think they are about arguments . . . They think when politicians speak it's an act of sense. But it's not. It's an act of strategy. It's taking up a position. It isn't like debate. We're not actually debating . . . The only true analogy is with waging war. (p46)

In theory George, the hero of the play, should challenge Oliver at this point in the play. After all he is asking George to abandon some of his most cherished beliefs for the sake of the Party. But Oliver is also offering George more than the 'showmanship' of the Bishop in *Racing Demon* or the idea of right 'behaviour' commended by Sir Ian Charleson in *Plenty*. He is offering George the chance to win a war. Winning is more important than holding on to his integrity. George's spirits remain high and, at the end of the scene, he remembers the last general election and the war campaign that began in Preston. 'Those sausages. Those beans!' someone recalls. 'I ate the beans', George says. 'Every one of them . . . Those beans, I'd say, were the best of my life. Eat! Eat!' (p49). In fact George will go on to lose this election, too, precisely because he cannot hold on to the belief in himself and the generosity of spirit he displays during the early meal in his flat.

Skylight is not normally regarded as one of Hare's more political plays. Yet it contains a clash of values as strong as any portrayed in *Plenty* or *Racing Demon*. On a winter night in north London, a teenage boy calls on a young teacher, Kyra, and asks her to be reconciled with his father. His mother has died of cancer and Tom, his father, is full of guilt and remorse about having been unfaithful. Scene 2 begins with the arrival of the father, Tom, in Kyra's flat. He has indeed come looking for comfort. Interestingly, Kyra has just laid out the ingredients for a spaghetti sauce – '*onions, garlic and chilli, none of them yet chopped*' (p15). Throughout her long encounter with Tom, Kyra will be preparing a pasta supper for them both. In Richard Eyre's production at the National's Cottesloe Theatre, this meal was cooked with complete naturalism on stage. The spaghetti sauce smelled delicious.

The meal, of course, is never eaten. Tom and Kyra have too many angry things to say to each other. Later, when it becomes clear that Tom will be invited to stay the night, the couple forgo supper and make love instead. The attraction they have for each other does not include the possibility of sitting down to a meal together. Interestingly, Tom is the owner of restaurants in London on a Conran scale. As he paces the stage like a hurt animal, he remembers with affection the financial opportunities offered to him by Mrs Thatcher's government during the 1980s:

> I tell you, there was a time . . . what was it? Four years? Five years? Just through that little opening in history you could feel the current . . . You walked into a bank, you went in there, you had an idea. In. Money. Thank you. Out. Bang! They gave you the money. (p25)

Kyra of course feels quite differently about banks. She is a teacher at a sink school in north-west London and despises the materialism of the Thatcher years. David Hare likes to tell the story that during the play's run at the Cottesloe audiences tended to side with Lia Williams' social-minded Kyra during her arguments with Tom. However, when the play transferred to the Wyndham's Theatre in the West End, there was much warmer support – and indeed applause – for Michael Gambon's pro-capitalist Tom. The point is that both characters hold their own on stage, and our sympathies shift between them as the play develops. Part of the reason that Hare's political plays have been so successful in the theatre since the late 1960s is that he has consistently anticipated and reported on the changes taking place on the top rung of British society as well as the bottom. The Foreign Office which Sir Ian defends at the end of *Plenty* is not the same institution which presided over the empire, or even England, during the Second World War. At the climax of *Racing Demon*, the Bishop rages about having to defend the ordination of a woman bishop, an appointment which would have been inconceivable just a few years before. He tells Lionel:

> Today I am in a position to command a schism in the Church. If I leave the Church of England because of this heretic woman, then hundreds of thousands will follow my lead. They look to me but I shan't. I shall stand on the brink. For a long time. All the time, shaking with anger. (p80)

So, too, does Tom rage against the passing of his capitalist utopia in *Skylight*: 'And then of course everything slipped back to normal. The old "are you sure that's what you really want to do." The "wouldn't it be easier if we all did nothing at all?" They always have new ways of punishing initiative. Whatever you do, they think up new ways' (p25). This constant revising of the rules, the thinking up of 'new ways' to play the game, often enrage those who hold on to power in Hare's plays. Susan in *Plenty*, Lionel in *Racing Demon*, George in *The Absence of War* and Kyra in *Skylight* are all on the receiving end of that anger. Whether it's Sir Ian in *Plenty*, or the Bishop in *Racing Demon*, the strong blame the weak for the changes taking place around them. In his anger against Lionel, the Bishop puts forward a decisive criticism:

> You bring it on yourselves. All of you. Modernists. You make all these changes. You force all these issues. The remarriage of the clergy. The recognition of homosexual love. New bibles. New services. You alter the form. You dismantle the beliefs . . . You witter on until you become all things to all men. (p77)

Which, of course, is just what Lionel Espy thinks he should be.

In *Skylight*, there is a difference. Kyra is in love with Tom. But with the uneaten meal abandoned on the table, the couple wake up in the middle of the night and have to come to terms with the fact that they have no future together. As Tom makes his exit, he suddenly turns back:

> At least, if nothing more, come to one of the restaurants. There are one or two which are really not bad. I promise you, you know on a good night, it's almost as nice as eating at home. (p97)

The one thing Tom is unable to do, of course, is to eat a meal at home. He is no lover of domestic routine. However, there remains another meal to be served in the play. The following morning, Kyra wakes up to a new visitor ringing the bell. Edward, Tom's son and a student in his gap year, returns with breakfast. From an enormous polystyrene box, he produces a linen tablecloth, which he spreads over her table, followed by a set of silver from the Ritz (he has a friend who works there). Knives and forks, pudding spoons, salt and pepper pots and an ornate butter dish are all plucked miraculously from the treasure chest. Then comes the food: 'Charentais melon. The orange has been freshly squeezed. Marmalade. And there are croissants. At least I know the coffee is hot. The eggs are scrambled.' Edward pulls up a chair.

> KYRA: Are you ready?
> EDWARD: Yes. Yes, I'm ready.
> KYRA: Then sit.

The stage directions read: '*Edward goes round to his side of the table, Kyra standing behind her chair waiting until he is ready as well, observing the formality.*'

> KYRA: This looks terrific. Come on, Edward, let's eat.   (pp98–102)

These are the last words of the play. Clearly this is a very special breakfast, the kind of occasion Kyra might have once enjoyed with Tom. But it's happening in her home, not in a restaurant. This breakfast represents a moment of generosity on the part of Edward, which does something to heal the divisive relationships of the play. Kyra, we sense, will be a stronger person as a result.

David Hare's earlier political plays, particularly those written in the 1970s, do not end on such an optimistic note. Consequently food and, more commonly, drink are treated very differently. *Teeth 'n' Smiles* (1975) describes the anarchy unleashed by the arrival of a rock band at a Cambridge May Ball who are booked to play a gig but are hell-bent on self-destruction. The lead singer Maggie (played by Helen Mirren in the original Royal Court production directed by Hare) is first seen being carried on to the stage by Snead, a college porter in top hat and black tails. Maggie is out cold. Arthur, the songwriter and her ex-lover, immediately asks what she's been 'on'. He's told:

> She starts drinking at breakfast, she passes out after lunch, then she's up for supper, ready for the show. Then after the show she starts drinking. At two-thirty she's out again. Morning she gets up. And drinks. She's a great professional. Never misses a show.   (p109)

Maggie is not a drug addict, however:

> No goofballs, no dexies, no dollies . . . No one in the world but her and Johnnie
> Walker. (p109)

When Maggie does order food, she asks for hamburgers, vanilla ice cream with hot chocolate sauce, onion rings, frankfurters and tomato sandwiches on brown bread ('I'm a health freak' – (p141). In response to this, Snead the porter fetches a trolley of hot food from the college kitchen. Maggie doesn't touch it. Like the other members of the band, she has no truck with regular meals.

Bass guitarist Peyote, for instance, prepares a very special meal for himself during the play. He first enters with an electric kettle, which he plugs in and turns on. He then arranges a plastic funnel and two glass tubes carefully on a bench. When told that there are a couple of girls outside ready to do a blow job on the bass guitarist, he abandons his preparations for a while and leaves the stage. When he returns, he's holding a piece of gauze. He sterilises the tubes on the bench, takes out a hypodermic needle ('The cleanest needle in showbiz' – p117) and melts some twenty pills in boiling water, pouring them through the funnel and gauze into the tube. He then ties a rubber tube round his upper arm, teases the liquid into the hypodermic and shoots up.

Peyote's meal is background action to the main action of the scene. But his self-destructive and delinquent behaviour mirrors the lifestyle of the entire band, including, surprisingly, its middle-aged and acerbic manager Saraffian (played by comedian Dave King in the original production, and partly based on Michael Codron, Hare's first supportive West End manager). Saraffian enters carrying a crate of champagne and a chicken which he has proudly stolen from the dining tent at Jesus College: 'Loot from the ball, my dears . . . Just in case we don't get paid' (p151). It turns out that Saraffian's formative experience in life was in witnessing ordinary people pilfering and looting from dead bodies after the bombing of the Café de Paris during the London Blitz in 1941. The ballroom at the Café de Paris (where people were enjoying a glorious supper in 1941 just as the undergraduates at Jesus College do in *Teeth 'n' Smiles* in 1969) was of course modelled on the *Titanic*. It is no coincidence that the final number in *Teeth 'n' Smiles*, beautifully scored by Nick and Tony Bicât, is 'Last Orders on the Titanic'. *Teeth 'n' Smiles* is Hare's portrait of the 1968 generation who came, like the band in *Teeth 'n' Smiles*, to equate revolution and rock 'n' roll. It also suggests a decline into disillusionment and adulthood. It is not simply that, as the *Daily Express* would have it, the 'acid dream is over'. It is also that Maggie, Arthur and others in the band are growing up. Even though Maggie burns down the dining tent at the May Ball, Cambridge is going to survive her assault. At the end of the play, Snead hands Arthur the bags he left there as an undergraduate at the college. We learn that everyone will survive their time with the band apart from Peyote, who is to die of an overdose in a hotel room in San Antonio, Texas, in 1973. Earlier in the play, Arthur expresses his frustration at the way the rules and regulations change in Cambridge:

> They invent a few rules that don't mean anything so that you can ruin your health trying to change them. Then overnight they redraft them because they didn't really matter in the first place. One day it's a revolution to say fuck on the bus. Next day it's the only way to get a ticket. That's how the system works. An obstacle course. (p124)

This is a frustration which Arthur shares with several other Hare protagonists, including the Bishop in *Racing Demon* and Tom in *Skylight*.

Plenty (1978) opens with its leading character, Susan Traherne, at her lowest ebb. The room, in her Knightsbridge home, has been stripped bare and her diplomat husband, Raymond Brock, is lying face downwards in front of her fast asleep. A friend, Alice, walks in off the street carrying a small tin-foil parcel. Susan tells her that Raymond's 'had a couple of Nembutal and twelve fingers of scotch . . . nothing else. Don't worry' (p378). Alice opens the tin-foil parcel, which turns out to be a Chinese takeaway. She offers some of the sweet and sour prawns to Susan, who declines. Then Susan walks out, leaving Alice to contemplate the sleeping Brock on her own. Suddenly he wakes, mistaking Alice for his wife. 'What's for breakfast?' 'Fish', she replies (p379). The bare room, the failed diplomat Brock lying drunk on the floor, career and marriage in ruins: of all the abandoned meals in Hare's plays, this takeaway counts as the most miserable.

The play is a postwar kaleidoscope moving back and forth between the 1940s and the 1960s. During the autumn of 1956, we find Susan and Raymond hosting a diplomatic party in the same (now elegantly furnished) Knightsbridge house. Dinner has been eaten and they are at the coffee and brandy stage. Present are the Burmese Ambassador and his wife. Then a man called Darwin arrives. He is Brock's boss at the Foreign Office. Darwin has learned that night of the British government's duplicity over the Suez invasion. 'I would have defended it', says Darwin. 'I wouldn't have minded how damn stupid it was. I would have defended it had it been honestly done. But this time we are cowboys and when the English are the cowboys, then in truth I fear for the future of the globe' (p435). He leaves the party resolved to resign. Susan, having insulted almost everyone in the room, is suddenly elated. 'Isn't this an exciting week? . . . Everything is up for grabs. At last we shall see some changes' (p440). Then she remembers that Darwin did not eat any dinner:

> I made some more dinner [for him] . . . A little ham. And chicken. And some pickles and tomato. And lettuce. And there are a couple of pheasants in the fridge. And I can get twelve bottles of claret from the cellar. Why not?
> There is plenty.
> Shall we eat again? (p440)

This is a very different occasion from the breakfast served in Kyra's flat at the end of *Skylight* or the unpacking of the supermarket food at George's flat during *The Absence of War*. The contents in Susan's fridge represent post-war excess and self-indulgence. In *Plenty*, upper-middle-class social events are viewed with a sense of asceticism and even disgust. By the end of *Plenty*, as we have seen, Susan's cupboard in her Knightsbridge home is literally bare. There is nothing to celebrate during this dinner party other than the unmasking of Britain's greatest postwar lie. What *Plenty* honours is the austerity of life during the war years and the sacrifices people sometimes make for a cause. There is a similar admiration shown for the peasants who consistently have to change and rearrange their lives in *Fanshen*, Hare's 1975 account of the Chinese Revolution, based on William Hinton's book on the inhabitants of Long Bow. It is also underlies the compassion shown for the survivors of the St Pancras rail crash in *The Permanent Way* (2003). This drama, wholly shaped from interviews with the survivors and railway personnel, begins with a dazzling projection of coloured slides on stage – nostalgic posters from the prewar era where trains were clearly part of a nation's pride rather than a measure of its decline.

I am not, of course, suggesting that Hare is entirely dependent as a playwright upon scenes which involve food and drink. The plays are by no means as schematic as that. Each play has its own particular atmosphere and contrasting style. But he does consistently draw audiences into a consideration of his main themes by dramatising very accessible social occasions. A political playwright has to entertain as well as inform. He or she needs to engage us in ways which a purely documentary drama or even the best journalism cannot. Several of the scenes discussed above provide fascinating, if also ironic, points of contact with the audience. Hare has been described by a contemporary as the most talented journalist of his generation. But there is more to the plays than that. A journalist, even one of the best, is unlikely to create a Susan Traherne or a Lionel Espy; characters who take us through a historical moment but who also engage and frequently make us laugh. In *The Absence of War*, George makes a telling point about language: 'To tell the truth even . . . that would be wonderful. If words were only their meaning. But words are their effect also' (p48).

This is perhaps the major difference between a dramatist and a journalist or politician. However truthful a character may be on stage, his words may still have a negative effect on those around him. A successful play shows us the 'effect' words can have on others, including the audience, as well as their meaning. The most fascinating character in *A Map of the World* (1982) is undoubtedly the outspoken Indian novelist Victor Mehta. The opening scene of the play is set in a vast old colonial hotel in Bombay. Mehta is there to attend a conference on Third World poverty. He immediately clashes with an English left-wing writer in the lounge, Stephen Andrews, who is also attending the conference. Stephen has not stopped for lunch, but for a drink in the spacious lounge, and has been trying to attract the attention of a waiter. 'Why are there no waiters?' asks a friend. Stephen replies:

> Because the bar is nowhere near the lounge. In India no bar is anywhere near any lounge in order that five people may be employed to go backwards and forwards between where the drinkers are and where the drink is. Thus the creation of four unnecessary jobs. Thus the creation of what is called a high-labour economy. Thus low wages. Thus the perpetuation of poverty. (p158)

In contrast, Victor Mehta has no problem in attracting the attention of the waiters. On his arrival, they follow him into the lounge carrying a bottle of champagne. It turns out to be very bad champagne, and it is Stephen, the Englishman, who eventually drinks it. Meanwhile Mehta dazzles us with his unconventional and, for Stephen, shocking views on the Third World. In Roshan Seth's urbane performance at the Lyttelton Theatre, Mehta's eyes danced with impish delight at the prospect of upsetting the liberals gathered before him. Rather like the Nobel Prize-winning novelist V. S. Naipaul, Mehta refuses to blame the West for the problems of India and Africa. 'Nobody can help', he claims. 'Except by example. One is civilised. One is cultured. One is rational. That is how you help other people to live' (p165). Also, like Naipaul, he admires old civilisations and is horrified by the new ones. 'That's why I have been happiest in Shropshire. They are less subject to crazes. In younger countries there is no culture' (p164). In contrast with Patrick in *Knuckle*, Mehta is a genuinely cultured man, whom the playwright admires enormously. His views, however, cannot be accommodated within the conference. There are other more urgent issues at stake here. Ironic views of civilisation are not a priority. The individual voice of the writer counts for little. During a public debate between the two men towards the end of the play (the winner will get to sleep with the American, Peggy Whitton), Stephen accuses Mehta: 'You will fight tomorrow for the right to make fiction. And why? Why do writers insist on their right to distort reality? You demand it in order to make better jokes' (pp212–13).

Now, this is a criticism which has been levelled at Hare himself. Are there too many jokes in the plays? The criticism that writers distort reality is also pertinent here, for it turns out that the events we are watching are actually scenes from a film that is being shot around the characters. *A Map of the World* is a play-within-a-film-within-a-play. The very notion of the playwright's art, the purpose of fiction, is being questioned. This is perhaps why Hare occasionally seems to abandon fiction altogether in pieces like *Via Dolorosa* (his 1998 monologue about Israel in which he played himself) and *The Permanent Way*. But I think a statement by Victor Mehta in *A Map of the World* is closer to the truth. 'How do you write a book?' he is asked. 'I mean when you start out, do you know what you think?' 'No', replies Mehta. 'The act of writing is the act of discovering what you believe' (p204). I do think this is true of Hare's work. Writing plays is how he finds out what he believes. Watching them, perhaps, makes an audience think about what it believes.

The Secret Rapture (1988) begins and ends with a funeral. At the beginning of the play, two sisters arrive from London to mourn the death of their father at his house in the country. Their stepmother is a recovering alcoholic, so only lemon squash and coffee are offered to them after the service. During the course of the play both sisters find out what it is they believe. Marion is the high-flyer, recently appointed as a government minister in a new Conservative cabinet. She crackles with confidence. 'You know they were expecting an idiot', she says of a recent meeting with a group of environmentalists:

> That's the first mistake. Because you're a Conservative. And a member of the Government. They expect you to be stupid . . . You blast them out of the water. Hey . . . the gloves are off. That's what's great. That's what's exciting. It's a new age. Fight to the death. (pp37–8)

Despite her confidence, Marion is angry, like so many of Hare's protagonists who get to the top of their professions. Her husband Tom tells us: 'She gets angry. Why? I mean she's got everything she wants. Her Party's in power. For ever . . . I just don't see why she is angry all the time' (p7). In fact, she is angry at her sister Isobel, who simply won't conform in the way Marion expects. Isobel is a partner in a small design firm. She has absolutely no interest in Marion's new age of competitive struggle. When Isobel's firm is given money to expand by Marion's husband Tom, Isobel simply withdraws. She goes back to the house in the country. Marion is exasperated: 'We live in this world. We try to make a living. Most of us just try to get on with our lives.

Why can't we? . . . Why does there have to be this endless complication?' (p65). It is Isobel's idealism and grasp of complexity which enrage Marion.

By the end of the play, Isobel is dead, murdered by her lover, who also cannot bear to lose her respect. Marion returns to the same country house as at the play's opening for her sister's funeral: 'I've stood at the side. Just watching. It's made me angry. I've been angry all my life. Because people's passions seem so out of control' (pp82–3). Marion is consumed with grief because her sister chose a different path in life to her own. Throughout the scene, covers are being taken off the furniture, the room is being restored, furniture, carpets, curtains, ornaments, to what it was at the start of the play, a perfect English sitting room. Marion is delighted by the result. Tom tells her: 'Well done. It's lovely. A perfect imitation of life' (p83).

In some ways, of course, 'a perfect imitation of life' is a definition of great theatre. But here Marion's imitation is an artifice, an illusion, a home that is removed from anything real. In *Racing Demon*, Tony, a young evangelical priest, argues that people need to find true religion again, not the watered-down version served up by Lionel Espy. The Rev Harry Henderson, Lionel's friend and supporter, tells him:

> There's a dream there, Tony. Today you've expressed that dream. It's a dream that has haunted the church for two thousand years . . . Does it have a name? It used to. In the Inquisition they called it something else . . . I'd say of all temptations it's just about the most dangerous on offer. The illusion of action.
>
> (p54)

Once again 'the illusion of action' may stand as a description of drama. Yet the perfect action, Marion's 'perfect imitation of life', can also be dangerous. Like the perfect meal, it may only exist in the mind of its creator.

In *Stuff Happens*, George Bush, having stopped for lunch, also dreams of a perfect action. Colin Powell argues with him:

> Sometimes I think all the trouble in the world is caused by intellectuals who have an 'idea.' They have some idea of action with no possible regard for its consequences. We need to get a balance here.　　(p50)

During the scene an audience comes to realise that Colin Powell will lose the argument about the invasion of Iraq. There is a comparison here with the scene in *Racing Demon* where the Bishop of Southwark dismisses the doubts of Lionel Espy about the Church, or even in *Plenty*, where Susan Traherne learns of the treachery of the Foreign Office.

Condoleezza Rice is also present at the meeting with Colin Powell and Bush. She says very little, as does the President. At the end of the scene, Powell rises and offers her a lift home. It is late at night and there is a poignancy in the fact that the Bush regime has appointed these two black Americans to such high positions. Rice is tempted to accept the lift home. Then she changes her mind. 'I'm going to take a rain check. I'm going to work a little longer.' Powell nods with a sense of defeat. 'Sure. You do that. Goodnight, then' (p55).

Before the meeting Powell has had dinner in the President's quarters. It is not a meal he will have enjoyed.

NOTE

1. David Hare, *Stuff Happens* (London: Faber, 2006), pp4–7. All subsequent quotations from the play are taken from this edition. Other quotations in the essay are taken from the following editions: *Plays: One* (London: Faber, 1996) for *Teeth 'n' Smiles* and *Plenty*; *Racing Demon* (London: Faber, 1990); *The Absence of War* (London: Faber, 1993); *Skylight* (London: Faber, 1995); *The Asian Plays* (London: Faber, 1996) for *A Map of the World*; and *The Secret Rapture* (London: Faber, 1988).

II
Working with Hare

7

CATHY TURNER

Hare in collaboration

Writing dialogues

What humanity is can be properly grasped only in its reciprocity.[1]
I feel that the debate itself is what is interesting.[2]

Playwrighting can be a more sociable art than its popular image might imply. Perhaps the isolation of the writer's role is its most obvious feature: Hare himself writes of realising, at the end of the 1970s, 'what more intelligent writers know from the start. I remember thinking: "Oh I see. I'm alone."'[3] He reflects on the provisional nature of relationships with other theatre makers, such as actors and directors. Yet if it was during the 1970s that Hare had most sought, as he puts it, 'to reconcile some kind of group impulse with the task of writing individual plays', this openness to dialogue continues to be evident in his work, particularly in more recent theatre writing.

Perhaps because of its frequent, though by no means inevitable, association with collective authorship, the idea of playwrights working in 'collaboration' (whether with each other, or with an ensemble, or with others) can sometimes be associated with notions of artistic compromise or of inept 'theatre designed by a committee'.[4] It may alternatively arouse suspicions of exploitation of a group by an author who takes credit (and royalties) for work done by others. As the playwright David Edgar comments, 'We live in an age when, if we hear the word "collective", we reach for our copyright lawyer.'[5] Consider, for example, the fury excited by fairly recent discussions of the role of Brecht's collaborators in the development of his work. Such discussions are made more problematic by the difficulty of our ever really being able to gain an objective insight into a collaborative process or of being able to disentangle the various contributions from members of a collaborative team. Yet there are clearly as many ways of engaging in collaboration as there are of engaging in dialogue, many of them extremely productive.

An examination of David Hare's collaborations suggests that, even when dealing with such a strongly individual writer, his capacity for *listening* and *exchange* might be important to acknowledge. In looking more closely at what listening can entail, we may first need to lay aside its association with passivity, which is at the heart of many of the negative views of collaborative work.

This chapter borrows the term 'dialogic listening' from communications theory, and will, in particular, reference John Stewart and Milt Thomas's essay 'Dialogic Listening: Sculpting Mutual Meanings',[6] which is underpinned by the philosophies of Martin Buber and Hans-Georg Gadamer. The term is here coined by Stewart and Thomas to distinguish their approach from 'active' or 'empathic' listening, as outlined by Carl Rogers and others. Whereas 'empathic' listening emphasises '*one* person grasping the *other* person's meanings',[7] 'dialogic' listening, as their title suggests, highlights the productive and mutual qualities of communication *between* people. Whereas in 'empathic' listening you attempt to 'lay aside yourself', in 'dialogic' listening you remain present and acknowledge your own position and responses.

I'd like to suggest that Stewart and Thomas's descriptions of 'dialogic' listening in many ways mirror and so draw attention to aspects of Hare's role as a writer who listens and dialogues. I will focus on some of the clearest examples of collaboration in Hare's writing career, including his co-writing of *Lay By* (1971), *England's Ireland* (1972), *Brassneck* (1973) and *Pravda: A Fleet Street Comedy* (1985), his work with the Joint Stock company on *Fanshen* (1975) and his later work with Joint Stock's successor group, Out of Joint, on *The Permanent Way* (2003). However, although there is not room for detailed discussion here, I suggest that similar qualities inform other works, such as *Via Dolorosa* (1998) or even, less obviously, his trilogy, *Racing Demon, Murmuring Judges* and *The Absence of War* (1993), which are underpinned by the extensive research documented in *Asking Around*.[8] The ability to dialogue with collaborators may be linked to a close attention to the many voices of society and to a sense of dialogue with an audience.

This chapter looks particularly at the rewards and demands of the collaborative *process* – there is scope for much more detailed, if necessarily speculative, discussion of the impact of collaboration on the content and structure of the plays themselves. However, my intention is to point to sources of energy and creative development in the experience of the playwright working as, and with, a responsive dialogue partner (or partners), rather than primarily to critique the works produced.

In each collaboration, as we might expect, the dialogue unfolds differently.

'Focus on "ours"': the potter's wheel

Stewart and Thomas use a metaphor of joint artistic creation to illustrate the process of 'dialogic' listening, as they stress the importance that the focus is on 'ours' rather than on 'mine' (which might mean monopolising the conversation) or on 'yours' (as in 'empathic' listening). They compare it to an image of two people working at the same potter's wheel, sometimes playfully 'co-sculpting' a vague mass, sometimes working carefully on 'detail and refinement'.[9]

The image that Hare uses to describe *Lay By*, one of his earliest collaborations, is that of 'a sort of cancerous growth that just grew and grew'.[10] Just as the sculptors each add clay to the wheel, the playwrights (Howard Brenton, Brian Clark, Trevor Griffiths, Hare, Stephen Poliakoff, Hugh Stoddart and Snoo Wilson) added words to their growing script. In the same interview, Hare and Brenton explain that the play, which grew out of a newspaper article about a rape trial, was initially written with crayon on rolls of wallpaper, giving the writing process an unusual materiality and maintaining a scale that allowed the work to be continuously shared. This method, initiated by Brenton, made it impossible for writers to work alone in corners of the room. Again, the approach is not dissimilar to that of the co-sculptors, whose work is laid out before them, to be added to as it evolves. The process may have produced the shape of the work, which is episodic, revisiting the subject matter (spinning the wheel?) as it is explored from a number of different perspectives. It may also have produced something of its energetic brashness, its elements of caricature. Its methodology ensured that project was, in a real sense, a creative dialogue, rather than an assemblage of disparate contributions.

Hare's role at the Royal Court Theatre and his connection with Portable (he was artistic director until 1971) involved him in the commissioning and production of both *Lay By* and a subsequent co-writing project, (the unpublished) *England's Ireland*. He suggests that he initiated *Lay By* since he 'wanted to write a script with a lot of other people'[11] and proposed a group project during a gathering at the Royal Court, where he was then Literary Manager. He was also responsible for producing *England's Ireland*, which was toured by a company set up as an offshoot of Portable and which addressed the controversial subject of British involvement in Northern Ireland. David Edgar has commented on the vitality that engendered the play, which was co-written by Tony Bicât, Howard Brenton, Brian Clark, Edgar himself, Hare, Francis Fuchs and Snoo Wilson, holed up together in the isolation of a Pembrokeshire farmhouse. He suggests that it was effective in generating debate about 'what plays should be about and how those aims should be reflected in form . . . *England's Ireland* constructed me as a playwright'.[12]

Thus Edgar indicates that perhaps one of the most significant achievements of both projects was the debate itself and the productive process developing between playwrights. He suggests, interestingly, that 'the principles of collaboration' seeped into the mainstream, via writers previously involved in group writing and collaborative play-making. He also proposes that it allowed a group of playwrights to share certain strategies which gave rise to the influential 'State of the Nation' plays, enabling playwrights to establish a rich and productive common ground, so that, even as each developed individually, their plays remained in dialogue with one another. Both Brenton and Edgar have suggested that the earlier and the later projects, respectively, could be seen as 'manifestos' for the group of writers.[13]

Hare is a little more critical of these writing processes, suggesting in 1974 that it was necessary for himself and Snoo Wilson to complete *England's Ireland* after the others had gone.[14] He also comments, as he does of collaborations with Brenton, that there is a point at which, 'if you are involved in a collaborative work . . . you stop short at the minimum agreeable statements',[15] although he points out that even such statements went further than the theatre establishment of the time was prepared to countenance. For both plays proved to be controversial. Indeed, both Hare's and Edgar's descriptions of the projects suggest that they were designed to be so. Edgar even writes that 'Both [*Lay By* and *England's Ireland*] were written on the principle that any individual writer could deny responsibility for the most outrageous scenes.'[16]

The Royal Court, which commissioned *Lay By*, declined to produce it, though it was shown at the Edinburgh Festival in 1971. As early as 1974, Hare associates *England's Ireland* with a time when 'a sense of solidarity on the fringe was lost'.[17] Theatres across the country refused to host it; it was performed in only five cities and remains unpublished: 'the English theatre as a whole, and with more resolution than I'd ever seen them muster, got together and said no in thundering tones to the idea of a show about a British civil war. We were totally exhausted by this reaction.'[18]

Hare's role as a producer meant that he was less protected by the collective process than Edgar may have been. Whereas Edgar associates these projects with an energy that fed into the mainstream, Hare associates the latter, at least, with the struggles of the 1970s that led to the bankruptcy of Portable and eventually to the fragmentation of the Fringe, attacks from both the political Left and Right and increasing administrative pressures, in part exacerbated by the competition for Arts Council funding. Speaking in 2004, thirty years after the *Plays and Players* interview quoted above, he again uses the word 'exhausted' when describing his experience of the creative struggles of the 1970s.[19]

The two perspectives are not incompatible. The vitality of such experiments surely did inform the development of the work of these writers, most of whom went on to enjoy considerable success. Hare recognises that the plays produced were not to be compared with those of Brenton or Griffiths individually,[20] but it may be that such projects should not be measured solely by product or acclaim; their value is at least as much in the engendering of debate and the event of their making.

Perhaps, too, it is not surprising that such an enthusiastic and exuberant 'focus on "ours"' should turn out, like so many Fringe ventures, to run into its biggest difficulties when the attempt was made to open out the dialogue to the wider world. Brenton, involved in both projects, comments in 1974 that he believes 'the fringe has failed. Its failure was that of the whole dream of an "alternative culture" – the notion that within society as it exists, you can grow another way of life, which, like a beneficent and desirable cancer' (cancer again) 'will grow throughout the Western world and change it . . . a ghetto-like mentality develops'.[21] The group relished the idea of being uncompromising, aggressive, lacking the required 'balance' or 'humanity', daring each other to push the boundaries of post-censorship British theatre. Yet, as Hare has suggested above, and as a mere glance at the names might suggest, this tight-knit group was not without its own limitations. Though it could have been enormously energising, perhaps one can understand why the work was not met with wider enthusiasm.

While this was intensely disappointing, it does not negate the value of the creative dialogue *within* the group and Hare was able, in later collaborations, to find modes of engagement that seemed more acceptable to, or perhaps more directly in touch with, its producing venues and audiences.

Open-ended and playful: 'We genuinely do not know what the outcome of the conversation will be'[22]

Harold Hobson identifies in *Brassneck* the 'third person' spoken of by Maeterlinck, who is 'present in every dialogue . . . the unconscious but powerful idea that the dramatist has of the universe, who gives to his plays their resonance and reverberations'.[23] In *Brassneck*, a play about postwar capitalism, Hobson suggests that the 'third man' is a malicious and enigmatic presence.

Richard Eyre and Nicholas Wright write of a similarly vibrant presence in Hare's work, something above and beyond the significance of an individual character – an 'imp' that makes an early appearance in the second Brenton/Hare collaboration, concerning Fleet Street, *Pravda*: 'Every playwright has an imp. It's the unofficial, unacceptable part of the writer's psyche . . . Once the imp is released, it becomes uncontrollable: it goes rampaging from play to play . . . Hare's imp is an emotional tyrant and a right-wing charmer.'[24] Eyre and Wright's description, however, does not allow for Brenton's joint discovery or unleashing of this 'imp', at least in the case of Le Roux. Yet Hare recollects that *Pravda* was the source of a new energy for a period of intense activity: 'Those weeks of argument with Howard about how we could satirise this nihilist . . . were incredibly important. From that I began to get an energy that then produces *The Secret Rapture*, and then I'm away with *Racing Demon, Murmuring Judges* and the rest.'[25] As with Edgar's recollections of the earlier collaborations, we find that they have a significance that goes beyond the immediate production and has the potential to fuel the participants for some years to come. It is notable that both these collaborations came at crucial points of transition for Hare and energised new phases of his career. *Brassneck* was part of a move into more mainstream venues and an exit from the Fringe. Richard Eyre, who commissioned it for Nottingham Playhouse, remembers it as a chance for Hare 'to do a play on a bigger scale'.[26]

Both Hare and Brenton have used Hobson's image of a 'third person', jokingly termed 'Howard Hare', to characterise their joint, collaborative 'voice'. Though they have co-written on several group-written plays, including both those discussed above, Hare and Brenton have only written two jointly authored plays. A third, about the BBC, was discussed but never materialised.[27] Hare has commented on the two plays' similarity of tone, despite a gap of twelve years.[28] This tone is nevertheless quite distinguishable from that of either writer's separate creations: 'Howard Hare's interests aren't really either mine or Howard Brenton's . . . And he writes in a tone of caustic, abrasive, satirical confidence, a tone without doubt, if you like.'[29]

Who or what is this mysterious 'third person'? Brenton, in words that echo Eyre and Wright's description of the 'imp', suggests that he could be 'a psychological entity' and comments that he operates 'like a mask in a way'.[30] However, by envisaging him as a 'third person', placed *between* the two writers, they avoid pathologising him as a projection of either's psychological preoccupations. In Jungian terms, he may exhibit aspects of the 'Shadow' figure, but this 'shadow' is not the sole product of either consciousness. Stewart and Thomas emphasise that in 'dialogic listening' the focus is on what is 'in front of or between the conversation partners', not on unearthing what is hidden 'behind' the words of one or the other. The emphasis is on forward momentum, not self-revelation, moving towards a productive outcome in which 'the whole actually can be greater than the sum of its parts'.[31]

Perhaps Brenton comes closest to accounting for the enigmatic 'third person', whose presence seems so tangible to Hobson, when he identifies the collaboration between the two writers as crucially revolving around a shared theme, a character who is 'a monster': 'there was definitely a team of monster-writing. We only had one theme as a collaborative team there.'[32] Though the 'third man' is not himself the monster, the monstrous male character

(Bagley in *Brassneck*, Lambert Le Roux in *Pravda*) exemplifies the worst of capitalist Britain for both writers, providing a mutual focus. Both *Brassneck* and *Pravda* are at their most effective when their central 'monsters' are on stage. In fact, Hare, Brenton and reviewers have all commented on the plays' dependence on these figures.

Stewart and Thomas identify a key strategy of 'dialogic listening' as a readiness to 'run with the metaphor', extending those of the dialogue partner, developing your own and encouraging each other to share and build on these metaphors: 'when people hear their metaphors coming back at them, they can get a very quick and clear sense of what's being heard.'[33]

Brenton reflects that one of the best techniques for collaborating is to 'say things aloud to each other'.[34] Hare writes, 'the ingredient which makes all plays is metaphor'.[35] Brenton and Hare, then, were able to 'run with the metaphor', develop a vision of postwar and contemporary England around their monstrous central characters. In one sense, neither Bagley nor Le Roux are solely 'metaphorical' – they had (and have?) their real equivalents; however, they come to represent a particular malignant spirit, representing the times, rather than *The Times*, gathering momentum from the political environment. As Hare says of *Pravda*, the play is not fundamentally driven by an interest in Fleet Street, specifically: 'We wanted to re-write *Richard III* and ask again the old question about why and how evil is so attractive.'[36]

Both Hare and Brenton recognise that their collaboration had limitations. Hare comments of *Brassneck*: 'Howard and I stopped short at exactly the point where we began to diverge politically in our approach to the subject . . . on how exactly the system will be transformed, how the future would shape, we couldn't agree.'[37] *Pravda* also fails to offer a vision of social change. The metaphor of the 'monster' who epitomised so much of capitalist Britain was sufficient to sustain a satire; however, the elusive Howard Hare seems to have had no vision, no metaphor for expressing the future. As Hare comments, a little ruefully, 'Modern plays have seemed, perhaps unintentionally, to end up celebrating malign energy.'[38]

'Metacommunication': *Fanshen*

Fanshen, with Joint Stock, involved a whole company in the initial creative process (though not in the writing). In such work, the company becomes a research engine, a sounding board and provides tremendous security through its demonstrable skill and through a common understanding of the work's theatricality and politics.

Hare jointly founded the company in 1973–4, with David Aukin and Max Stafford-Clark, as an 'umbrella organisation', which would 'provide work on a one-off project basis for those who had been associated with fringe groups'.[39] *Fanshen* is based on the book of the same title by William Hinton,[40] which documents the process of revolution in a Chinese village.

In entering the project, which was proposed by the director, Stafford-Clark, Hare suggests he was 'very keen to work in a workshop. I sensed that multi-authored plays were losing their energy . . . I was very eager to have my doors kicked open again.'[41] Yet he also notes that the play itself remained very much his own. Joint Stock seem to have been unique in the ability to make writers feel that their individual contribution was not compromised in any way, while also creating a genuine sense of group ownership of the production, its themes and its modes of realisation. The pattern of working seemed to allow time, space and freedom for all to make their contributions. This, of course, was immensely time-consuming (and therefore expensive), which may be one reason why it has not been more widely imitated.

Fanshen was an early project and so the company's working process had not yet had time to become well established, though Bill Gaskill, who co-directed, recollects that the basic pattern of 'workshop–gap–rehearsal' was conceived after the first production, *The Speakers* (1974).[42]

The process for *Fanshen* comprised a five-week workshop period, followed by a four-month writing period, succeeded by six weeks of rehearsal. Hare comments that the initial workshop did not influence him directly, in terms of the discoveries made, but that he 'was crucially affected by its spirit'.[43] However, notes made by Stafford-Clark[44] during the workshop process do prefigure, in simple ways, a number of decisions that remain in the final script, particularly in relation to the opening section: for instance, the suggestion that the cast should be seen as actors before becoming characters and that the simple actions of daily agricultural work should be established in the opening sequence. Above all, this workshop provided a space for what Stewart and Thomas call 'context-building';[45] that is, establishing the circumstances and desires which underpin the creative dialogue – in this case, both the context of the story and this specific adaptation of it.

Hinton's book, in seven sections and over six hundred pages long, could, as Hare has commented, yield a number of different plays. It is interesting that, through their struggles to find points of connection between their own experience of London and that of peasants in agricultural Communist China, the company found in the play a way to explore the very concerns they had to address as a company: the process of negotiation, dialogue and group organisation. It seems to have been Bill Gaskill's suggestion, prior to the workshop, that the company should make all decisions communally, 'to reflect the character of the book'.[46] Stafford-Clark was less than enthusiastic and records discussing this on the first day of the workshop: 'Spent the whole day discussing whether we were to be a democratic body. In the end we decided we were. Big deal. Talk, talk, talk.'[47] A company ethos and ways of working were gradually established in relation to this project and it served to politicise the company structure, which became that of a collective, seeking to make decisions democratically. In a way, the book was an active partner, invited into the emerging dialogue of the new company.

If this project developed *through* dialogue, it is also a play *about* dialogue and that *invites* dialogue. As Stewart and Thomas suggest, 'metacommunication', communication about communicating, may be an essential part of facilitating a productive dialogue.[48] In some ways, the open ending of *Fanshen* seems to imply that democratic dialogue is more important than any specific outcome it produces. This open-endedness did not entirely please the book's author; Hinton, unlike Hare, was a committed Marxist and demanded a number of small changes, many of which were made.

This dialogue was envisaged as self-critical. Taking up the pattern of the Chinese peasants' self-classification and self-criticism, the company engaged in a process of critiquing their own roles and behaviour. This led towards an equalising of roles, as well as to an evaluation of their own personal contributions. This could all sound very introspective, but, as Bill Gaskill points out, the purpose of these discussions and this self-analysis was not therapy, but the way in which it helped to inform the joint work.[49] As discussed earlier, in 'dialogic' listening, as opposed to 'empathic' listening, the focus is on what is developing between the participants, rather than on analysing the psychological states of participants.

This emphasis on shared decision-making, rather than on individual psychology, is something that was also mirrored in the approach to the subject matter. Stafford-Clark acknowledges that it was relatively late in the process that he recognised that the play did not work through the emergence of character, but through the dramatics of dialectics.[50] What matters to the play is what happens, what is debated and what changes, rather than what motivates individual characters.

Fanshen is not typical of Hare's working process (or of his writing generally) and he did not work as a writer with Stafford-Clark again until *The Permanent Way* with Out of Joint (Stafford-Clark's more recent company), co-produced with the National Theatre in 2003. The *Fanshen* approach had never been envisaged as an ongoing methodology for Hare, though it became one for the company. Hare has suggested that the 'dialectical technique' was only really appropriate for 'dialectical material and companies come to grief when they try to be co-operatives with more bourgeois subject matter'.[51]

In his controversial lecture of 1978, he contrasts the successes of the Chinese revolution with the failure of European Marxism. He continues to value the positive example proposed by *Fanshen*, but seems to suggest that, in tackling the climate of contemporary Europe, it is dishonest not to acknowledge the despair and inertia of the times, which are not to be convincingly resolved through a simplistic Marxist ideology or, indeed, any political manifesto. He suggests, in fact, that the key dialogue partner is not the theatre company, but the audience, which means that theatre is 'something we cannot calibrate because it is in the air and nowhere else' and that writers must face the 'real and unpredictable dangers of a genuinely live performance'.[52] The dialogue with collaborators is only part of the story.

Hare's more obviously collaborative projects are more thickly distributed through the 1970s, with a long gap between *Pravda* in 1985 and *The Permanent Way* in 2003, yet they represent significant achievements and stepping stones at the start of his career, rather than being peripheral works. Through them, Hare discovered themes, political concerns and fertile conversations which he continued to pursue in more solitary work. While *Fanshen* did not provide a model for later work, it helped to establish Hare as a political playwright and, through the difficulty, as well as the success, of its dialogues, to clarify his own choices and positioning as such.

'Paraphrase plus': verbatim theatre

The Permanent Way, like Hare's one-man show, *Via Dolorosa*, is based on documentary material that has not been integrated into a fictional story. A play about the state of the British railway system, Stafford-Clark again proposed the project, having experience of work based on documentary material and interviews (for instance with *A State Affair* by Robin Soans, produced in 2000). Meanwhile Hare had become dissatisfied with aspects of contemporary theatre and recently excited by 'verbatim' theatre such as Richard Norton-Taylor's *The Colour of Justice* (1999), based on the Stephen Lawrence inquiry. He also mentions the influence of performance art:[53] such practice tends to avoid the fictional 'matrix' and, broadly speaking, to work with found material, the autobiographical, the living body and the 'real' action or interaction.

Both *Via Dolorosa* and *The Permanent Way* provide channels for other voices to be heard, with minimal filtering through the writer's imagination. Hare has described the writer's role as that of 'witness'. While he is also able to 'bear witness' through stories, this documentary style places an emphasis on the voices he hears, rather than on his own: 'What my attitude is, is hardly relevant. What matters is what they've got to say.'[54] In *The Permanent Way*, dialogue has been prioritised from process through to outcome. A dialogue (or 'dialogic listening') with the interviewees has formed the basis for dialogue within the company and is eventually brought before the audience, to initiate new listening and new dialogue.

One of the techniques suggested by Stewart and Thomas for 'dialogic' listening is simply the invitation to the dialogue partner to 'say more'. They suggest that one can make a contribution to the dialogue just by encouraging your partner to keep talking, to clarify what is presently 'fuzzy or incomplete . . . in effect "I can't continue our sculpture until you add some definition to the form you began."'[55] This strategy of soliciting further comment, particularly from those whose statements remain underacknowledged or incomplete, is a key element of the Out of Joint process.

In this project, Hare and the company come closest to trying to set their own views aside. However, in the final outcome, all acknowledge that this cannot entirely happen. This poses an ethical dilemma for the company, as discussed in Bella Merlin's contribution to this volume (Chapter 8). At times, all members of the company seem uncertain about how much of themselves they bring to the material, hovering between a desire to step back from it and a realisation that, as artists, they are inevitably giving it new shape. What takes place is highlighted in the subtle shift from 'empathic' to 'dialogic' listening.

In fact, the 'empathic' listener may be in an ethically more problematic relationship to the dialogue partner. Firstly, 'empathic' listening is 'based on a kind of fiction . . . you cannot actually "get inside" the other person's awareness and it can be confusing to think, feel and act as if you could'.[56] Secondly, whereas in 'empathic' listening paraphrase becomes a useful strategy with which to demonstrate an understanding of the other's viewpoint, 'dialogic' listening proposes 'paraphrase plus', in which the intention is 'not to re-produce the other's meaning but to pro-duce a fuller conversation text between you'.[57] Stewart and Thomas go on to explain that a listener who focuses exclusively on understanding the other person isn't fully sharing 'the conversational load'. They suggest that in 'dialogic' listening the goal is to go beyond 'fidelity' to 'creativity', 'beyond reproducing to co-producing'.[58] Thus, to think of the dialogue as mutual is to pay respect to your dialogue partner as a collaborator, with whom new meanings can be created.

The idea of 'paraphrase plus' suggests that, in order to become its own creative work, a 'verbatim' play must and invariably will go beyond mere paraphrase or citation of what is said – at the very least, the statements are edited and arranged in order to produce a certain effect. A key strategy in *The Permanent Way* is the way the characters occasionally refer to the audience as 'David', thus placing us in the writer's position and highlighting his role in interpreting their words. In this way, Hare makes himself present in the work – and 'presentness', in all its complexity, is also suggested as an aspect of 'dialogic' listening.

The Permanent Way may be seen as having been partly prepared for in Hare's one-man performance about the Middle East, *Via Dolorosa*, in which the writer himself is literally present before us, placing himself clearly in relation to the material. Though much of the work records the statements of others, it is impossible not to be aware that these words are filtered through the writer's imagination and that what we witness is very much his own account. This is not an attempt to be 'objective'; nor is it a purely 'subjective' view without reference to the conflicting views of others. Others are represented to us, but indirectly; they are not enacted but are narrated.

Via Dolorosa is paradoxical, in that it places a cast of thirty before us, yet remains a monologue. We see a uniquely individual performance, yet we see a performance that openly mediates for a whole range of other, distant voices. This quality can be found in many of Hare's works, however. While the strategies and approaches outlined by Stewart and Thomas are often discovered instinctively and may sound self-evident to those used to collaborative work, the active qualities needed for dialogue are often under-emphasised, while receptivity and adaptability are stressed. This may be one reason why writers sometimes hesitate before engaging in collaborative creation. However, the mutually productive 'focus on "ours"', the playful ability to 'run with the metaphor', 'metacommunication' that enables action, rather than mere introspection, 'paraphrase plus' and 'presentness' are all aspects of communication that involve creative initiative and are involved in all kinds of playwrighting.

Indeed, perhaps to insist on the importance of considering a writer's ability to listen and to engage in creative conversation with others is to do no more (and no less) than to ask that we acknowledge the paradox of every theatre writer's position: however strong our sense of an individual authorial voice, we are always hearing dialogues.

NOTES

1. Martin Buber, 'Elements of the Interhuman', in John Stewart (ed.), *Bridges Not Walls: A Book About Interpersonal Communication*, 6th edition (New York: McGraw-Hill, 1995), p517.
2. David Hare in 1977, quoted in David Bradby, Louis James and Bernard Sharratt, 'After *Fanshen*: a Discussion with the Joint Stock Theatre Company, David Hare, Trevor Griffiths and Steve Gooch', in David Bradby, Louis James and Bernard Sharratt (eds.), *Performance and Politics in Popular Drama* (Cambridge: Cambridge University Press, 1980), p298.

3. David Hare, *Obedience, Struggle and Revolt: Lectures on Theatre* (London: Faber, 2005), p27.
4. Michael Patterson, *Strategies of Political Theatre: Post-War British Playwrights* (Cambridge: Cambridge University Press, 2003), p128.
5. David Edgar, 'Come Together', *Guardian*, 10 January 2005, p2.
6. John Stewart and Milt Thomas, 'Dialogic Listening: Sculpting Mutual Meanings', in John Stewart (ed.), *Bridges Not Walls: A Book About Interpersonal Communication*.
7. *Ibid.*, p186.
8. David Hare, *Asking Around: Background to the David Hare Trilogy*, ed. Lyn Haill (London: Faber, 1993).
9. Stewart and Thomas, 'Dialogic Listening', p188.
10. Quoted in Richard Boon, *About Hare: The Playwright and the Work* (London: Faber, 2003), p67.
11. Quoted in Malcolm Page (comp.), *File on Hare* (London: Methuen, 1990), p15.
12. Edgar, 'Come Together', p2.
13. See David Edgar, 'The Italian Job', *Guardian*, 26 October 2005, p1; and Brenton, quoted in Catherine Itzin, *Stages in the Revolution: Political Theatre in Britain since 1968* (London: Methuen, 1980), p190.
14. Quoted in Page, *File on Hare*, p18.
15. David Hare, interviewed by Peter Ansorge, in 'Current Concerns', *Plays and Players*, July 1974, p19.
16. Edgar, 'Come Together', p2.
17. Hare, 'Current Concerns', p19.
18. *Ibid.*, p19.
19. Hare, *Obedience,* (date of lecture 2004), p27.
20. Georg Gaston, 'Interview: David Hare', *Theatre Journal* 45, 2 (May 1993), p217.
21. Quoted in Itzin, *Stages in the Revolution*, p188.
22. Stewart and Thomas, 'Dialogic Listening', p189.
23. Quoted in Page, *File on Hare*, p22.
24. Richard Eyre and Nicholas Wright, *Changing Stages: A View of British Theatre in the Twentieth Century* (London: Bloomsbury, 2000), p291.
25. Quoted in Nicholas Wroe, 'The *Guardian* Profile: David Hare: Makeover Artist', *Guardian*, 13 November 1999, http://books.guardian.co.uk/departments/artsandentertainment/story/O.,103076,oohtml#top (accessed 26 February 2007), p3.
26. *Ibid.*, p3.
27. Cathy Turner, unpublished interview with Howard Brenton, London, 17 January 2001.
28. Quoted in Boon, *About Hare*, p295.
29. Gaston, 'Interview: David Hare', p224.
30. Turner, interview with Brenton.
31. Stewart and Thomas, 'Dialogic Listening', pp185–92.
32. Turner, interview with Brenton.
33. Stewart and Thomas, 'Dialogic Listening', p195.
34. Turner, interview with Brenton.
35. Hare, *Obedience* (date of lecture, 2004), p31.
36. David Hare, *Writing Left-Handed* (London: Faber, 1991), p135.

37. Hare, 'Current Concerns', p19.
38. David Hare, interviewed by Graham Hassell, 'Hare Racing', *Plays and Players*, February 1990, p7.
39. Quoted in Rob Ritchie (ed.), *The Joint Stock Book: The Making of a Theatre Collective* (London: Methuen, 1987), p100.
40. William Hinton, *Fanshen: A Documentary of Revolution in a Chinese Village* (Berkeley: University of California Press, 1996). First published 1966.
41. Gaston, 'Interview: David Hare', p219.
42. Quoted in Ritchie, *The Joint Stock Book*, p105.
43. *Ibid.*, p108.
44. *Ibid.*, p. 110–16.
45. Stewart and Thomas, 'Dialogic Listening', p196.
46. Quoted in Ritchie, *The Joint Stock Book*, p105.
47. *Ibid.*, p111.
48. Stewart and Thomas, 'Dialogic Listening', p199.
49. Quoted in Michael Coveney, 'Turning over a New Leaf: *P & P* Investigates the Background to *Fanshen*', *Plays and Players*, June 1975, p11.
50. Quoted in Ritchie, *The Joint Stock Book*, p111.
51. Quoted in Carol Homden, *The Plays of David Hare* (Cambridge: Cambridge University Press, 1995), p47.
52. Hare, *Obedience* (date of lecture 1978), p119.
53. David Hare, 'Why Fabulate?' *Guardian*, 2 February 2002, pp4–5. Also published in Hare, *Obedience*.
54. David Hare, cited in Richard Boon, 'Platform Interview with David Hare on *The Permanent Way*', National Theatre, 27 January 2004, www.nt-online.org/?lid=8304amp;cc=1 (accessed 24 March 2005), p8.
55. Stewart and Thomas, 'Dialogic Listening', p194.
56. *Ibid.*, p186.
57. *Ibid.*, p196.
58. *Ibid.*, pp. 196–7.

8

BELLA MERLIN

Acting Hare

The Permanent Way

Acting Hare under the direction of Max Stafford-Clark must be akin to playing a Beethoven sonata conducted by Simon Rattle: so sure are the hands in which you find yourself as a performer, it is nigh on impossible for your 'instrument' to sound out of tune. In the course of this chapter, I explore my involvement with Hare's play *The Permanent Way*,[1] a co-production between Stafford-Clark's Out of Joint theatre company and the National Theatre, London. However, the structuring and writing of *The Permanent Way* was not necessarily the way in which Hare would traditionally work: far from being a solitary task, the process of assembling the material included a number of actor-researchers, as well as the director himself. Indeed, my own involvement with the play began with the early research in February 2003, when I first met Hare, and continued through to the production's final performance in Sydney during March 2005.

I begin by concentrating on the collation of the original material, and thereafter examine the ethical issues involved in a play that essentially draws upon living people's accounts – an area which particularly provoked both me and Hare – and the impact on the acting choices raised by those issues.

How it all began

It was during a discussion in November 2002 that David Hare as playwright and Max Stafford-Clark as director determined that they should work together on a new play, having not collaborated directly since the 1978 production of *Fanshen* for the Joint Stock Theatre Company. In a manner not dissimilar to *The Permanent Way*, *Fanshen* had involved a group of actors working with Hare as the writer to adapt for the stage William Hinton's book, *Fanshen* (see Chapter 7), and indeed Stafford-Clark's passion has always been to engage collaboratively with a creative team, be they actors, writers, designers – he craves 'the ensemble'. And so, in November 2002, Hare and Stafford-Clark agreed that, if a mutually intriguing subject arose, their reunion would be forthcoming. Thereupon Stafford-Clark – whose personal interest in trains and railways stretched back to his boyhood – gave Hare a small book by the journalist Ian Jack entitled *The Crash that Stopped Britain*.[2] This was a pithy account of the Hatfield train crash in 2000 (which, by dint of a faulty rail, brought Britain's railways to a halt). Having read the book overnight, Hare telephoned Stafford-Clark, and instantly the wheels whirred into motion. Three months later, in February 2003, a group of nine actor-researchers (Pierce Quigley, Lloyd Hutchinson, Sally Rogers, Nigel Cooke, Matthew Dunster, Maxine Peake, Paterson Joseph, Peter Wight and myself, all of whom shared an interest in the material but who might not necessarily form part of the final cast) was brought together along with the director, the writer and the assistant director, Matthew Wilde, to embark on a two-week research period.

In response to Hare's requirements at this early stage in the play's development, the two weeks of research were to consist predominantly of interviews with people whose experience of the railways covered a broad spectrum – from train operating company executives, investment bankers, politicians and entrepreneurs (the 'Men in Suits') to those who had survived or lost family in the four crashes which followed privatisation (the 'little people'). Some interviews would take place in the National Theatre Studio in Waterloo, although the usual practice would be for two or more researchers to interview individuals in their homes, workplaces or local watering holes. As we embarked upon the detective work, no one – including Hare – had any idea of plot or character. Indeed, both Hare and Stafford-Clark were unclear as to whether there would be any play at all: the interviews would reveal all.

Stafford-Clark had engaged in this kind of research before, most recently with Robin Soans' *A State Affair* (2000), and was to do so again with the same writer's *Talking to Terrorists* (2005),[3] and the unique aspect to such a process is that the writer and the actors develop a delicate and nuanced relationship. It requires a creative team with an openness, an innocence, and the awareness of a kind of metaphorical empty space into which the information they are about to uncover can flood. As Stafford-Clark put it:

> The embarkation point is that both actors and writer are going to surrender themselves to the words that they find [and] surrender themselves to the material in terms of the story.[4]

From this surrender, the new play would emerge. Therefore an extreme degree of trust and collaboration had to exist between Hare and the actors in terms of how the information was garnered, as the investigation of character and the development of dramatic plot would rest quite considerably on the

shoulders of the actor-researchers. This relationship was particularly important, as the method of collecting material was not through the recording
and subsequent transcription of interviews. The usual format was for two
or three actors, with or without Hare or Stafford-Clark, to undertake the
interview and thereafter return to the National Theatre Studio, where they
fed back the collected information to the assembled company *in character*.
In other words, our roles as actor-researchers were not only journalistic in
the sense of finding out the information and 'digging' for stories; we were,
in Hare's phrase, 'hunter-gatherers'. From the very beginning, we were literally shaping the drama with our own bodies in a deeply psycho-physical
way.

Without doubt, this sort of work carries with it a particular weight of
responsibility. As Neal Ascherson describes in his article, 'Whose Line is it
Anyway?':

> It's asking a lot of actors to use them as a research team, as if asking them
> to become journalists. But Stafford-Clark had no anxieties. 'You're getting
> real commitment from the actors, because you are asking them to take real
> responsibility.'[5]

One degree of 'responsibility' arose out of the 'condensation' of material (as
Stafford-Clark called it) or 'theatrical distillation' (a term coined by actor-
researcher Matthew Dunster), which was an inevitable part of the feeding
back of information. Most of the interviews for *The Permanent Way* were of
an hour's duration, sometimes longer. Our improvisations were subsequently
condensed to between twenty and thirty minutes. What Hare might draw
from that condensation would probably constitute only a matter of minutes
of stage action. Therefore, as actor-researchers we were determining to a
large extent what we considered to be theatrically interesting enough to feed
back to Hare in the first place. We were subconsciously editing and filtering
the material through our own creative sieves, based on the extensive notes
we had made during the interviews and in response to the impact that our
interviewee had initially had on us – and therefore how we might now impact
in a similar fashion upon our own listeners. Hare in turn heavily notated
our improvisations, with a keen ear for turn of phrase and idiosyncratic
speech patterns as much as for the facts and figures, and he probed us (as
we remained in character) about areas of particular interest for him as the
dramatist. He, too, was filtering our feedback through his own craftsman's
ear for character and structure.

It is important to note that at no point during the two-week research
period was the nature of the emerging play discussed. Certainly no indication
was made by Hare that the play might be orientated towards direct-address

monologues, which was in fact the format that the final draft eventually took. Nonetheless, I found my own responsibility as an actor-researcher and what might make for theatrically provocative material was particularly challenged when in the final few days of the research period I was sent to Cambridgeshire to interview a mother whose eldest son had been killed in the 1999 Ladbroke Grove crash.

The fact that the interview took place in the mother's house, with photographs of her deceased son and the regalia of family domesticity surrounding us, shifted for me personally the perspective of journalist-researcher. When fellow actor Matthew Dunster and I returned from the interview to give our feedback, we experienced a strange confusion in terms of what information to include and what to edit out, to the extent that we felt very strongly that Hare himself should meet the subject. At the heart of this bereaved mother's disturbing story was how she had heard that an article had been written by one of the survivors of the Ladbroke Grove crash describing the potent smell at the disaster site as being like that of a 'human barbecue'. Since her son had been 'totally literally destroyed'[6] in the fire, the description carried overwhelmingly distressing implications. The mother had subsequently rung the survivor in question requesting that this detail should not be included in the article, only to find in bold print in the next day's newspaper the words 'I woke to the smell of human barbecue'. The mother had started to tell us this story in a state of emotion-recalled-in-tranquillity; halfway through, her composure cracked and she began to weep, leaving Dunster and me in a state of chronic discomfort.

The public revelation in the newspaper of the 'human barbecue' detail had been extremely painful at the time for all the members of the family, and the prevailing thought in my mind as Dunster and I returned to the National Theatre Studio was whether we should offer up to Hare the mother's moment of agony as dramatic material, or was it something to which we had been privy that should remain within the confines of her kitchen? Yet at the same time I believed, as a 'hunter-gatherer', that by sharing this moment of emotional breakdown with Hare, Stafford-Clark and the other actors, we would be injecting a deeply human aspect to the unfolding story, one which would counterpoint many of the facts and figures discovered to date as presented by the 'Men in Suits'. As Dunster and I fed back our interview in character (it was common practice for all the actors who had conducted an interview to feed information back collectively, regardless of age or gender), I suddenly took a deep breath and began the 'barbecue' story, echoing the manner in which the mother had told it, stopping exactly as she had stopped, with her voice cracking mid-sentence before saying, 'I'm sorry . . . this is very difficult for me', and weeping as she struggled to regain composure.

Having been on the receiving end of the mother's breakdown, I attempted to convert my observations and experiences into something psycho-physical through which I could then attempt to elicit the same response from Hare and my other listeners as the mother had elicited from myself and Dunster. It struck me as significant that Hare should witness a moment of pain amidst all the clarity of expression. By that I mean that most of the people we interviewed – including the survivors and bereaved – had become very adept at telling their stories: they were almost raconteurs. Perhaps through a process of therapeutic counselling or simply telling their stories to a myriad of different inquiries and committees, many were surprisingly articulate and even witty. To see a moment when the enormity of a bereaved mother's pain might break through the astonishing composure with which we were frequently presented struck me as a significant offering to Hare's evolving narrative palette. Of course, his craftsmanship saw all that, and indeed, the moment – almost exactly as I had re-enacted it – was included as a part of a draft which was presented at the end of the two-week research period.

In fact, Hare wrote like a demon during that fortnight. On the first day, Stafford-Clark had described how the aim was to turn fact into art, and Hare worked remarkably fast, as if developing a photograph from a negative. By the beginning of the second week, nine pages of a Prologue for nine actors had been written, comprising a montage of sound-bites on 'State of the Nation' themes and perspectives. By the end of the fortnight, he had written a fifty-page script essentially presenting 'verbatim' extracts from the interviews undertaken to date, revealing the direction in which the play might go and presented to the producers of Out of Joint and the National Theatre. And yet there was still no definite decision that *The Permanent Way* might be a strongly 'verbatim' piece: as far as the research team was concerned, the new play might well have emerged as a fictionalisation of facts in the fashion of *Racing Demon* or *The Absence of War*.

At what point, therefore, did the 'verbatim' style of the writing become concretised? As Stafford-Clark described:

> I got an inkling of it after the workshop when David assembled his material and then the subsequent drafts didn't change. I suppose a couple of weeks, maybe a month subsequent to the workshop when the final draft came in, I thought, 'Oooh, it's still verbatim!' So not 'til then, and David didn't discuss it with us. In fact [at the end of the two-week research period] he'd said the opposite: 'This is the story we want to tell, but this is not the way we want to tell it.'[7]

So at what stage did Hare decide that this *was* the way in which he wanted to tell it?

The manner in which people were talking was so compelling. It was so obvious they'd organised their thoughts in their own heads in ways that made the narrative so vivid, that I then thought, 'What would it mean for me to interpose myself?' Also, it became clear to me that it was a ten-year story, and once you say it's a ten-year story, you can only do a little bit of each section because you want to get everything in. What's the point of fabulating when you've got to cover ten years like that? It felt like it did with *Via Dolorosa* [Hare's one-man piece about Palestine and Israel]: that to start inventing characters would just be a convention. What would they add to what was being told directly?[8]

Strictly speaking, however, *The Permanent Way* is not a piece of 'verbatim' theatre, a term which really came into circulation in the 1970s with the advent of the portable cassette recorder. In his article on '"Verbatim Theatre": Oral History and Documentary Techniques',[9] Derek Paget cites the words of writer Rony Robinson (a pioneer in this aspect of documentary theatre):

It is a form of theatre firmly predicated upon the taping and subsequent transcription of interviews with 'ordinary' people, done in the context of research into a particular region, subject area, issues, event, or combination of these things. This primary source is then transformed into a text which is acted, usually by the performers who collected the material in the first place.[10]

While the material for *The Permanent Way* was not 'firmly predicated upon the taping and subsequent transcription' of the interviews we undertook, it did share other significant elements of verbatim theatre. As Paget puts it:

In common with other manifestations of documentary theatre, Verbatim Theatre can . . . offer its actors a greater share in the *means* of production, in the Marxist sense – it offers the ensemble method of working.[11]

In other words, as we've seen, the actor's role directly connects the *collation* of the material with its *embodiment*. Paget goes on:

The inclusion of all members of the company in the process of interviewing people was seen by everyone consulted as a fundamental precept of Verbatim Theatre. This not only sets up a circle of direct interaction with the community which achieves completion in the performance of the play, but also gives actors an input into the very creation and shaping of the theatre pieces – something more usually denied to them as 'interpreters' rather than 'makers'.[12]

Hare was acutely aware of the unwritten negotiation between actors and himself as the writer in this process of 'making' rather than 'interpreting', and he treated the 'hunter-gatherer' status bestowed upon the actors by Stafford-Clark with great respect:

> The fundamental idea of what Max is trying to do is to give actors status and dignity. In other words, they're not simply vessels into which the author can pour his stuff, but they're creating the work alongside the author. When we did *Fanshen*, this attempt to give the actor status was complicated by political questions about whether actors should be acting, directors should be directing, and authors should be writing, and were these roles creating stereotypes? And indeed people questioned why I was getting royalties and actors weren't, when in fact the actors created the work and all the money was coming to me and so was it wrong for me to be getting royalties? . . . But what seems to me to have happened in 25 years is that modern actors now come with a much more innate sense of their dignity, and it absolutely astonished me in the first week of that workshop for *The Permanent Way* that none of the actors didn't regard that process of going out and researching and coming back and being responsible as a completely natural part of their function as actors.[13]

As well as acknowledging the contribution of the actors in the process of creating an essentially 'verbatim' piece, Hare was also keenly aware of his own ethical responsibility in shaping real people's lives into a dramatic format, at the same time as balancing that responsibility with a certain political bite. Some weeks into performance, after Hare had ensured that the survivors and bereaved were 'at peace' with the script of *The Permanent Way*, he reported:

> As far as I know, nobody's unhappy with the way they are represented in *The Permanent Way* because I don't think anyone is unfairly represented – except perhaps John Prescott, who is presented from the point of view of people who have only seen his *public* side, and I have no interest in exploring his *private* side . . . But having said that, the process of writing the play involved an infinite amount of ethical worry. I don't think you can do this kind of work without responsibility to the people involved and that will either be in consultation with them – which is what I did on both *Via Dolorosa* and *The Permanent Way* – or through the artistic balancing of what you're trying to say. But that's an artistic process which is very hard to explain to anybody who doesn't *understand* the artistic process. The sense of 'this feels fair' has to be a personal stance . . . And this to me is really a fundamental misunderstanding about playwrighting – the idea that fairness and balance creates a better play, and that there is such as thing as a non-judgemental playwright. The very act of writing is an act of judgement. Chekhov is one of the *most* judgemental playwrights: . . . Shakespeare is incredibly judgemental about people's failings. And this idea that good playwrighting consists of withholding judgement is totally mistaken.[14]

Discoveries through rehearsal

During the course of the rehearsals, Hare's relationship to the material and his position of 'judgement' subtly shifted in terms of defining what he thought the play was about, and these shifts impacted quite significantly on the overall temperature of the piece. (The cast for the first production comprised Flaminia Cinque, Souad Faress, Kika Markham, Matthew Dunster, Nigel Cooke, Ian Redford, Sam Graham and myself.) Hare had initially described the play as being about the privatisation of the railways; in the process of rehearsals, he modified this to being about the disillusionment of Blairite Britain, and – although he didn't change that idea – shortly before the production opened he did take his thoughts on further: for him, the play became about honour and dishonour, and how those who felt dishonoured (in particular, the bereaved) were seeking to find honour for those whom they had lost. The author's own discovery of the play through the process of rehearsals revealed his evolving 'superobjective' – that is, what his motivating reason for writing *The Permanent Way* might be – as he disclosed in discussion some time after the play had opened:

> For me, there are two axes in the play which became very interesting: one is the question of honour and dishonour – what it means to behave honourably and what it means to behave dishonourably, and the excitement of the contrast between the two is what animates the play. The other is suffering: it's the degree to which human beings distinguish . . . between suffering that's avoidable and suffering that's unavoidable, and what they should be doing about suffering that's avoidable. I wanted to study how these accidents could have been avoided, and how people dealt with the results of these accidents. And once those two ideas became clear to me as the subjects of the play, then I was away. The 'superobjective' is quite simply to express the anger of people who have suffered unnecessarily and been humiliated basically by the way they've been treated.[15]

This 'superobjective' notion of anger was to fuel much of the play's inner rhythm as rehearsals unfolded, and was particularly true for me around a section in the play involving a re-enactment of Lord Cullen's Inquiry into the 1999 Ladbroke Grove crash. Both Hare and Stafford-Clark impressed upon me that the Cullen Inquiry was the Second Bereaved Mother's avenue for anger: she could allow herself to express anger here because the main point of focus was facts and figures, not close relatives. She could channel private anger into public outrage, and various expressions of that outrage during the Cullen Inquiry became moments of triumph for both her and the other bereaved. Within their 'very Englishness', the bereaved succeeded in threatening the stability of the Inquiry with their acts of anarchy in the courtroom, even if those acts were little more than shouting out 'Judas' when the Chief Executive of Railtrack was asked for his name as he took the stand.

Allied to this anger, we discovered in rehearsals that the storytelling device of *The Permanent Way* demanded a certain sense of bravura, which the actors had to own. Right from the start of the Prologue, Stafford-Clark encouraged us to be – in effect – 'egotistical'; to grab the attention at the top of each beat. Indeed, the play would only work if we adopted a sense of 'Look at me, look at me!' That bravura involved each actor possessing a sense of command, as well as a physical and vocal energy and attack. That said, when the moments in which the drive was not so desperate, not so anger-driven – as in the scene immediately following the Prologue and involving an Investment Banker, a Senior Civil Servant and a High-Powered Treasury Thinker (a scene which became known colloquially as 'The Three Wise Men') – Nigel Cooke, Ian Redford and myself could afford to enjoy the solidity of composure experienced by these three 'Men in Suits'. Thus, by juxtaposing 'Look at me' anger (Prologue) with 'Look at me' confidence (Three Wise Men), the inherent rhythm of the play revealed itself.

To some extent, a simple, technical trick was required to embody the necessary quality of bravura: as actors, we needed to keep our eye-lines high. And herein lay a technical paradox: we had to embrace the whole auditorium, while retaining the illusion that we were talking quite intimately to a handful of individuals – or perhaps only one, David Hare – in a small room. To fill this technical demand with inner connection, Stafford-Clark proposed that with each character there had to be a bigger 'want' to tell our stories. In other words, volume, size and 'Look at me' bravura would not suffice on their own: we needed to amplify the inner desire to tell each and every individual story, and send that desire beyond the walls of the rehearsal room into the expanse of an auditorium.

Stafford-Clark revealed where the inner conflict for us as actors resided: while each character wanted to 'charm' the audience into hearing his or her story and thereby ally the listener with his or her personal perspective, we constantly had to be aware that the majority of the characters were middle-class, and their inner tension lay in their 'middle-classness' battling against the anger with which the experience had endowed them. Hare was forceful in his desire that the acting timbre should be

> Visceral and raw: that's what the play's all about – it's not intellectual polemic . . . A performance . . . where the actors do not have the experience of expressing that anger is an inadequate performance of *The Permanent Way*: the anger has to be there.[16]

The experience of performance

This 'visceral, raw' style certainly impacted on the way in which I played the Second Bereaved Mother, especially when the real-life mother came to see a preview at the Cottesloe Theatre in January 2004, to which the survivors, the bereaved and their legal representatives had been invited.

My own connection with the play that evening was (to some degree, inevitably) fractured. I had the strange sensation that I was holding the Second Bereaved Mother's life story in my hands like a fragile crystal ball, and consequently I was incredibly scared of dropping it or even breathing on it for fear that I would mist it over. When I met the mother in the foyer after the performance, her response was muted and cautious. On the one hand, this was to be expected as she and her husband had just sat through a re-enactment of their very personal tragedy. On the other hand, I felt a certain sense of failure. This was exacerbated when eventually she admitted that she felt I had been rather 'hard' in my portrayal of her. To some extent, I connected directly with what she was talking about, as the blanket 'anger' note had caused me some concern. Throughout the run of previews at the Cottesloe Theatre, I had felt that my interpretation of the Second Bereaved Mother was becoming somewhat shrill, a little highly strung, and that that timbre didn't feel wholly appropriate. Consequently, I somehow felt that I had failed the mother: that I had inadvertently betrayed the very qualities which I so wanted to honour in her – her integrity, her dignity, her bravery, her 'perkiness'.

My quandary as an actor was whether or not I was right to 'forsake' the real person to some degree in order that the theatricality of the subject matter and the play's overall visceral quality was maintained and in order that Hare's 'anger' superobjective was honoured. Was I right to compromise the mother's truth – or should I remain faithful to her 'centredness'? Or was there indeed a middle ground, a nuance which I had yet to discover? It was important to hang on to the fact that Hare's characters as montaged in *The Permanent Way* were artistic creations – they weren't impersonations. In his process of 'theatrical distillation', he had chosen to condense several hours of interviews into twenty minutes of on-stage montage between the survivors, the bereaved and the Cullen Inquiry. In a similar way to that in which he had no desire to show John Prescott's personal side, he sought here to highlight the Second Bereaved Mother's emotional, angry side, in order to juxtapose the cold-hearted facts and figures surrounding the railway industry with the flesh-and-blood pain and dishonour surrounding the disasters. In other words, he had no wish to show her temperate side; he had other characters to demonstrate temperance at other places in the play.

Although the mother whom I was playing had read the script prior to performance, it seemed that she had not fully comprehended the play's emotional impact once it became embodied by living actors on a stage in front of several hundred audience members. She possibly hadn't comprehended on the black-and-white page the anger underpinning much of the action. Perhaps she wanted to appear more temperate, less angry, more three-dimensional, less a dramatic function. It was arguably the visual and psycho-physical potency of the montage of the characters which affected her and caused her some initial concern having seen the play, and subsequently caused me a parallel concern in assimilating her reaction to the performance.

Curiously, I was not alone in my concern. Throughout rehearsals of *The Permanent Way*, whenever I had thrown up issues of ethics, David Hare had teased me saying that he was a writer with a sliver of ice in his heart. However, the adjective that he chose to describe the preview at which the survivors and bereaved were present was 'harrowing', revealing within himself a profound sensitivity. When I quizzed him as to why it had been so 'harrowing' for him, his answer was particularly insightful:

> The reason that art is so potent is because it parallels the process that goes on in our own heads. We tell ourselves stories. It's what [the writer] Wally Shawn calls 'that bzz bzz bzz' that goes on in our heads, where you say, 'I'm telling myself this and I'm telling myself that, and I'm doing this for a good reason, and I'm doing that for a wrong reason.'
>
> If you confront a very grave event, then that 'bzz, bzz, bzz' becomes almost unbearable. And you can see that the survivors and bereaved have gone through five years of 'bzz, bzz, bzz' – 'How do I make sense of this event?' In the case of [the Bereaved Mother, played by Flaminia Cinque], it obviously relates to religious faith: 'Do I lose faith in God? Do I keep my faith in God? Why is God doing this to me? Why is God killing my son? Giving me cancer? Killing my dog? Putting tensions in my marriage?' So the 'bzz, bzz, bzz' that goes on in their heads is at an unbearable pitch. If you meet either of the bereaved mothers, you know they've been to such terrible places inside their own heads that you pray – in your own life – you'll never have to go there.
>
> But what you inevitably come up with is a version of events, a story, a narrative, with which you can be at peace. You organise events inside your head to say, 'Well, plainly this happened, that happened'. If you have a love affair, then plainly you ask, 'Why did the love affair end?' You organise events inside your head, so that you say, 'Well, probably she felt this, and I felt that, and that's probably the reason.' And it troubles you for a while, until you organise it into a place where it's peaceful in your head. Until somebody arrives with a disrupted version of events and says, 'Well, she was going out with so-and-so all the time she was with you.' And you go, 'Ah, fuck! There goes my version of events!'

> So art is a version of events that is organised by the artist in a particular way. And of course I was worried that I would disrupt the way [the survivors and bereaved] had these events in their head. And the Second Bereaved Mother *was* disrupted by it: she said, 'That's not how I see it.' And because you know the cost at which they've been able to organise the events in their head, you feel a heel for doing anything that disturbs what peace of mind they have been able to achieve through suffering.[17]

Quite soon after the preview in question, possibly due to the fact that the public and critical responses to the play were so positive and enflamed, the Second Bereaved Mother's family contacted Hare and Stafford-Clark, in effect acknowledging the dramatic power injected into their story. They seemed to have found a sense of peace with *The Permanent Way*: their 'bzz, bzz, bzz' had evolved.

Art or journalism? Mixed responses

I felt very strongly that my style of performance with the character of the Second Bereaved Mother was most successful if there was a kind of Brechtian storytelling, in the sense that the character was in effect the puppet, I was the puppetmaster, and my task was to manipulate the puppet as simply and 'unencumberedly' as possible. The process was reminiscent of Grotowski's *via negativa*:[18] there needed to be the *elimination of blocks* between me and the words of the text, rather than the *accumulation of characteristics*. I, as an independent individual, had to 'get out of the way' of the character's words; there was no room for my *own* emotional response. To replicate technically my observation of the mother's breakdown – when to hesitate, when to falter, when to crack my voice – was the required acting strategy. Any emotion, any tears, had to be *her* emotions, *her* tears, and not *my* pity suffered on her behalf: it was a subtle, but significant nuance. As Paget writes in his article on 'Verbatim Theatre', 'It is not, entirely, a question of the actor constructing a character, nor is it, exactly, that they are playing themselves.'[19] He goes on to cite director Chris Honer's connection between verbatim theatre and Brecht's 'Street Scene':

> It seems to me that the shows always work best when you've got a kind of attitude that . . . Brecht talks about, actually. It's a slightly detached thing on the part of the actor . . . very *lightly* sketched in, but very *precise*.[20]

Curiously, this light, precise and technical approach to a very emotional moment elicited particular attention, especially with regard to what was considered 'real' and what was considered 'art'. In response to *The Permanent Way*, director Richard Eyre wrote:

The desire to make that experience of simulated reality more 'real', more like life as it is rather than how it's supposed to be, is the motor of modern theatre. Which is possibly why the most powerful plays I've seen recently are *The Permanent Way* and *The Hutton Report*, both taken directly from life. They both have dialogue [steeped in] artful artlessness and both demand performances that do justice to the circumlocutions and eccentricities with which real people lard their speech . . . would an actress relating the nightmare of her son's death break down and stop speaking with a silence of unbearable length without the authority of the observed event from which the moment was transcribed? The obligation of actors playing real people to honour their subjects leads to a naturalness and transparency that has the effect of making performances in plays not based on real events seem insincere.[21]

Grounding his argument securely in Stanislavsky's ideas of the 'magic if' and emotion memory, Derek Paget makes the following point regarding 'reality' in his article 'Acting a Part: Performing Docudrama':

For the audience, the founding principle [of docudrama] in psychological terms is the 'testing of reality' or 'realities'. Audiences are drawn to dramas by the question of 'what if' . . . In the 'what if' situation of drama, audiences' imaginations are stimulated to consider what it might be like to be another person ('like me but not me') in another situation, in another place, at another time . . . Link this imaginative projection existing within performance to the ratification of a factual base and you have a potentially powerful cocktail. Acting, even moderate acting, uses experiential intensifiers drawn from emotion memory, and seeks to supply them to the audience. The documentary element, however weak, supplies the heavily indexical assurance: this did happen.[22]

To a great extent, the purpose of the 'what if' scenario inherent in this kind of political theatre is to create within an audience member an empathy, an imaginative and emotive connection with the events that 'did happen', which might then provoke social change. For me, therefore, an assessment of the audience's response to the Second Bereaved Mother's breakdown moment as recorded by writer Esther Freud served as a useful barometer for the play's efficacy:

Bella Merlin who played [Second Bereaved Mother] . . . had been very self-possessed, very amazing, and suddenly her voice cracked and actually I think everyone in the audience imagined what they would've felt if that had been them. What more can you want from theatre?[23]

This seemed to me to be evidence of the 'what if' factor, which underpinned Hare's structuring of *The Permanent Way* in its juxtaposition of events and voices. Not that it was always received with such rapture: another mention of this particular breakdown moment in the play suggested that some audience members misunderstood both Hare's dramatic intention and my acting strategy. David Aaronovitch subtitled his article 'Tracking Truth' with the words, 'Theatre can question where journalists often can't. But it must be a measured inquisition.'[24] He went on to stir up what was for me a particular ethical hornets' nest: 'I just think that we writers and journalists should note what we do, and how we use people. Consider this from *The Permanent Way*. A mother is speaking' – and Aaronovitch then quotes the Second Bereaved Mother's 'human barbecue' speech, before continuing:

> You can see the problem here. The very thing that caused so much offence in a newspaper can now be repeated in performance after performance of the play. Because it suits the playwright's purpose. *L'auteur*'s excuse.

Bearing in mind my own ethical issues in feeding back this particular moment after the initial interview in Cambridgeshire, I confess I was rattled by Aaronovitch's comments, but felt quite ardently that Hare's intention with the inclusion of this moment in the final script of *The Permanent Way* was political and artistic, not journalistic. Not only had the survivors and bereaved approved the script (as previously mentioned) so that they could (in Hare's words) 'be at peace' with the contents of *The Permanent Way*, but also the very exposure of the Second Bereaved Mother's breakdown enabled the aggrieved party to *reclaim* 'ownership' of the 'barbecue' story. It had been taken out of the realm of journalism and repositioned in the sphere of art through the structuring of Hare's play. By allowing an audience to understand the grotesque pain caused by the story, Hare was by no means jumping on the bandwagon of that grotesquerie. He was, through dramatic juxtaposition, revealing the levels and textures of suffering endured by individuals swept unwittingly into such disasters, and through the formal structure of the play he was 'containing' a morsel of that suffering. It was this containment of suffering and the ardent political provocation of the piece which marked out for me *The Permanent Way* as the most creatively lucrative experience of my acting career to date. Acting Hare truly felt like playing an important instrument in a powerful orchestra.

NOTES

1. David Hare, *The Permanent Way* (London: Faber, 2003).
2. Ian Jack, *The Crash that Stopped Britain* (London: Granta Publications, 2001).
3. Robin Soans, *A State Affair*, in Andrea Dunbar and Robin Soans, *Rita, Sue and Bob Too/A State Affair* (London: Methuen, 2000) and Robin Soans, *Talking to Terrorists* (London: Oberon Books, 2006).

4. Bella Merlin, interview with Max Stafford-Clark for the Royal National Theatre educational website (www.nationaltheatre.org.uk/education) on *The Permanent Way*, March 2004.

5. Neal Ascherson, 'Whose Line Is It Anyway?', *Observer*, 9 November 2003, http://arts.guardian.co.uk/politicaltheatre/story/0,,1082019,00.html (accessed 3 December 2006).

6. Hare, *The Permanent Way*, p45.

7. Merlin, interview with Max Stafford-Clark.

8. Bella Merlin, interview with David Hare, March 2004.

9. Derek Paget, '"Verbatim Theatre": Oral History and Documentary Techniques', *New Theatre Quarterly* 3, 12 (November 1987), pp317–36.

10. *Ibid.*, p317.

11. *Ibid.*, p318.

12. *Ibid.*, p327.

13. Merlin, interview with David Hare.

14. *Ibid.*

15. *Ibid.*

16. *Ibid.*

17. *Ibid.*

18. Jerzy Grotowski, *Towards a Poor Theatre* (London: Methuen, 1976), p207.

19. Paget, '"Verbatim Theatre"', p332.

20. *Ibid.*

21. Richard Eyre, 'Speech Impediments', *Guardian*, 21 February 2004, www.arts.guardian.co.uk/features/story/0,11710,1152652,00.html (accessed 2 December 2006).

22. Derek Paget, 'Acting a Part: Performing Docudrama', *Media International Australia Incorporating Culture and Policy* 104, August 2002, p37.

23. *Saturday Review*, BBC Radio 4, 17 January 2004.

24. David Aaronovitch, 'Tracking Truth', *Observer*, 15 February 2004, www.observer.guardian.co.uk/comment/story/0,6903,1148420,00.html (accessed 3 December 2006).

9

RICHARD EYRE

Directing Hare

Paul Scofield once wrote this to a friend of mine who'd had been rash enough to write to ask him to give a lecture on the subject of acting. 'I have found that an actor's work has life and interest only in its execution', he said; 'It seems to wither away in discussion, and become emptily theoretical and insubstantial.' If discussing acting is difficult – 'writing on water', Garrick called it – imagine the folly of trying to describe directing, an activity of which audiences are largely unaware unless it's intrusively self-advertising, and which even its practitioners find hard to define and harder still to describe. It's something you do, like gardening, and, like gardening, you only learn about it by doing it.

Directing is the process of understanding the meaning of a play and staging it in the light of that knowledge, underscored by a view of what the writer is trying to say and why. In the case of a play by David Hare the 'why' is as important as the 'what' – the politics and attitudes to class and gender are seamlessly woven into the writing. But even the most innocent of comedies reflects a view of the world that a director endorses or indicts by his or her choices in casting, design, costume and performances: they demonstrate a view about how people live, how they behave and how they are influenced. What do the characters earn? Where were they were born? What do they believe in? Answering these questions is central to deciding how a director physicalises the world of a play and how the actors speak and move and dress.

Beyond that, as David Mamet has observed, 'choice of actions and adverbs constitute the craft of directing': get up from that chair and walk across the room. Slowly. Add to this the nouns 'detail' and 'patience' and the maxim 'Always remember tomorrow is not the first night', and you have said more or less all that can be said of the craft of directing.

In rehearsal the writer provides the actors with the territory to be explored and the director draws the map of the journey they are to take together. He or she encourages the actors to approach their project with the innocent optimism of new settlers, bound by the same social rules and sharing a common aim, and exhorts them to bury their egos for the good of the whole, however clamorous and individualistic they may be. The actors have to work to a common pulse, even if each chooses a different tempo. That pulse will always be derived from the play: water doesn't rise above its source. Hidden in the heart of every theatre director lies the desire to be an *auteur*. However, theatre directors cannot play God: they are negotiators, diplomats, mediators, suspended between the writer's need to impel the play forward and the actor's desire to stand still and create a character, obliged to interpret the blueprint, not to redraw it. They are the builders, not the architects.

Nevertheless the tension between the recognition of this truth and the desire to dispense with the architect remains, and it accounts for the fact that many directors are drawn to directing the classics exclusively, where the author is obligingly not present at rehearsals. With a new play there will always be a tension – more often than not a fruitful one – between the author and director. In spite of the obvious advantage of having the author present to ask for advice and refer to for meaning, and the obvious distinction between the roles of writer and director, there will always be an implicit (and sometimes explicit) competition for territory that has to be negotiated by both parties with a blend of self-effacement and self-assertion.

'The playwright has two alternatives', said Tennessee Williams, 'Either he must stage the play himself or he must find one particular director who has the very unusual combination of actively creative imagination plus a true longing or even just a true willingness to devote his own gifts to the faithful projection of someone else's vision. This is a thing of rarity.'

Many playwrights direct their own work because they are fearful that their vision will be blurred or diluted when mediated through other hands. David Hare is not one of these. He is a first-rate director, who became a writer when he ran his own theatre company because he wanted material to direct. His own productions of Trevor Griffiths' *The Party*, Christopher Hampton's *Total Eclipse* and Bernard Shaw's *Heartbreak House* possessed an exemplary and passionate lucidity. He directed his collaborations with Howard Brenton – *Brassneck* and *Pravda* – with a fearless bravura and, among the many productions of his own plays, *Plenty* stands out still as one of the most significant productions in the life of the National Theatre. Staged with a paradoxically lush austerity, it provided theatrical images – and performances – that remain luminously vivid twenty-five years later.

David Hare knows what the craft of directing is and what it demands of all parties, which begs the question as to why, on most occasions in the last fifteen years, he has chosen not to direct his own work. The answer is probably a weariness with the business of bringing a play to life, the barter and the diplomacy involved, and perhaps a writerly desire to preserve his objectivity by avoiding the politics of the rehearsal room: watching the furnace, but not putting his hand in it.

In his memoir *Acting Up*, he describes two kinds of director – the interventionist and the editor: 'Crudely, interventionists possess a vision of the work towards which they are, at all times, working. The show is already conceived before they begin, and they have an idea of the production which they need the actors to help them achieve. They have, in short, a Platonic show in their heads. Editors, to the contrary, work pragmatically, looking all the time at what they are offered, refining it constantly, and then exercising their taste to help the actor give of their best.'[1] The two directors who have directed the bulk of his work in recent years are Howard Davies and myself. Davies he categorises as an interventionist; me as an editor. The truth, in my experience, is somewhere in between.

The first play of David Hare's that I directed was *The Great Exhibition* at Hampstead Theatre Club in 1972. After that – or was it because of that? – he directed his own work until he wrote *The Secret Rapture* in 1988 and offered it to me when I had just started to run the National Theatre. I was directing an ill-advised revival of a production of Ben Jonson's *Bartholomew Fair* which I had staged successfully at Nottingham Playhouse, and I asked Howard Davies to direct *The Secret Rapture*. Was it an 'interventionist' production? Possibly, in that the stage was dominated by a large and very beautiful oak tree and haunted by the ghostly presence of one of the characters – neither of which gesture was indicated in the script.

But is this any more interventionist than the design that Bob Crowley and I evolved two years later for *Racing Demon*, when we presented the play in the Cottesloe Theatre on a raised stage in the shape of a cross that ran the length of the auditorium? No walls, no decoration, just the actors and furniture and light. This was our response to a play which had a series of soliloquies in which the characters addressed God, and had twenty-three scenes set in streets, housing estates, a bedroom, a kitchen, a study, the garden of a bishop's palace, the lounge of the Savoy Hotel, a cathedral, the General Synod and more, and yet was an intimate and warm-hearted study of failed love – of God as much as man – as much as an exploration of an institution.

In all Hare's plays, the sense of place is a prime ingredient. No playwright creates more evocative rooms: whether they're in echoing country houses or on factory floors, cheap two-room conversions or basements glowing dimly in the London blackout, they share a sharp density of atmosphere. The tattiest seaside boarding house or the emptiest provincial nightclub have a desolate magic about them, just as they would in a novel by Graham Greene or Patrick Hamilton.

The world of *Racing Demon* is one of dirty south London streets, bicycle-clips, *Goon Show* jokes and Tony Hancock tapes, empty churches and clarinet lessons, devoid of metropolitan swagger and shot through with a sense of loss. 'Is everything loss?' asks the defeated Lionel Espy in the last scene. An epilogue follows, a sort of optimistic epiphany, as Frances imagines herself flying off to the sun:

> I love that bit when the plane begins to climb, the ground smooths away behind you, the buildings, the hills. Then the white patches. The vision gets bleary. The cloud becomes a hard shelf. The land is still there. But all you see is white and the horizon.
> And then you turn and head towards the sun.[2]

Bob Crowley and I matched the sense of hope with a glare of white light, an image that we thought of as both literal and transcendental. Others saw it as 'interventionist' direction.

Working with Bob Crowley begins slowly in casual discussion, aided by sketches, anecdotes, photographs and reference books. The design always starts as a tone of voice and of colour, formless as a moving shadow, and through discussion and illustration the play starts to come off the page and acquires a three-dimensional shape. It's at this stage that there's the danger of imposing specious order, of tidying everything up to conform to a design conceit. The director has to guard against this by continuing to ask the questions: What's this for?, What does this mean?

In the five plays of David Hare's that I've worked on with Bob, we've always tried to find a staging that allows the physical world to breathe in the mind, that conjures up the required environment but dispenses with walls and ceilings and decorative elements; that is, in a word, iconographic. We weren't inventing a style; rather inheriting what Caspar Neher did at the Berliner Ensemble, Harley Granville-Barker and, later, Jocelyn Herbert at the Royal Court Theatre and John Bury at the Royal Shakespeare Company – making scenery expressive and metaphorical, rather than decorative and literal. We wanted everything we placed on stage to be specific and real, while being minimal and iconographic – like the cart in *Mother Courage*, and the large dining table, the heartland of the upper-middle-class family, in *The Voysey Inheritance*. As Granville-Barker said himself: 'To create a new hieroglyphic language of scenery. That, in a phrase, is the problem. If the designer finds himself competing with the actors . . . then it is he that is the intruder and must retire.'

The second play of the Hare trilogy, *Murmuring Judges*, required us to find a way of unifying the three universes of the judiciary, the police and the prison system. Bob devised a beautiful unifying device – a metal floor on to which a vast metal pillar descended that became the hub of the three worlds. With the help of giant projections on the back walls of the Olivier Theatre, we sped from the lobby of the High Court to a police charge room to a prison hall to the auditorium of the Royal Opera House with vertiginous ease. We defined the space with furniture, light fittings and actors, sometimes combining the three worlds in a multiple image only achievable in the medium of theatre – simultaneous action in separate areas of the stage occurring in the same time continuum. Probably the weakest of the trilogy from the author's point of view, from the director's and designer's it was the most exhilarating to stage.

With *Amy's View* we had the problem of staging a four-act play that for three of its acts was set in the spacious drawing room of a large house near the Thames owned by the widow – a successful actress – of a painter, and then it moved to a poky dressing room in a West End theatre. It set out to establish, and subvert, the upper-middle-class world of the four-act 'country-house' play. The establishing stage directions at the beginning of the play read as follows:

> *The living room of a house in rural Berkshire, not far from Pangbourne. The year is 1979. To one side there is a large summer-house-cum-veranda, full of plants. At the back, a door leading to a hall and staircase. The room has an air of exceptional taste, marked by the modern arts movement of the 1920's and 30s . . . This was once the home of an artist, Bernard Thomas, and all round the room is evidence of his work, which is rather Cezanne-like and domestic in scale.*[3]

And more.

It's a very specific description and one that we decided to distil into its essentials rather than attempt to reproduce. For instance, we thought that if the paintings were put on the wall the audience would be distracted by considerations of what school of painting they belonged to and how good they were, and they would become dominant objects that upstaged the actors. Our solution was to have barely perceptible ghostly images on the walls of the room and to make those walls of gauze, relying on the audience to imagine the paintings. By making the walls diaphanous and semi-translucent, the room suggested the beauty and the resonance prescribed in the stage direction, and dispensed with the heavy baggage of stage 'reality' – cornices, ceilings, door frames, light fittings.

The end of *Amy's View*, again a sort of epiphany, provided a different sort of challenge. We had to change the set from the dressing room to the stage of the theatre and then suggest that we were backstage just before the opening of a play. In the rehearsal draft of the play there was an explicit stage direction of the setting of the play – a shipwreck had taken place, spars and tattered sails remained, and there was the suggestion of a desert island – and the first line of the play was spoken: 'Who's there, tell me who's there'. Bob and I argued for a simple and, we thought, more expressive theatrical gesture.

Of this moment David said to me, only half-facetiously, that he expected something brilliant of me, a coup de théâtre. We decided to reverse the image, so that the actors walked away upstage rather than towards us. We wanted to create a gesture, innocent of technology, that would highlight the vulnerability of two actors walking on a bare stage towards an imagined audience. It had to be an image that would draw together the play's use of theatre as a metaphor for the endurability (and vulnerability) of human relationships and at the same time act as an assertion of the power of theatre itself. And it had to avoid being an attention-grabbing piece of bravura staging. We achieved it in the simplest possible way, with the sound of breaking waves, two huge pieces of white silk, music and lighting. The magic – as with most things in the theatre – was in the timing.

In essence what Bob and I have tried to do consistently is to find a physical style for presenting the plays that exploits the 'theatreness of theatre', the poetic property of theatre in which everything is metaphorical, everything stands for other things – a room stands for a house, a group of people for a society – and the audience fills in the gaps with its imagination.

The end result – the mise en scène – is always the result of a dialogue, a dialectic even, between designer, author and director. There is generally a difference of emphasis rather than substance, and only on one occasion – directing *Skylight* – have the differences become fundamental. The play was designed by John Gunter, with whom I've worked many times, and in our early discussions we decided that we would like to stage the play (in the Cottesloe Theatre) in the round, or as a traverse production with the audience on both sides of the action. I've done other productions like this – *The Voysey Inheritance, Vincent in Brixton*, for instance – and I was attracted to the potential intensity of the emotional debates happening within touching distance of the audience. David was opposed to this. He repeatedly stressed his desire for the set and the staging to be 'painterly'. He had written, as always, very specific physical details which he wanted translated into a stage reality. So we created this – every detail of Kyra's life from the age of the frying pan to the choice of the books on the shelves – with scrupulous accuracy, making a painterly whole that fulfilled the author's description:

> A first-floor flat in north-west London. There is a corniced plaster ceiling and underneath the evidence of a room well lived in: patterned carpets which have worn to a thread and a long wall of books. The kitchen area at the back of the room looks cluttered and much used. (p1)

Apart from moving the kitchen area, where much of the action was set, down-stage, nearer the audience, we conceded to David's views without regret. This, from Tennessee Williams, should be the director's credo: 'Just as it is important for a playwright to forget certain vanities in the interest of the total creation of the stage, so must the director.' And its corollary, from Howard Brenton: 'Knowing when to speak and when to shut up is nine-tenths of being a playwright in the theatre.' It's an article of faith with David Hare who, after the initial close examination of the text, invariably retires from the rehearsal room for a week or ten days. It allows the actors and director an opportunity to take 'ownership' of the play, and to stumble and shuffle around with scripts in their hands free of the judgement of the author. The play gets staged during this period; in my case, an empirical process without too many explicit instructions. The choreography of a scene should emerge from character and narrative rather than from pre-conceived design.

For a man who is never uncertain of his opinions and never shy of express-ing them, David Hare is a highly tactful collaborator. He acknowledges that there is an area of choosing actors where judgement is subjective, and occa-sionally, but only occasionally, our tastes differ. Actors in his plays need to be technically adept, be witty, intelligent and respond to his rhythms. His dialogue is deceptively non-naturalistic; it resists paraphrase and actors can sometimes find it surprisingly difficult to learn. Like all good playwrights, while he simulates natural conversation, his dialogue is highly structured and highly musical. There is nothing that pains him more than an actor who is unable to 'hear' the rhythms.

No less painful to him are actors who are unable to get his jokes. They're sometimes elusive on the page. None of us in rehearsal for *Murmuring Judges* imagined that this exchange – between a Home Secretary and a High Court Judge (Cuddeford) – would be a literal show-stopper at the top of the second act.

CUDDEFORD: ... (*He nods, suddenly incisive.*) Now it's *this*, it's this sort of thing, Home Secretary ...
HOME SECRETARY: Charles ...
CUDDEFORD: What would you call it? This slow *silting* of tradition, this centuries-long building-up, this accumulation of strata, which makes the great rock on which we now do things. It's infinitely precious.
HOME SECRETARY: (*Frowns*) Yes, but it must also be open to change.
CUDDEFORD: (*Enthusiastically*) Open.
HOME SECRETARY: It must not become hidebound.
CUDDEFORD: Hidebound?
HOME SECRETARY: Yes.

CUDDEFORD: Small chance of that! (*He leans forward, sure of himself.*) Remember, all the time judging brings you in touch with ordinary people. In our courts. We see them every day. Ordinary, common-as-muck individuals. Some of them quite ghastly, I promise you that. (*He nods.*) This makes us alert to public opinion. We're closer to it, perhaps, than you think.

HOME SECRETARY: Are you?

CUDDEFORD: It's reflected in the way we sentence. Everyone claims it's our fault if we sentence too high. But the tariff for rape . . .

HOME SECRETARY: I know . . .

CUDDEFORD: . . . has shot up from what?

HOME SECRETARY: I know this . . .

CUDDEFORD: . . . Maybe eighteen months deferred to over five years. It's not at *our* wish. It's because we have listened to what the public, at least the female part of it, wants us to do.

(*The* HOME SECRETARY *is smiling, familiar with this argument.*)

HOME SECRETARY: Yes, I admit. But it's a rare exception. There are figures from – Germany. Did you read those?

CUDDEFORD: (*Frowns*) Germany? No.

HOME SECRETARY: I sent them over. I circulated all High Court judges.

CUDDEFORD: I read little from Germany.

(*He turns to* SIR PETER, *diverting, but the* HOME SECRETARY *is not letting him off the hook.*) Like most judges, I have no time to read, off the case. Maybe, if I'm lucky, a thriller.

HOME SECRETARY: There they've reduced all prison sentences radically, by up to one-quarter, even one-third, without any effect on the criminal statistics.

(CUDDEFORD *looks at him warily.*)

CUDDEFORD: Really? Germany?

HOME SECRETARY: The same is true in Sweden.

CUDDEFORD: Sweden? (*He turns to* SIR PETER.) Peter, had you heard this?

SIR PETER: No. No, actually. (*He looks down, feeling himself on thin ice.*) Word hadn't reached me.

CUDDEFORD: It hadn't reached me either. (*He frowns.*) I think it's to do with the mail.[4]

The effectiveness of this exchange in performance illustrates a maxim of David Hare's: 'If the audience are with you for the first half, you have ten minutes for free at the beginning of the second.' The 'for free' passages in his plays contain some of his most exhilarating and skilful comic writing: the Savoy Hotel scene in *Racing Demon*, Tom's post-coital monologue in *Skylight*, Esme's story about her fictional nursing career in *Amy's View*.

His jokes are almost invariably effective in performance; if they fail they are honed, replaced or cut. He is never unaware that in writing for the theatre the words on the page are only half the story. He places jokes judiciously at the beginning of his plays – 'bumsettlers', he calls them – which allow the audience to feel that they're being let into the play, that they can be assured that they're in the hands of a writer who is aware that the point of theatre is that the audience and the actors occupy the same space and time.

At the core of every play of David Hare's is a debate, and in order to present a debate it's necessary to present two sides to an argument. Without debate, any form of political play – and his plays are indelibly political – becomes frozen in polemic. In all his plays Hare shows that he possesses the fiction writer's Philosopher's Stone: the ability to empathise with and to create characters wholly opposed to his view of the world and to endow them with life and vibrancy: Lambert Le Roux in *Pravda*, Marion in *The Secret Rapture*, Tom in *Skylight*, Victor Mehta in *A Map of the World*, the Bishop of Southwark in *Racing Demon*, Frank Oddie in *Amy's View*.

In the plays of the trilogy the scenes in which there is a confrontation between two opposing characters embodying two conflicting ideologies emerged late in the writing process: they were written after readings of a rough draft of each play in the National Theatre Studio. It was part of the process of directing the plays to participate in the readings and the discussions that followed them. In each case the reading was an essential step towards evolving a bringing together of the themes of the play. In terms of the 'music' of the plays and their themes and meaning, these scenes are essential: they are what David Hare refers to as the '*scènes à faire*'.

It's part of the joy of directing his work that there is a sense of inevitability about these substantial dialectical encounters which detonate with such satisfying eloquence and emotional force. And it's part of the joy, too, to collaborate with a writer who has the ability from time to time to surprise himself with his advocacy of a life far removed from his own. Take this wonderful defence of the ordinary by the young evangelist, Tony, in *Racing Demon*:

> Like everything in England it turns out to be a matter of class . . . Educated clerics don't like evangelicals, because evangelicals drink sweet sherry and keep budgerigars and have ducks in formations on their walls. (*Nods, smiling.*) Yes, and they also have the distressing downmarket habit of trying to get people emotionally involved. (*Stares at them.*) You know I'm right. And – as it happens – I went to a grammar school, I was brought up – unlike you – among all those normal, decent people who shop at Allied Carpets and are into DIY.

And I don't think they should always be looked down on. And tell me, please,
what is wrong with ministering to them? (p59)

It's a voice not often heard in his plays, a voice that emerges from his childhood – pure Bexhill-on-Sea.

He has a very considerable knowledge of actors and of their processes
(even more so since his adventure in *Via Dolorosa*). Occasionally he becomes
impatient with actors who appear to be treading water, exploring character
at the expense of playing a scene, and on occasions we have argued about
the need to intervene (his instinct) against the need to let an actor find their
way (my instinct). Above all, he's aware that the actors have to mine their
emotions – a sometimes untidy and haphazard process – and that the director's most important job is to enable them to do this successfully. And he's
aware that sometimes the absence of the playwright is as important as his
presence.

David Hare understands the ecology of theatre – how difficult ensembles
are to maintain, how anxiety is actors' daily bread, how necessary it is for
leading actors to assert their leadership. In the early stages of rehearsal, when
the play is anatomised and eviscerated by the actors and director scene by
scene, line by line, word by word, he's an exemplary companion: curious
to see how actors respond to what he's written; curious, too, to discover
whether he has written the play he thought he had. At this stage he's generous,
droll, entirely collaborative – collegiate, even – swapping advice and taking
suggestions: Do we need this line? Could this line be better? Is this speech too
long? Do you mean to say this? Then, as the performance draws closer, the
easy relaxation declines into tension, the body becomes taut as a wire, the
skin becomes almost translucent, the knuckles become white and the notes
hail down on the director by fax or email, voluminous, highly detailed,
specific, remorseless, run-through after run-through, preview after preview,
until the first night, and then, as in silence after a storm, you can hear the
dust falling between the walls.

At the first performance, with inspiring courage, David sits in the body of
the audience listening to them as much as to the actors. Subsequently, after
this bloom of boldness, the fear returns and he watches the show curled in
a foetal position in the stage manager's box, or crouched behind the back-
row seats. Nevertheless, however hermetic and paranoid he appears, he's
always ready, if not eager, to know what the objections are to the play and
production, whether, as he puts it, it's 'him' or it's 'me' – the writer's job or
the director's to fix the problem.

When David asked me to direct *Racing Demon*, I asked him what he
thought I'd bring to it. 'Another point of view', he said. What this point of

view consists in is probably a stubborn persistence to examine fiction against reality. Is this truthful? How does this measure against my experience of the world? These are questions that I ask of a writer just as I ask of an actor, an invitation to examine the only model available to us: Is this what you would do in real life? 'He and I are well suited', he writes in *Acting Up*, 'playing to each other's strengths. People usually said that it was because I was romantic and over-reaching, whereas Richard was careful and classic' (p179).

No director of his work can ignore David Hare's romanticism: it runs like an artery through all his work. It's partly expressed in a belief in the possibility of fulfilled love and in its redeeming power. Partly, too, in the belief – a far from naive one – that things can be changed, that it's possible to create a better life, and that Britain – or more particularly England – in the postwar period has squandered the opportunity to do so by deceit, cowardice, complacency and greed. 'There will be days and days and days like this', says Susan Traherne at the end of *Plenty*. Of course it's ironic, but then again it's not: the hope is real.

If a romantic view is always present in his work, so too is a political one. The belief in the possibility of radical change, of revolution, in his early work has not decayed with the death of socialism into a cynical belief in the immutability of man. His plays remain concerned with social justice, with the question: How should you live your life? In its public form, expressed in the trilogy, the questions were asked of our public institutions: How does a good person change people's lives for the better? Can an institution established for the common good avoid being devoured by its own internal struggles and contradictions? Is man a social animal interested in justice, in equality, in love? It's a moral view, but for all his mordant criticism he's far too self-aware to become a Shavian moralist. He has the pen of a polemicist but the soul of a romantic.

If his appetite for moral debate and inquiry remains undiminished, so too does his love – unquestionably romantic – for the medium of theatre itself. In its communal aspect – its ability to tell stories to a live audience – and its indissoluble reliance on the human form and human voice, it acts a model of social possibilities.

The director Jonathan Kent, who knows David Hare and me well, often says, particularly when we're bickering, that we're like an old married couple. It's not a bad image of the relationship between a director and author. Directors are ever hopeful of making a successful marriage of actor and character, of text and design, of play and audience. They have to be dogged yet pliable, demanding yet supportive. And if this sounds like a prescription for a perfect marriage partner, it's because it is.

NOTES

1. David Hare, *Acting Up: A Theatrical Diary* (London: Faber, 1999), p142.
2. David Hare, *Racing Demon* (London: Faber, 1990), p98. All subsequent quotations are taken from this edition.
3. David Hare, *Skylight* (London: Faber, 1995), p1. All subsequent quotations are taken from this edition.
4. David Hare, *Murmuring Judges* (London: Faber, 1991), pp54–6.

III
Hare on screen

10

JOHN BULL

'Being taken no notice of in ten million homes'

David Hare's adventures in television

DOMINIC: Do you do television also?
ESME: Oh, television, really!
AMY: She hates it.
ESME: I do.
AMY: She doesn't even watch.
ESME: Working your guts out while people do something else. There you are,
    working. What are they doing? Eating. Or talking. Just great! Being taken
    no notice of in ten million homes . . . Television? No I don't want to do
    it. For as long as London has its fabled West End . . .

David Hare, *Amy's View*, 1997

A fore-word

It is 1979, and Amy is in conversation with her partner, Dominic – a
journalist-critic, soon to be television producer – and her mother, Esme –
an actress of the old school[1] who will, by 1995, her stage career on the
slide, be playing Nurse Banstead in a television soap. There is possibly a
political significance in the fact that David Hare should open his play in
the very year that Margaret Thatcher first ascended the Westminster throne,
but, given the play's foregrounding of a live theatre/television debate, it takes
on a more personal significance when it is realised that the year is immediately bookended by the first broadcasts of two of the only three original
plays directed by him for television: *Licking Hitler* (1978) and *Dreams of
Leaving* (1980). Furthermore, when it is remembered that the first of these
existed in an effectively symbiotic relationship with his stage play *Plenty*
(1978, and in 1985 released as a self-adapted film), it is apparent that the
nature and potential of the different mediums was very much a current
preoccupation.

Reference to the play is, then, a useful way of introducing a central problem
in any discussion of Hare's work for television. It is a problem of definition,

and it would be as well to tackle it at the outset. Nine of his 'plays' have appeared on television. Five of these were television versions of stage works. In chronological order of screening, they were: *Brassneck* (with Howard Brenton) – BBC 'Play for Today', 22 May 1975; *Fanshen* – BBC, 18 October 1975; *Knuckle* – BBC 'Theatre Night', 7 May 1989; *The Absence of War* – BBC, 1995; and *Via Dolorosa* – BBC, 2000. That *Knuckle* should be incorporated into the 'Theatre Night' series and that *Brassneck* was screened as a 'Play for Today', as were Hare's first two original works for television, is significant. These generic descriptions owe much to the way in which early television drama appropriated both the kudos and, to a varying extent, the techniques of live theatre. Thus, of the original television works, the first is shaped very much like a stage play, with easily discernible act breaks. As in the second original work, *Licking Hitler*, the scenes are all in internal locations and, as Carol Homden points out, its essential three-act structure is very easy to detect.[2] However, the fact that *Licking Hitler* was subtitled a 'Film for Television' gives added point to Homden's description of the third original piece, *Dreams of Leaving*, as 'a film that happened to be produced for television rather than a television play'.[3] There is no longer an exclusive concentration on interior locations, and it is clearly a very different animal from the first two efforts.

Now, as it happens, the years between its first transmission, 1980, and that of his final original TV piece, 1991, are dominated by Hare's first efforts at film directing, producing *Wetherby* (1985), *Paris by Night* (1988) and *Strapless* (1988), all three of which, interestingly, were part-produced by television's Film Four. With hindsight it is difficult not to now think of the earlier efforts as moves towards his taking on the role of movie director. However, it is not as neat as this, and the same years also saw him have considerable stage success with *Pravda* (1985, with Howard Brenton), *The Secret Rapture* (1988) and *Racing Demon* (1990), all of which were produced at the National Theatre, London.

Given that a further new work, *Saigon: Year of the Cat* also premièred on Thames Television in 1983, it is important to attempt some distinction between what may truly be regarded as part of Hare's adventures in television and what may not. In general, I have considered the television versions of his stage plays only when it seemed useful to do so. To look at *Via Dolorosa*, for instance, would provide an opportunity to discuss the way in which the cameras capture so well his casual yet biting stage presence. *Saigon*, too, is omitted, for it is in no sense a work for television and, furthermore, was not directed by Hare. *Heading Home* is clearly a film also, as a brief examination of the first scene in the Soho pub would graphically demonstrate; but it was produced for television transmission exclusively and it was directed by Hare, and so must find a place.

***

Given the multi-faceted, multi-talented nature of the man, it comes as no surprise to realise that, as well as his highly successful work for both alternative and mainstream theatre, as a writer and director (of his own and others' works), and his acclaimed film work (again as both writer and director), David Hare has also enjoyed a considerable career as a writer and director for television. It comes as no surprise, perhaps, because for many playwrights of his and the previous generation television (and before and alongside that radio) had frequently acted as a launch pad to introduce the playwright to a wider audience. It was in this sense that Osborne's *Look Back in Anger* (1956) only started to enjoy real box-office success at London's Royal Court Theatre after a long extract from it had been screened on the box. And if that signalled the beginning of the power of that medium to confer favours on its performative elder, many playwrights were quick to understand the potential of enormous viewing figures unmatchable by even a long West End run in the theatre.

For, there was once, or so the story goes, a golden age of television, long before the proliferation of channels both terrestrial and non-terrestrial, when a play not attached to a serial format could reach the kind of viewing figures not even dreamed about by the most optimistic executives as yet another hopeful appearance by the England team in the football World Cup looms. It was a time when a Trevor Griffiths play, *Through the Night* (1977), could attract over 11 million viewers; and, even earlier, when a play by the still relative newcomer Harold Pinter, *A Night Out*, was screened on 24 April 1960 in ABC Television's 'Armchair Theatre' series, and was seen by an estimated 18 million people. That it was scheduled to be screened immediately after the commercial channel's flagship weekend show, *Sunday Night at the London Palladium*, may have done something to boost these figures, but the fact that it should have been so positioned bears witness to the (then) perceived popularity of the single play. Indeed, such was the importance of television as a medium for new writers, as had radio been before, that it provided a launch pad for many a stage career, that of Pinter not excepted.[4]

However, David Hare is very much the exception to what can almost be regarded as a rule, in that his early writing career owes virtually nothing to his contributions to television. In part this is a matter of timing: his theatrical career dates from 1968 and was initially concerned very much with an alternative theatre world that was antipathetic towards mainstream theatre, let alone television; and, unlike, for instance, Trevor Griffiths, he did not regard the medium as providing the audience that he wished to reach.[5] There were other reasons, however. Hare in 1982: 'For some years I didn't try to write for television. I had two main objections. First, I thought the studio process was harmful to good work and, second, I didn't like the censorship. I had started writing for the stage long after the Lord Chamberlain had been discredited, so it never occurred to me that a writer should be anything but free.'[6]

His first television play, *Man Above Men*, was screened as a BBC 'Play for Today' on 19 March 1973. As was standard practice at the time, it was recorded very quickly; and, since the text has never been published and the play was recorded on to videotape that was later wiped, the nearest we can get to re-creating the production is via the shooting script.[7] It appears to have been a mixed experience for the writer. On one hand he was given a young director, Alan Clarke, whom he later wrote of 'as one of the greatest British film directors . . . [though] he barely worked in the cinema at all',[8] and to whom he dedicated the published text of a later television play, *Heading Home*, 'in memory'. And on the other hand, the experience of watching his text take dramatic shape clearly created unhappy memories:

> My original feeling that standards were so low that it was not worth working in television at all was based on my early experience of videotape. The play is cast, rehearsed in a couple of weeks, then slung on through a three-day scramble in the studio which is so artistically misconceived that excellence is rarely achieved except by accident. The eye is always on the clock. The pressure of time and the cost of over-running are so great that a director justifiably feels he has done well if he has got the play made at all. 'Good' directors in the studio are therefore, as far as the management are concerned, those who get the shows in on time.[9]

Man Above Men was, indeed, videotaped over three days (11–13 November 1972), although in the absence of the completed play it is impossible to assess the effect of this haste. The play's title refers to the figure of the Judge: in his own words, 'The law is a fascinating game. And a hard rewarding mistress. It is a necessity – the very basis of society – and so you must administer it with all the wit and courage you can muster. The very best men of each generation' (scene 20, p52 of the shooting script). It is this same Judge who, in the opening sequence – after a nostalgic Fred Astaire song has accompanied the credits and opening placement of the action in the courtroom – makes a foolish mistake over the length of the sentence handed out to a prisoner, and is rewarded for his efforts by being struck by a clock (time being thrust upon him) thrown from the public gallery by the man's wife. The play's title also predicates a division, a division that is reinforced by the narrative. If, as the Judge argues, the machinery of the law is run by an elite, then its deliberations concern men at the other end of the social spectrum. The two cases presided over by the judge are concerned with men who would precisely not be thought of as a part of his world. Not only are they presented as straightforwardly lumpenproletariat, but the details of their offences are offered for comic approval. The first case involves a 20-year-old, Andrews, who with his friends had brutally attacked the Mayor of Wimbledon on the common bearing his name. Questioned further, he claims that the 'queer bashing' was prefaced by his rendition of the Boy Scouts' signature tune, and that they were only performing a public duty that the police ought to be attending to. All this is interwoven with the Judge's own memories of racial empowerment in the East ('The last time I swam – was in the Gulf of Suez in 1942 . . . Shahiz brought us Pimms Number One. Waded in in his white cotton trousers . . . You could have said Shahiz put your head under and hold it there till we said take it out'; scene 1, pp4–5).

The play is, then, a somewhat strange mixture of pointed, if scarcely original, observations about class struggle and borrowings from a by-then-well-established English absurdist tradition.[10] So that, when the second case is brought into court, concerning a mechanic, James Kelly, who is found guilty of murdering and stealing from a money lender to whom he is already in hock – the Judge's Clerk commenting that the 'class of clients' has not changed – the cut and thrust of the questioning is punctuated by an inserted filmed sequence of a matador 'elegantly placing a stick in the neck of a bull'. This sequence is repeated and then, after the Prosecution's last attack, the final sword goes in, there is a gush of blood and the crowd roars (scenes 13 and 14, pp41–3). The overall effect is one of non-naturalism, with melodrama merging into parody.

However, what is most interesting about the play is the way in which the absolute assurance of male dominance suggested by the title is continually undercut, and it soon becomes apparent that the real centre of interest for Hare was not with the Judge or the prisoners – for all of the men are seen in some way as inadequate, as incapable of fulfilling their roles in a patriarchal world – but with the women and, in particular, with the Judge's daughter, Susan (played by Gwen Watford). Although she is in her fifties, Susan is the first of two recurrent types of women in Hare's work. She is sexually independent – embarking on a brief affair with the Judge's Clerk, the latest of a string of weak men to whom she has felt attracted – but vulnerable to the point of attempting or committing suicide at the end of the play. This is linked to her role as an innocent who is used to carry the burden of discovery, much as is Anna in *Licking Hitler*: the first scene in the play is the first time that she has been to see her father at work, but by scene 16 she has a fully articulated critique of the system and the Judge's part in it:

What do you think when you sentence them? The same people over and over. Coming back for more. Popping up in court in four yearly intervals . . . My father's watched this pageant of horror and poverty and violence and blood go by in his courtroom, and systematically – once a week, twice a week – he kicks out a leg and says it's all too difficult for me – smother it – we don't know how to deal with this, but a kick in the teeth should do it.   (p45)

Man Above Men is, ultimately, an apprentice piece, but it gives strong indications of the way in which Hare's work for the medium would develop. Remarkably, it was only a further five years before he was to produce what is one of his most important plays, *Licking Hitler*, a play that demonstrates an ease with working for television quite unheralded by this first effort. First, however, came adaptations of two of his stage plays. In 1975, *Fanshen* was broadcast on BBC TV (18 October). Overall, it was an extraordinarily honest attempt to transpose the stage original on to the screen but, like the original, it is a one-off in Hare's career, his increasing interest in the world of the individual being sublimated into a drama of community and national political struggle where the individuals have, in Brechtian terms, to introduce themselves in order to acquire any sense of identity.

Immediately before this came an adaptation of his and Howard Brenton's stage play, *Brassneck*. The play, which was directed by Mike Newell on this occasion, was put out on 22 May, also as a BBC 'Play for Today'. *Brassneck* (Nottingham Playhouse, 19 September 1973) is a surreal account of post-war history and local council corruption in a Midlands town – very much a 'State of the Nation' play. The original production had been a very complicated affair technically, with barrages of back-projected slides being used to create the series of essentially non-naturalistically conceived, and frequently quite bizarre, backdrops to the action. The television version retained the surrealism of the dialogue, but relocated it in naturalistically conceived sets and outside locations, so that, for instance, our first sight of Alfred Bagley's family (Act 1, scene 6) occurs on an actual station platform, and the preceding scene in the stage play, with Bagley being crowned as Pope, is omitted altogether. At the Nottingham Playhouse, Act 2 had opened with a calculatedly absurd fox-hunting scene. On television this became a cricket match, again with a surface naturalism being played against the dialogue. There are other examples that could be mentioned, but all of them support the way in which television sought to reclaim a contextualising naturalism, as though the deliberately symbolic nature of the narrative could be re-presented in terms of conventional storytelling. The one significant exception to this came with the opening scene, where the club location of the final scene is visited briefly for a part of the police raid, the discovery of the heroin, and Sidney's conspiratorial address to the camera, 'You're not going to believe this. (*PAUSE*) But . . .' Following this, the '*screen peels*', and there is a caption that takes us back to the start of the chronology of the play, '1945' (p84), before the '*screen peels*' again and the play picks up from where it had on stage. What is particularly significant about this change is that, not only does it provide a framing device for the narrative, but, by virtue of the fact that it was shot on telecine, it creates a more grittily film noir opening, reminiscent of parts of Nicolas Roeg's film *Performance* (1970).

Although three extra days were allowed for filming on telecine (readily convertible to video format for television screening), the studio work on video again took place in the statutory three days, between 5 and 7 February. It was evidently a rushed affair, although the final product seemed, to me at least, a thoroughly admirable attempt to capture much of the excitement of Richard Eyre's magnificent production of the play at the Nottingham Playhouse in 1973. David Hare: 'My own last memory of the recording of *Brassneck* was of leaving the box forty minutes after "time" had been called, with an unrehearsed scene of a hundred extras and four unplotted cameras still going on chaotically downstairs, and the director crying help-lessly to a random cameraman, "Go in. Number Four, anything you can get."'[11]

It is tempting to see this experience as pivotal. Although Brenton and Hare were to collaborate on stage one more time, with *Pravda* in 1985,[12] their theatrical and political strategies began to diverge quite significantly. By the time that Hare's next original television play was broadcast, both writers had made their debuts at the newly completed National Theatre on London's South Bank. They both used a modified version of the epic model that they had begun to develop with *Brassneck*, but to very different ends. Where Brenton's *Weapons of Happiness* (1976; published in *Plays: One*) seeks to engage directly with political struggle at a public level, Hare's *Plenty* (1978) does so at a more directly personal level, and it was in this direction that the latter's work would increasingly go. That the 1978 play should be directly associated with Hare's next venture on television makes the significance of the distinction the greater. For not only had his previous experience taught him the necessity to take control of his own production, as director, but it consolidated for him the importance of working with film rather than video: and he was prepared to wait a whole year in order to achieve these ends. *Licking Hitler*[13] also allowed him to strike up a good working relationship with the producer, David Rose, who told him, 'When-ever you've got another, let me know.'[14] This led to a third television play, *Dreams of Leaving*,[15] again written and directed by Hare and produced by Rose.

Plenty had opened in 1962 before briefly flashing back to 1943 and the arrival of the play's chief protagonist, Susan Traherne, in France, trained to work with the Resistance. It then follows Susan's progress, and her growing disillusionment with postwar Britain through the subsequent years, in a series of jumps through history, concluding with a return to France in 1944 and her final euphoric but unconsciously ironic words of the play, 'There will be days and days like this.'[16]

The television play *Licking Hitler* does not attempt a comparable sweep through history, but concentrates the action into a brief period during the Second World War that is the chronological starting point in *Plenty*. This reduction in the narrative scale is matched by a narrowing of the focus of the locale. In his construction of the setting, Hare drew skilfully from television's long-established borrowing of an emphasis on domestic interiors derived from their continual deployment in postwar theatre – a connection made evident in the description of television fictional narratives in terms of theatre-based experiences[17] – but with the added versatility of easy movement from one interior to another. This can be seen in the way in which the directions for the two brief opening scenes lead the viewer from an outside world that is initially rooted in a tranquil past world of class privilege and then is rudely interrupted by evidence of warfare, before he or she is pulled inside and into the action. It is a visual journey that is anticipated, and thus in a sense impelled, by the soundtracked voice-over:

> *An English country house. Perfect and undisturbed. Large and set among woods. The sun behind it in the sky. Loudly a bird tweets . . . A convoy of military vehicles comes noisily up the long drive . . . A corridor inside the house. At the end . . . we can see through to the large hall . . . sound of the convoy arriving . . . All the time the camera is tracking back, drawn by the voice of* ARCHIE MACLEAN.[18]

That it should be Archie's voice that we first hear, and that it should be he who sets the action on its way, acts as a deliberate cue, for what I excluded from the above directions is the portrayal of the evidence of the traditional inhabitants of the country house – its '*elderly chauffeur*' and '*even older maid*' – on their way out in every sense with the luggage of the past. For, as we soon learn, Archie is a working-class Glaswegian hostile to all that is represented by the house's ousted owner, a Lord Minton whose declining faculties – established by the chauffeur's use of deaf and dumb language to his master in scene 6 – reinforce the sense of a change in the social ownership of all that might be represented by the house. However, the ease of this interpretation, though not the class antagonism, is immediately called into question as Archie takes his leave of the Lord:

ARCHIE: Very kind. Of you. To lend us. Your place. (*MINTON turns and gets into the car, the door of which is held open for him by his CHAUFFEUR.*) Tell him we appreciate his sacrifice. Having to spend the rest of the war in that squalid wee single end in Eaton Square . . . That's right Minton, you bugger off. (p14)

That this transparently symbolic parting of the ways should be witnessed by the arriving 19-year-old Anna Seaton, whom we have briefly seen struggling unaided along the road with her luggage, renders the episode the more ironic. For Archie, having seen off the old representative of the old order, is immediately presented with a younger version, an Anna whose uncle is Second Sea Lord and who has so little contact with ordinary life that (scene 13) she attempts to make tea by pouring cold water over the entire week's ration.

Because of this continual cross-cutting at the outset it is left to the viewer to realise by degrees that the country house has been taken over for the duration of the war as a make-believe German radio station, intent on demoralising the troops that it claims to be supporting. The director of the radio station, and thus of the house, is Archie.

> His brilliance at his job stems from his absolute lack of belief in any lip service to the moral tenets of the class that he sees as the real enemy. In the country house, as in the Diplomatic Service in *Plenty*, the lie reigns supreme, but for Archie it is unencumbered by any sentimental attempts to pretend that there is a larger morality. He argues successfully that, instead of propagandising against the German invasion of Russia on the demoralising grounds of its evident stupidity, they should be aiding it because it *is* stupid.[19]

For Archie there is, then, a double enemy and when, inevitably, he makes sexual advances on Anna, he does so in a directly aggressive manner, breaking drunkenly into her bedroom, ousting the teddy bear of her childhood innocence, and effectively raping her: 'The Scot makes love wi' a broken bottle' (p34). Although Anna comes to understand much of what fires Archie, any real communication across the class barrier proves impossible and, when he believes that there is the possibility of a real relationship developing between them, he has her taken off the project.

The country house, although relocated as a bureau of 'untruths', still functions as a battleground for Archie, and neither the political nor the personal narrative are ever resolved in the play. Having established the complicatedly symbolic nature of both the location and the project, Hare carefully denies the viewer a resolution. Instead, a voice-over describes the various ways in which the play's central characters occupied themselves after the war: 'Many of the most brilliant men from the Propaganda and Intelligence Services went on to careers in public life, in Parliament, Fleet Street, the universities and the BBC' (p51). Unlike Susan Traherne in *Plenty*, whose war had been the one euphoric moment in which all things seemed possible – and whose subsequent mental disintegration is clearly meant to mirror Hare's sense of the moral decline of postwar Britain – Anna has learned a bitterer lesson, as is clear from her (the last) words in the play, from an unanswered letter to Archie:

> Whereas we knew exactly what we were fighting against, none of us had the whisper of an idea as to what we were fighting for. Over the years I have been watching the steady impoverishment of the people's ideals, their loss of faith, the lying, the daily inveterate lying, the thirty-year-old deep corrosive national habit of lying, and I have remembered you. (p54)

Anna's words are complemented by those of Hare in his 'Cambridge Lecture' (published with the play), where he talked of himself as a history writer: 'if you write plays that cover passages of time, then you begin to find a sense of movement, of social change'; and the change that he sees most fundamentally in the postwar years is evidenced, as it had been by Susan and by Anna, 'in the extraordinary intensity of people's personal despair, and it is to that despair that as a historical writer I choose to address myself time and time again'.[20] Later in the same lecture, he argues that, in addition, 'I write love stories. Most of my plays are just that.'[21]

This conjunction, between the worlds of the public and the private, was to become ever more important in Hare's work and it is arguable that the particular potential of film as a dramatic medium for the articulation of emotional intensity allowed the playwright to explore this relationship in ways that gave increasing emphasis to the personal; the public becoming the context rather than, as previously, the main text. And this helps to explain the particular power, as well as the particular significance, of his next (and last) two plays for television,[22] for in both of them Hare's starting point is this sense of public malaise and personal despair.

Hare's next self-directed play for television, *Dreams of Leaving* (BBC, January 1980) is in many ways a departure from the fictionalised account of history offered in *Licking Hitler*. It appears to be gesturing towards the personal/biographical rather than the historical/biographical, with a voice-over not provided by the 'innocent' Anna but by a young man who might be thought to have significant connections with Hare himself. For a start, the William who arrives in London in 1971 is 24, the same age as Hare, and he has come from Nottingham, familiar to the playwright from his important sojourn there as resident dramatist from 1973 during Richard Eyre's directorship. The probable connection with Hare is most important in relation to the use of the voice-over. This is a feature of all Hare's television plays, but here deployed very differently. In *Man Above Men* it had simply operated to allow the Judge to look back on his past and for us to note his innate class and racial prejudices; and in both *Licking Hitler* and *Heading Home*, the voice-over is that of a woman whose progress we have followed through the play, and whose judgements we have come to trust. In *Dreams of Leaving* it is as if the character were always aware of an audience for whom he or she must perform wittily – rather than telling the truth as best the character knows it – demonstrating his or her detached coolness. For example, within about a minute of the start of the play William informs the viewer of his loss of a girlfriend: 'I was living with someone called Angela, or thought I was, because she was never there . . . It was six days before I realised she'd left me and another six before I could get over it.'[23] That each of these VO sentences should not only take place in separate locations where he is shown to be in a frantic rush (the outside of the Fleet Street office, William running for a bus, and 'hastening' up the stairs to his flat) forces the viewer to see the clear gap between the way in which the speaker chooses to interpret his life and its more probable reality.

A further effect of this continual use of William's VO is that we are denied any insight into the object of his hopeless affections in the play and (as we learn) his entire life, Caroline: she is created as an enigma for us. That Caroline was played by Kate Nelligan, who had also created the part of Susan Traherne, has acted as a prompt for Homden to construct an almost literal biographical scenario for the play, down to the fact that the actor playing William, Bill Nighy, was the same age as Hare and bore 'a startling physical resemblance' to him.[24] However, this is perhaps of more interest to potential biographers than to viewers of the play.

Hare is in agreement with Homden that the continuing preoccupation of the piece is sex.[25] However, it is essential to consider the context in which William and Caroline play out their hopeless relationship, ending in madness for her and the ongoing continuity of suburban married life for him – as we are made to observe in the magnificently staged final VO. William and his wife and mother of his children, Laura, are in bed. They kiss briefly and there is a long pause as *'they look at each other'*. Before the light goes out and the play ends, William gives us his last sad words: 'Our lives dismay us. We know no comfort. We have dreams of leaving. Everyone I know' (p41).

Different though it is from *Licking Hitler*, the play starts historically pretty well where Anna's final unrolling of postwar history had ended. But, whereas her break with the 'straight' world in 1968 had been accompanied by a series of stills of the Grosvenor Square demonstration against the American presence in Vietnam, William enters London in the very different context of the 1970s. His chosen profession of journalism is precisely one of those picked out by Anna to illustrate the 'thirty-year-old deep corrosive national habit of lying' as William, hoping to impress Caroline, points out at an editorial meeting (pp306–7). In her turn, Caroline is as cynical about her initial occupation in the art gallery and, significantly, her later success as a photographer is predicated on her work with London prostitutes, where money is as much to the forefront as in the world of art.

Although the drug case involving a cockney musician named Keith, the aftermath of which figures importantly in the play, is probably intended to echo that of the 1967 bust of the Rolling Stones, the action is solidly located in the next decade, something that is emphasised by Hare's deliberate running together of the events of the years 1971–3. At the start of his journalistic career, William appears to be writing about the 1972 miners' strike, and later reference is made to the negotiations over Britain's membership of the EEC, something that finally happened in 1973. However, the specific mention of the British Leyland strike means that the real context is the long period of industrial action initiated on 1 May 1973, when nearly 2 million workers protested against the Conservative government's economic policies, action that led ultimately to the 'three-day week', the downfall of the government and the long spiral of industrial discontent that was to lead eventually to the first electoral victory of Margaret Thatcher in 1979, a process that would have been very much in Hare's thoughts at the time of writing the play.

Heading Home (BBC, 13 January 1991) starts approximately where *Brassneck* had, in 1946. Given the obvious links between Ian Tyson, the slum property would-be tycoon and the get-rich schemes of Bagley in *Brassneck*, that the working title of the play should have been 'Safe as Houses'[26] points to a significant tension in the work; and one already apparent in *Dreams of Leaving*. Its original title is a piece of conscious political irony: the houses that Tyson peddles are neither safe nor in any meaningful sense homes, let alone ones fit for heroes.

At the centre of the play is another of Hare's innocent young female protagonists, Janetta Wheatland. Her very surname evokes the pastoral southlands from which she originates and to which she continually wishes to escape from London. The beach location that not only opens and concludes the play, but provides the scene for the two sexually significant visits with each of the men she is attracted to, ironically recalls her own 'innocent' childhood in Weston-Super-Mare. Both men are products of the war. Her chief protector, Leonard Meopham, is an aspiring writer, attempting to make sense of the dreadful experiences of the conflict in his poetry. He is passive where his rival, Ian Tyson, a slum property landlord who is later linked with the activities of the notorious Peter Rachman, is aggressively active, forcing his attentions on Janetta. These personal qualities are linked with their class origins. Ian is from the other ranks, whereas Leonard has clearly been bred as officer material. He tells Janetta, in one of his rare moments of self-revelation,

> Before the war . . . I was brought up. I was trained to be brilliant. Like the rest of my family. I played cricket, I would have a proper career. Running the country. It was simple, I was English.[27]

Instead, changed by his wartime experiences, he has become a writer. That he is one, and employed by the BBC as a part of its cultural arm, is important for Janetta, as acknowledged by her recognition of her qualities as muse for him, and reinforced by her acceptance of a job in a library, dispensing books. This is further stressed by the manner of their meeting. Attracted to the voice of a male poet on the wireless, she had written a letter and arranged a visit to the studio: 'Only somehow, I don't know, I arrived to see Charlie, and I left with Leonard' (p215).

In the winter of 1946–7, in the immediate aftermath of the war, Leonard introduces her to Soho and a bohemian group of writers and artists. She is confronted straight away with the fact of a single mother, and with somewhat unusual, although at this juncture, quite innocent, sleeping arrangements at the newly met poet's flat. On the second night of their acquaintance, she has with her photographs of her securely middle-class family, with five English rosebud sisters, a father who is the proprietor of a large haberdasher's and a mother who is a 'Mummy [who] said, go to London, learn shorthand typing so you can help Dad with the paperwork until . . .'. In answer to Leonard's reaction to her pause, she continues, 'Well, obviously, until I get married' (p222).

In contrast to the lifestyle offered by Leonard, Ian inhabits a world of murky property auctions, wheeler-dealing, shady clubs where he conducts his business and underworld acquaintances who will subsequently brutally assault his friend and associate, Juliusz, and murder the developer for his incursion into the property world. Janetta has met Ian at the library, which he uses for access not to poetry but to property surveys, and she is soon drawn into working for him on a casual basis as a rent collector.

The way in which she is used as another innocent abroad in a postwar world of alternative possibilities – as was Susan in *Plenty* and Anna in *Licking Hitler* – is reinforced by the way in which Hare deploys her voice-overs. There are sixteen in all and, although they all operate to link the strands of the narrative, the first eight are specifically linked to her sense of her awakening sexuality, an awakening that is linked, as so often with Hare's female protagonists (and most disturbingly for Anna), with the growth of a political understanding of the world. Her gradual progress towards Edward is described by her in the voice-overs as 'like the phoney war' (p226) and then, at last, 'the phoney war was over . . . that night I took Leonard to bed' (p228).

Thereafter, the voice-overs concentrate on her connections with Ian's business dealings, and on his insistence that, as a woman, she can be something other than just a muse: 'I believe women can actually do it . . . I believe in you' (p250). Then there are three more concerning Leonard's successful poetry reading and his leaving the flat in recognition that she has another life elsewhere, before, finally, her voice returns us to the same beach that she had visited with Leonard, but now with an Ian about whom we learn that 'I never heard from him again' (p271).

The only direct reference to the title of the play is made by Ian's ex-army colleague and bagman, Juliusz, whom Janetta discovers in her newly acquired flat (given to her by Leonard, but the lease bought by Ian to emphasise the distinction) after his beating. She patches him up and he announces that he is 'heading home' to his native country, Poland. He asks her if she too has a home, and she replies, 'Yes . . . Weston-Super-Mare . . . but I've left it. And I think it may be hard to go back' (p267). For the other characters there is no home to return to, no way of recovering the past (save in the memories of Janetta that constitute the play's narrative). Ian's properties are only laughably describable as homes and, towards the end of the piece, Janetta's voice contrasts the past with the present. Curiously, the scenic description given in the script is not fully realised in the production, but there can be no doubt about the import of Janetta's words:

> There used to be spaces. You took them for granted. In England, there were views. Everywhere you turned you saw countryside, stretching away and beyond.
> *We turn a corner. Beyond this row of houses, another row. Beyond that, another.*
> Now the South Coast of England is one long stretch of bricked-in dormitory town. (p272)

In one sense Ian has been proved right ('Everyone's gonna want property . . . build a little box, shut yourself in it'; p238). But the weight of the ending falls on Janetta's final visitation of her memories, seen in a montage of quick flashbacks, and to her nagging, but false, belief that 'This is not the only chance you get at living your life' (p274). What is ultimately most remarkable about this piece is the way in which Hare has brought to maturity the process that he started in *Plenty*, where the interrelationship of thematic cultural/political/ social material is perfectly linked to the relationships between his protagonists. If the play causes us to care about the fate of postwar England, much more than this it involves us in caring about this small group of characters who adapted, or failed to adapt, to these changes in very different ways. The play walks a brilliant tightrope of intellectual debate and emotional involvement, and is one of the playwright's greatest achievements to date. His adventures in television have led inexorably to film, but of late his interests have returned solidly to the stage, and in 2002 he expressed a weariness with the time taken to produce a film: 'as I got older I felt less willing to give up the huge amount of time you need to direct a feature film . . . the two or three years it now takes to see a film through from conception to home rental'.[28] With David Hare, however, it is always wise to take nothing for granted.

NOTES

1. I say of the 'old school' because Hare's decision to locate the play in 'rural Berkshire' is surely a playful echo of Kenneth Tynan's famous diatribe against the well-made play: 'its setting is a country house in what used to be called Loamshire but is now, as a heroic tribute to realism, sometimes called Berkshire' (Kenneth Tynan, *Curtains* (London: Longman, 1961), p83). The point is not only that Esme actively supports precisely this kind of play, but that in *Amy's View* Hare acknowledged that he had set out to write a four-act play in the tradition of Ibsen and Chekhov (see Richard Boon, *About Hare: The Playwright and the Work* (London: Faber, 2003), p145).
2. Carol Homden, *The Plays of David Hare* (Cambridge: Cambridge University Press, 1995), pp60–1.
3. *Ibid.*, p104.
4. See John Bull, *Stage Right: Crisis and Recovery in Contemporary British Mainstream Theatre* (London: Macmillan, 1994), p61.
5. On Griffiths' ideas on the possibility of the strategic penetration of television politically and on its 'basic leakiness' as a medium, see 'Author's Preface to *Through the Night*', in Trevor Griffiths, *Through the Night & Such Impossibilities* (London: Faber, 1977). See also John Bull, *New British Political Dramatists* (London: Macmillan, 1984), pp134–41.
6. David Hare, 'Ah! Mischief: The Role of Public Broadcasting', in Frank Pike (ed.), *Ah! Mischief: The Writer and Television* (London: Faber, 1982), p41. 1968 was the year that the censorship power of the Lord Chamberlain's office was abolished and, certainly, his role may have been discredited; but that power remained until the very end, something that strengthens the sense of the importance of the timing of the start of Hare's writing career.
7. For access to this and to all other BBC scripts of Hare's television work, I am very grateful to the institution and to the staff of the BBC Records Office at Caversham. Unless otherwise stated, all subsequent quotations are taken from these original scripts.
8. David Hare, 'Introduction', *David Hare: Collected Screenplays* vol. I (London: Faber, 2002), pvii.
9. Pike (ed.), *Ah! Mischief*, p46.

10. On this see John Bull, *Stage Right*, Chapter 3, 'Private Rooms and Public Spaces'.
11. *Ah! Mischief*, p41.
12. Technically it is twice more, because they collaborated with Trevor Griffiths and Ken Campbell on *Deeds* (1978), but this was really more of a celebration of Richard Eyre's wonderful regime at the Nottingham Playhouse, from which they had all benefited.
13. It was screened on the BBC on 10 January 1978.
14. David Hare, 'Introduction', *David Hare: Collected Screenplays*, vol. I, pvii.
15. It was screened on the BBC in January 1980.
16. David Hare, *Plenty* (London: Faber, 1978), p87.
17. 'The Wednesday Play', 'Play for Today', and so on: even today ITV refers to all its vastly different array of narrative series as 'drama' in its prefatory puffs.
18. David Hare, *Licking Hitler: A Film for Television* (London: Faber, 1978), p11. All subsequent quotations are taken from this edition.
19. John Bull, 'Adapting the Model: *Plenty* and *Licking Hitler*', in Hersh Zeifman (ed.), *David Hare: A Casebook* (New York: Garland, 1994), p153.
20. David Hare, 'A Lecture', in *Licking Hitler*, pp66–7.
21. *Ibid.*, p69.
22. I deliberately exclude *Saigon: The Year of the Cat*, as it is a film that simply happened to be first shown on television, an increasingly common phenomenon.
23. David Hare, *Dreams of Leaving: A Film for Television* (London: Faber, 1980), p12. All subsequent quotations are taken from this edition.
24. Homden, *The Plays of David Hare*, pp198–214.
25. Hare quoted in Boon, *About Hare*, p96.
26. *Ibid.*, p6.
27. David Hare, *Heading Home*, in *Collected Screenplays*, vol. I, p233. All subsequent quotations are taken from this edition.
28. David Hare, 'Introduction', *Collected Screenplays*, vol. I, pxii.

11

RICHARD BOON

Hare on film

An interview

Hare's career on film effectively began with Wetherby *in 1985, though, as John Bull points out in Chapter 10, 1983's* Saigon: Year of the Cat *blurs somewhat the distinction between cinematic and television work. Hare wrote and directed* Wetherby, *as well as* Paris by Night *(1988) and* Strapless *(1988). Two other screenplays,* Damage *(1992) and* The Hours *(2002), were directed by Louis Malle and Stephen Daldry respectively. In addition, the author adapted two of his most successful stage plays for film:* Plenty *(1985; directed by Fred Schepisi) and* The Secret Rapture *(1993; directed by Howard Davies). The interview took place in Hampstead in January 2007.*

I began by asking him about the relationship between his television and film work, and whether there was any significance in the fact that his attention turned so much to film in the mid-to-late 1980s.

What happened was that it became commercially possible for me to be a film director because of David Rose and Jeremy Isaacs and their patronage when they started Channel 4 in 1982. Isaacs was the Chief Executive, and Rose headed the film department. Their brief was that 'We're starting a new television channel and we want to make British films; we want to make films that look out toward British life, and which are contemporary.' I did it for as long as I could. More or less everything that was interesting on the screen in the 1970s was on television. It was not practical for us to make work for the cinema then, because there was no framework available: big British films – which were essentially aimed at the American market – had died. And then, quite simply, it was down to the genius of Isaacs and Rose, who set out to make a link between the distinguished tradition of British television plays and the cinema by nurturing writing and directing talent within the relative safety of television, then moving it on. My feeling has always been that the reason people left television was because of censorship. In the 1970s, problems of BBC censorship were very intense. The BBC was then run by establishment villains. So we all moved out to the cinema but, by and large, when I was making feature films I was working for the same person – David Rose – who had been my producer at BBC Birmingham.

Notwithstanding the infrastructural issues at that time, would you at some point have turned to cinema anyway?

The cinema was my first love. I ran the film society at Cambridge. It's where my real interests first lay. And remember I started as a director. If you direct, the film industry is the natural place to work. It's a director's medium, which the theatre isn't. But at the time when I finished university, you could not just start, in your twenties, making films as an *auteur*. It was impossible. It was not practical in those days for anybody without a background in cinema to make a career in it. So it became quite clear to me that I was not going to work in the film industry.

I didn't know I was going to be a playwright. I only discovered playwrighting when I tried to write a play.

When you talk about your cinema work, you always talk about your love of British films of the 1950s – the 'Doctor' movies for instance, or Genevieve – but at the same time you were interested in the French Nouvelle Vague.

Oh, very much so.

It seems an odd combination of influences . . .

I think I have always had a strange attitude about film, which is that I have always thought it was the medium you *dreamed* in. What that meant: I have tried to make films that had the intensity of dream. I can see that intention in most powerful films – the films that I love the most. If you ask me what my favourite films are, then they're: *Summer Interlude*, Bergman; Hitchcock's *Vertigo*; Fellini's *La Strada*; *Un condamné à mort s'est echappé*, the Bresson film; *Sweet Smell of Success* – Alexander Mackendrick; *Tokyo Story* – Ozu; Louis Malle's *Le Souffle au coeur*; Robert Rossen's *All The King's Men* . . . for me these are great movies. They are the movies I find myself wanting to see again and again. I find them inexhaustible. And what do they have in common? By and large, they come from the late 1940s to the 1960s, and of course that is my childhood. So my fascination is to do with the sense that films like that bring back the memory of your childhood.

Now, it is not enough, having said that, that a film simply be set in those years. For instance, I think that the 'Ealing Comedies' wear incredibly badly; to sit down now to watch *The Man in the White Suit*, or *The Lavender Hill Mob*, is torture. Nor is it sufficient that a film merely has images of what my life was once like. On the other hand, that sense of a life that . . . *seems more complete*, because it is how you imagined adult life was going to be when you were a child . . . that is the quality that I find in Bergman, in Louis Malle and in Fellini. So when I wanted to make films myself, I wanted them to have something of that attribute: I wanted them to have a pictorial intensity, a painterly quality, to be 'under a glaze'. It was not like my theatre work at all. Although I always use as a starting point visual images on stage, the plays tend be driven by ideas or characterisation or narrative. But when I wanted to make cinema, my hope was to make an intensely *visual* cinema. And if I felt that I failed as a director, then it was that I had failed, really, to make my own aesthetic in the cinema.

My films are peculiar; they're distinctive. I do not think anybody really made films quite like mine. But nor do I think I got anywhere near the visual intensity I dreamed of getting.

It's that sense that you are trying to represent a world 'polished' in its completeness?

That's exactly it: it's a world that's neither real nor not real. An extreme example would be in *Wetherby*, where I had a lot of conflict about the Chinese restaurant scene. I wanted to design a Chinese restaurant that did not look like any Chinese restaurant you'd ever been to, and I remember the producer standing on set and saying, 'This is ridiculous. It just doesn't look like a Chinese restaurant.' I said, 'No, but it looks something like what I imagined I wanted this strange, weird Chinese restaurant to look like.' I don't claim I brought it off. When I first saw Neil Jordan's pictures, they had something of the quality I was aiming for. I had a very strong response to his early film, *Angel*. I thought it was a very beautiful film, because it seemed to me to be doing roughly the same thing: here was a literary sensibility that was trying to invoke a surreal, dream-like quality, and create a world that was consistent in its own terms. That was the kind of stylistic ambition I had when I was directing movies – even the television movies – but if I'm honest I see very little of this in contemporary cinema. People just seem to plonk the camera down and think that making a film look like reality is all you have to do to be a director. But if you look at all those directors that I love – Fellini and Hitchcock and those people, the 1950s directors – they are incredibly selective about what they allow into the frame and what they don't. They want to make something that's internally beautiful, and not just through light, which I think is the mistake: I think that once cinematography became so self-conscious in the 1970s and 1980s, then the question of what you were actually *shooting*, what it was that was *in the frame*, seemed to stop being of as much interest to film makers as it was in that period that I love.

It's what Clint Eastwood learned from Don Siegal: 'Know what you want to shoot and know what you're seeing when you see it.'

And shoot it.

You say you never felt you found a consistent aesthetic as a film director . . .

Plainly those three feature films in the 1980s – *Wetherby*, *Paris by Night* and *Strapless* – are a failed experiment. I think each one was progressively worse than the one before! In all, *Wetherby* is the best of them, then *Paris by Night* and then *Strapless*. *Strapless* is in a way the most ambitious, because I am trying to do something which is purely filmic: it is a fable, but I don't think it has the power – well, I *know* it doesn't have the power – of my television film, *Dreams of Leaving*, which is also a fable. My memory is that *Dreams of Leaving* was not well received when it came out, though I may be wrong about that. To this day, people come up to me and talk about *Dreams of Leaving*: the novelist William Boyd was saying recently how deeply affected he had been by it, and I know Ian McEwan was too. You could say novelists were interested in it precisely because of that deliberate poetic intensity. But when I came to make *Strapless*, somehow realism had become an uneasy bedfellow with fable. Well, realism had never bothered Hitchcock at all; Hitchcock made his movies totally unrealistic. But I never quite had the courage to go that far. So I ended up in sort of a middle ground . . .

David Thomson [the film critic] talks about your mise-en-scène being rather severe . . .

What does that mean?

I think he's arguing that you felt you had to restrain yourself, because you were so aware of your own huge delight in the medium.

He may be talking about certain conscious decisions that I took. One of the reasons that *Licking Hitler*, another television film, is distinctive (Stephen Frears said it was a fluke that I made a film that good as my first!) is because I deliberately did only what the camera could do in the 1940s: in other words, there weren't any movements of the camera that were impossible in the 1940s. It is true that the language I use is not flamboyant. I did not have any desire to show off as a director, in terms of 'Look I can do this, or look I can do that', because that technical stuff is, in a sense, the easy stuff in film making. Yes, of course, you can pull off incredible shots where the camera does this or the camera does that, and that may well be pleasurable – usually more pleasurable for the crew than for the audience, but pleasurable all the same. But I think what he means by my 'aesthetic being severe' is that it is *what* is being looked at is important to me. A great director, say Scorsese as he once was, can do both things: technical wizardry and a focus on what the film's narrative demands. In *GoodFellas*, for example, there's the famous sequence when the camera tracks right through a nightclub: as a piece of technical film making, it's great. But Scorsese is also one of the people who knew that you were meant to be telling a story as well.

My other problem was that I do not think I ever found the right cameraman. Roger Pratt in *Paris by Night* was the nearest to understanding the kind of stylisation I wanted. But we were probably too much seduced by Charlotte Rampling: she is a brilliant person to photograph, but she is an *alluring* person to photograph. It is almost impossible to take a bad shot of her: visually, she is one of the great cinema faces, she is fascinating whatever you do. . . .

The sort of visual stylisation you are talking about seems to be to do with allowing the camera simply to look at figures who, at any one moment, might be doing very little – but there is a kind of sustained gaze which, especially if you are working with great cinema actors like Rampling or Vanessa Redgrave [in Wetherby*], enables you to slowly build a sense of the internal landscape of a character. Again, that's a very French thing, isn't it?*

That's right. That's it. There was a famous film editor who said to me, 'You know, you shouldn't give up on cinema because you're making films that aren't like anybody else's.' I have heard this said to me so often that it may even be true, but if it is, it comes from a naïve quality: I cannot explain why I wanted things to be the way I wanted them to be. I knew they came from my subconscious, whereas in the theatre I've felt much more in control. My plays have come to a greater degree from my conscious mind.

There was a wonderful moment where a focus puller told me that he had walked off somebody's film when the director watched the rushes and said, 'Oh, that wasn't how I thought it was going to look at all.' The focus puller was absolutely right to walk off, because it is the *job* of the director to know how the rushes are going to look. It is almost the definition of a film director: it is someone who knows what the rushes are going to look like, without watching them on the monitor. But my tragedy as a film director was that the images were rarely the images I'd dreamed.

Working with Roger Pratt was the nearest I got to achieving it. But then he was faced with a very brutal decision about whether to stay with me or to go and make a more lavishly funded Terry Gilliam picture – I've blocked out which one it was. I wrote Roger a letter. And Roger later gave an interview to the *New Yorker* where he said, 'Never quarrel with a writer, they write you such terrible letters.' Generally, I felt that it was difficult to find artistically ambitious people in the British cinema. That is not an excuse, and that is not the reason why I gave up, but my God, it was then a miserable industry. And I certainly had no welcome within it. One thing I found with the British film establishment: you have to be fast on your feet not to let them humiliate you. At the time I directed movies, British film culture was – I don't know enough now to know if it is still true – deeply conservative, and what I was trying to do was against the grain. It made me realise how lucky I had been in the British theatre – which is, by and large, supportive of innovation. Because of the history of subsidy, the question of failing and succeeding is not decisive: if you failed on one outing, you could be trusted to succeed on another. It is understood that a theatre may be making an investment in a talent. How genuine artists like Mike Leigh and Ken Loach withstood for thirty or forty years the sort of ruthless, pallid commercialism of British cinema, I do not know. The British film industry provides a deeply depressing and philistine atmosphere to work in.

Is that because it always appears to be looking towards the States?

Absolutely.

Where it should be looking towards Europe?

Of course it should be looking towards Europe.

For me it was all summed up by our experience of *The Hours*. For some months, life became a welcome but unending succession of awards cere-monies. When we went up for the BAFTAs, we were told, 'If you win, then on no account in your acceptance speech are you to mention the war.' It was exactly at the moment when Iraq was about to be invaded, and these BAFTA people said, 'You can make a speech about anything you like, but not the invasion of Iraq.' Then we went on to the Oscars and, of course, all anyone talked about was the war, in all the speeches – everybody. At least in America you have an industry that has the confidence to risk offending people; in Britain you have an industry that is so craven and right-wing that it does not want to offend *anybody*.

I am not saying that I gave up for lack of support; that is not the reason why I stopped. I stopped because I realised it would take up my whole life.

Stopped directing films rather than writing them?

Yes. Mind you, I've never quite been a screenwriter for hire. Remember, I have been lucky enough to work with Stephen Daldry and Louis Malle. It's spoiled me. I have just written a film for Michael Winterbottom. I'm nearly 60. I can't waste my life with anyone who isn't going to make a great film. Having said that, I did write a screenplay on [the photographer] Lee Miller that never got made, because I stupidly broke my own rule: I worked in a genre. And the biopic is the most contradictory of all genres, because it is essentially an intimate portrait of an individual. However, to re-create the life of Lee Miller you have to re-create, at the cost of 40 or 50 million dollars, the Second World War. The film was a financial contradiction, which is why, to my great sadness, it has never been made. I should also add that I have written another screenplay – of Jonathan Franzen's novel *The Corrections* – on which I have spent five years and of which I have written twenty-three drafts. Robert Zemeckis was on it for a year, then [Alejandro González] Iñárritu. I admire the hell out of him. But he walked. So I don't know what is going to happen to that one. It's the best film I've written.

As for directing, the path of any film director – and this is true of everybody, not just me – is that you can make your first film by luck and by vision, and then slowly you have to learn, and you have to devote your whole life to it. I think I would say, and Stephen Frears is the obvious example, that those friends and contemporaries of mine who have devoted their lives to being film directors have become incredibly fine film directors: when you see a Frears film these days, then the expertise behind it is the expertise of a lifetime of film making. Those directors who have dabbled, or flirted, or drifted in from the theatre have been much less accomplished. In my own life, there was a decisive moment in 1990 when Richard Eyre asked me to write three plays for the theatre, for the Olivier stage. It was at the same time as when I was being asked to direct a shedload of movies. Instead, I did five years of theatre work, and at the end of those five years I was no longer a film director.

What about the film adaptations of your stage plays?

I hate them. I just hate them. And I hate doing them, purely because I cannot judge them. All you have as a writer is self-respect. Your assessments, your judgements about your own work, may be wrong. But they are yours. But I cannot make the judgement about my adaptations: I cannot tell what's the film and what's the play. When people ask me, 'Do you like the film of *Plenty*?', which I guess is the most successful film adaptation of a play of mine, I really cannot say. I cannot tell what it *is*, because in my mind it is still conceived as a play and all the choices I made about how to write it as a play get in the way of my understanding of what it is as a movie. In the case of *The Secret Rapture*, I felt that my own work was so poor – not anybody else's – that at the end I vowed to never again adapt my plays for the cinema. On the other hand, I don't want to see other people do them.

It has always seemed to me that a good adaptation does not attempt a literal transliteration, but gets to the impulse behind the original work and reforms it, recasts it. It must be very difficult to do that with your own work.

It's impossible. You are completely dependent on the director saying to you, 'Look, we need this, and we don't need that.' That for me is not collaboration. Fred Schepisi was a fantastic film director and I loved working with him on *Plenty*, but in the end I couldn't judge it. I could tell Fred's work was brilliantly composed – you know, that singular use of the anamorphic lens which only Fred understands – and the dynamic width of the screen; he loves and understands composition. He's one of the few directors who can paint six and seven people perfectly into a shot – not just reduce everything to two or three. But if you ask me, does the film *Plenty* have the heft, the impact, that the play does?, I haven't the slightest idea. I can't tell.

Yet ironically, reviews of the original production of the stage play talked about its cinematic qualities . . .

I thought it was a very theatrical play. I've lived my whole life with the critical cliché that I introduced the techniques of the cinema to the stage. It's untrue. I just tried to find a kind of epic writing which used *parallels* to cinema. So, for example, you found ways on stage of doing a 'close shot' or a 'wide shot'. In fact, Stephen Frears, when he saw *Racing Demon*, said 'Well, it's a cinematic language, isn't it? You zoom in and the character's alone, and then you go wide: it's all in cinema language.' But it is a language that's the *equivalent* of cinema. It is not cinema language. It is a made language that is constructed for the stage, and it works very differently from the language of cinema. When I go to plays that have misunderstood what that language is, it drives me mad. Some playwrights think that you can make up plays from mosaics of scenes, each of which lasts an identical three minutes – and each of which has an identical weight. They have totally misunderstood what epic stage writing is.

I think it comes back to that very simple thing, that notion of 'wiping' the stage between scenes, of going to black, then coming up again into a new, different setting: it's how the old films shifted location.

My favourite scene of Howard Brenton's – I think it's the greatest thing he ever wrote! – is in *The Genius*, when the master of an Oxford or Cambridge college walks out on an empty lawn at seven o'clock in the morning and says something like, 'The first words of the day, the first words of the day . . . before it all gets messed up and spoiled.' That in a way is a metaphor for playwrighting, in that you empty the stage and on somebody comes – and it's clean until you mess it up. As an epic writer you do that twelve times in the evening, whereas a domestic playwright does it just twice.

I guess one of the best examples of that kind of epic writing is at the end of Plenty, *when you 'wipe' from a dark, dingy, monochrome bedroom in 1962 to a French hillside in summer 1944, and colour ignites as a brilliant sun comes up. That last scene, which contains all the hope for a future we know won't happen, has exactly that kind of polished 'glaze', of 'completeness', you wanted in your film aesthetic, doesn't it?*

Yes: completely. That's it. The thing that is true of us, after all, is that we contain many things in our heads at one time. A memory is not tarnished because it happened in the past. It is real to us, the optimism is there, the bud of it is there, even in the falling of the petals, the bud is still there. And that mixing of time is something that film does wonderfully. With *The Hours* we were really trying to follow and drive that idea as far as we possibly could, by jumbling up three different stories to a point where the audience . . . You know, one of the things I think about *Citizen Kane* is that, however well you think you know it (and I have certainly seen it twenty times), you are always surprised by the order in which the scenes come. You can never contain in your head the complexity of that structure. When the structure unrolls, it seems completely right. Yet when it goes to, say, Bernstein's point of view, you think, 'Oh, this is Bernstein's section, so we're going to have that scene . . . Oh. We don't have that scene. We have *that* scene. *Ah! It's put together like that!*' Similarly, at a question-and-answer session on *The Hours*, I was asked how long it had taken me to write it, and I said, 'Well, it took me three weeks to write the opening sequence, because it's so complex . . . But I think you'll find when you see the film, it's in the exact order in which I wrote it.' Then somebody wrote to me and said, 'I've seen the film, I've read the script, and it's all in a completely different order to how you wrote it!' Even I cannot contain in my memory the structural order of *The Hours*. I don't think Stephen [Daldry] could. None of us could. Nobody could sit down in an exam and say, 'This is how *The Hours* is structured', it's so complex. But once you get the structure of that complexity, it seems inevitable, and once you get it, you get something that's parallel to what's happening in our heads all the time.

Yes . . . you've spoken recently about how depressing you find the domination of the Star Wars *school of screenwriting, how relentlessly formulaic it has become.*

It is what George Lucas calls the 'scene-let'. Lucas believes that nothing should happen without it being foretold. Somebody must first say, 'I think something is about to happen.' (Hence he discovered that line, the most famous line in his work, which is 'I have a bad feeling about this.') And then something will happen. And then, he says, you must have a scene which explains what *has* happened, in order to reassure the audience that they have correctly understood it. He and I used to argue like students. He is a brilliant man: he can cut very deep, but he can only cut narrow. His cinema is like a plough which cuts a furrow straight across the field. He cannot 'go wide'.

But I think this formulaic screenwriting is part of a larger problem, which is that, as far as I am concerned, 'genre' is finished. Genre is what twentieth-century cinema traded in, but generic structures have now become so familiar that you can do no good work in them any more. Our expectations of genre have become so predictable that the audience is way ahead of us. All the contemporary work that I admire – like Iñárritu's *Amores Perros*, and *Babel* as well – is so powerful because it is outside genre. Maybe one of the reasons I am less keen on *Strapless* is because it veers too close to genre for my taste, whereas I think you would be very hard put to allocate *Paris by Night* and *Wetherby* to a genre; you can't say 'Well, it's a lonely schoolteacher movie' – there aren't that many others ... Similarly with *The Hours*. *Damage* is Greek tragedy and that is a very unusual genre for modern cinema.

Damage is the film where my opinion is most at odds with the public's – or the Saxon public, at least. The fact is that when I go to some countries – Spain, Italy, Mexico or anywhere Latin – *Damage* is remembered as a great movie. In Nordic countries it is thought to be a miserable movie! Stephen Daldry watched it again the other day and said, 'I still, even after ten or fifteen years, find its reception mystifying, because it still seems clearly to me to be one of the greatest British films.' It mystifies me, too. It may be partly that everyone taking part in it did not care for it: Jeremy [Irons] hated it, Juliette [Binoche] didn't care for it, and Louis [Malle] wasn't very happy with it. To my evident embarrassment, I was the only one of the team who really liked it. I'd always known that the best films made about Britain are made by foreigners; films like *Blow-Up* and *The Servant*. Antonioni is an Italian, Joseph Losey is a Canadian. And Malle's French, of course.

And one of the best films about America, Point Blank, *was made by a British director, John Boorman. He gives you an America you don't recognise from Hollywood product.*

Totally. It is brilliant. Brilliant. Again, Polanski's *Repulsion* is a wonderful film about Britain, but I think that the British resent the fact that it takes foreign film makers to come here and give us a view that is not the little parochial view that most British films give you.

That sense of the 'parochial' ... As is the case with your stage work, your films have always set out to relate private lives to the big social, political, historical issues. Do you see that scale of ambition in British film generally?

There was very little of that in the cinema back then, or now. What you see is habituated directors going through the motions with genres that you've seen a thousand times. As I said, it is very, very hard to mine anything more out of those genres. They're not yielding anything any more. The people I've loved, like [Rainer Werner] Fassbinder in the 1970s, and, more recently, Lars von Trier, at least tried to shake things up.

Cinema has become very decadent. Two things happened: first, genre (which we've talked about), and second, the shot began to become more important than the sequence. And all that boring talk about cinematography; from the moment you attended *Apocalypse Now* and they applauded [cinematographer Vittorio] Storaro's name, you knew you were into something terribly decadent. Today we hear directors go on and on about light, where the camera is and what the shot is, yet they don't pay nearly so much attention to what it is they are actually photographing! Louis Malle, on the other hand, always said that he was happiest with a lightweight crew, making *Vanya on 42nd Street* or his documentaries. When he was making his documentaries he was carrying his camera on his shoulder, and making great films. It drove him mad on *Damage* that [cinematographer] Peter Biziou would take an hour to set up a shot. He would say, 'This isn't film making. Film making has to have an impetus, it's got to have an impetus about what's happening. It is the cameraman's job to photograph it, not to make everyone wait around while he composes a frame.' And he's right. All the decadence in cinema comes from all this fascination with light and the loss of interest in the action itself.

Do you now see your film work as a career separate from your stage work?

No, it all belongs together, although it has been difficult for me to move easily between the two. I think that younger artists – Sam Mendes and Stephen Daldry, for example – are interesting because they have been able to move back and forwards with equal ease, and have done distinguished work in both media. Yet for some reason, my own generation found that movement much harder. I don't know why that was. Bergman is a master of theatre and cinema, but who else? If, like me, you're lucky enough even to have worked in both media, it's still impossible for your output to be seen singly. In the time I actually worked inside the National Theatre, I think I had one letter from the National Film Theatre, which is only just along the South Bank! The two institutions see each other across a gulf a mile wide. There is absolutely no contact between those two cultures.

Your current project is for Michael Winterbottom?

Winterbottom is a director I admire very much: films like *Wonderland* and *In This World* are outside genre. He is trying to do something completely different. *Wonderland* has exactly that quality you were talking about, of trying to let large thematic questions about the world into intimate subjects, and it is all done with hand-held camera, no lights, on location, and so on. *In This World*, which is the story of Afghan refugees travelling all the way from Pakistan to England, is as good as British cinema gets. For Winterbottom, I wrote the story of Craig Murray, our former Ambassador in Uzbekistan, whose undiplomatic honesty about human rights abuses led to his professional and personal humiliation by the Foreign Office. It's a great story. But sadly, I've been sacked. Winterbottom wanted a Steve Coogan farce. Genre, again, you see. I was writing something genre-free.

IV
Overviews of Hare

12

STEVE NICHOLSON

'To ask how things might have been otherwise . . .'

History and memory in the work of David Hare

ERNEST: Gilbert, you treat the world as if it were a crystal ball. You hold it in your hand, and reverse it to please a wilful fancy. You do nothing but rewrite history.

GILBERT: The one duty we owe to history is to rewrite it. That is not the least of the tasks in store for the critical spirit.

Oscar Wilde, *The Critic as Artist*

LAZAR: Did you know that sound waves never die? So every noise we make goes into the sky. And there is a place somewhere in the corner of the universe where all the babble of the world is kept.   David Hare, *Plenty*

In 1978, David Hare observed that 'It would be sad if this historical period had no chronicler', and one of the roles he has subsequently adopted has been to act as a witness of our times.[1] Indeed, the theatre critic Michael Billington characterises Hare's work as demonstrating a 'sustained conviction that writers have a Balzacian duty to record what is going on around them', and Blake Morrison agrees that 'When future historians come to study the state of Britain in the late twentieth century, Hare will be the playwright they turn to first.'[2] Hare's 'State of the Nation' trilogy of plays centring on the key public institutions of law, church and politics, which was staged at the National Theatre in the early 1990s, was significant in establishing his reputation in this respect; but some of his more recent work has also chimed with the rediscovery of 'documentary drama' and 'verbatim theatre', and the recognition of the potency of these forms as political theatre. Hare himself asks, 'Who, in a hundred years' time, will read the most interesting work of our period without exhaustive footnotes?'[3] Yet he rejects the notion that his plays should be judged in relation to criteria of accuracy and authenticity: 'I'm not interested in documentary as a form at all, and I find the vindication of work by the fact that it actually happened really depressing.'[4] Indeed, he delighted in endorsing a slightly bizarre response to *The Permanent Way* which saw it as a play about AIDS: '*The Permanent Way* is not about railways', declared Hare, 'any more than *Kes* is about a kestrel or *Moby Dick* about a whale. This is a play about grief.'[5] Hare is similarly insistent that, even though the process of writing them had involved extensive factual research, the plays in his trilogy (*Racing Demon*, *Murmuring Judges* and *The Absence of War*) were 'not in any way documentary' but 'works of the imagination'.[6]

In his theoretical analysis of historical drama from Shakespeare to Brecht, Matthew Wikander notes 'the classic distinction between mere chronicle, the record of facts, and true history, which organises the facts according to principles that may be called either scientific or literary'.[7] By this definition, it is clearly not sufficient to describe Hare as a 'chronicler' of his time, and Hare himself draws a useful distinction:

> To spell it out: the ingredient which makes all plays is metaphor. Journalism may be about only its ostensible subject and still be good. But of plays we ask something else, something more . . . the trick of playwrighting is to create density.[8]

As the author of a recent play about the war in Iraq puts it, 'the art of theatre is to build a story that's more true than fact'.[9] In his own Iraq play, *Stuff Happens*, Hare again has no compunction about mixing research with imagination, stating that the private scenes between leading public figures are 'based on what I believe to have happened'.[10] This raises important issues about the connections between history, reality and fiction, which have been the subject of much debate during the decades covering Hare's playwrighting career. After all, 'what I believe to have happened' both is and is not the same as 'fiction'.

At the start of Hare's 2000 play *My Zinc Bed*, Paul briefly addresses the audience from a disembodied 'black void' outside the narrative. Self-consciously paraphrasing Conrad, he tells us that 'inside every heart there burns a desire to set down once and for all a true record of what has happened'.[11] Conrad's original statement may itself have been intended with a degree of irony, and in a culture which has learned to question the absolute division between the real and the fictional, Paul's aspiration is likely to set alarm bells ringing. We must now doubt whether any recording of history can legitimately claim to be 'true', or whether such an ambition is doomed to fail. Writing in the same year that *Plenty* was first performed, the influential historiographer Hayden White made the case that all narratives of the past are necessarily verbal fictions, 'the contents of which are as much *invented* as *found* and the forms of which have more in common with their counterparts in literature than they have with those in the sciences'. White draws our attention to the ways in which writers of history are generally engaged in a process of shaping bare chronicles into coherent narratives and versions of the past, which make sense according to the ideological assumptions of the present.[12]

Much has been written about the relationships between history, playwright and 'truth'. For the nineteenth-century German playwright Georg Büchner, the dramatist was 'nothing but a historian', whose 'highest duty' was 'to come as close to history as it really took place'. Yet, in order that the theatre should be better able to fulfil the task of 'transporting us with immediacy into the life of the past, instead of offering a dry account', Büchner grants the playwright a licence to invent. In fact, for Büchner, the dramatist is actually *'superior* to a historian in that he creates history anew'.[13] Wikander agrees that the dramatist's duty is to occupy 'the gulf between the historian's "dry narrative" and the living bodies that once peopled the dead past'. However, he draws attention to the implications of the prologue to John Ford's 1634 play *Perkin Warbeck*, in which we are told that the playwright 'shows a history couch'd in a play'. Wikander notes that

> the word 'couch'd' is troublesome: history hides in the play, lurking in ambush, ready to pounce . . . As he pretends to be a historian, he concedes that he is not one. Thus he acknowledges . . . the wide gulf that opened up, early in the seventeenth century, between historian and playwright.

Wikander suggests that 'No such gulf had bothered Shakespeare', and that 'For Shakespeare and Brecht, the incompatible roles of dramatist and historian are one.' Citing a widely accepted definition of history writing as 'the imaginative re-enactment of past experience' – a phrase which is striking not least for its assumption of performance – he argues that Shakespeare unashamedly fictionalised the past to provide himself with the authority to moralise, and that Brecht 'poses as a historian' and 'recasts the events of the past to fit his vision of the future'.[14] It is interesting to consider this in relation to Carol Homden's anxiety about Hare's own fictionalising of history. In *Plenty*, *Brassneck* and *Licking Hitler*, complains Homden, Hare was 'explicitly determined to use that past to explain his/our present . . . and to reinstate a belief in change'. She is suspicious of what she perceives as a lack of authenticity in Hare's version of the past, insisting that Susan and Alice are 'out of their time, speaking the language of the seventies'. Claiming that Hare has himself indicated that research has been less important to him than 'instinct', Homden disapprovingly notes that 'one begins to suspect that history is a diversionary smokescreen cast by Hare to authenticate his imaginary creations'.[15] There are certainly grounds for resisting such criticisms, but it is perhaps not unreasonable to ask whether one should indeed be concerned that there may be difficulty in driving a secure wedge between what Shakespeare, Brecht and Hare do, and the practice of shredding and then fabricating the past of which Orwell warns in *1984*. One response to such a comparison is to recognise that Hare's history sets out to be more truthful than the narrative he seeks to supplant. In the case of the plays cited by Homden, Hare's analysis was based on Angus Calder's revisionist account of the Second World War and its aftermath:

> Reading Angus Calder's *The People's War* changed a lot of my thinking as a writer; an account of the Second World War through the eyes of ordinary people, it attempts a complete and alternative history to the phoney and corrupting history I was taught at school.[16]

Even though a level of invention is also allowed, Hare nails his colours to the mast of recovering 'true' versions of the past which have previously been suppressed.

> Most people's history is not in the history books. You can show the real under-history by taking an individual's experience. I did this in *Licking Hitler*, where I tried to show that the official history of the war is lies. Rewriting history is exhilarating. People have got a model, and you show them an alternative to it. It's tremendously exciting to show that the official version is untrue . . . I've been having a go at rewriting the account of the American evacuation . . . The difference between how the world perceived it and the reality of the evacuation is extraordinary.[17]

Hare has spoken often enough about the significance of a real and actual past to his plays, and to his political philosophy. In asserting its value, he has sometimes felt it necessary to counter less sympathetic stances than Büchner's: 'Dramatising history and the movement of society is mistakenly thought to be an activity more akin to journalism than to art', he writes.[18] He invokes significant precedents for his approach, suggesting that Shakespeare set his plays in the past rather than in contemporary England 'because he wanted to use the metaphor of history'.[19] Hare also acknowledges in relation to his own work that one reason he 'headed backwards'[20] was that 'I found it easier to get a hold on the immediate past than I did on the present.'[21] All tellings of history inevitably reveal as much about the teller and the time when they are being told as about the time described, but for Hare the past is more than a metaphor: 'One thing that the theatre tries to do is to explain to people how they have come to their present situation.'[22] With rare exceptions, the past to which he turns is not a remote one which would allow him, and the audience, to establish a Brechtian distance from our present reality, in order that we may then look at our own world afresh. Rather, it is a past very directly joined to the present – one which may be remembered, or even embodied, by characters and, indeed, audiences. Some of Hare's contemporaries and fellow playwrights – Howard Brenton and Caryl Churchill, for example – have achieved startling coups de théâtre by employing striking devices to physicalise a more remote past on stage, either by forcing different time periods to overlap or occupy the stage simultaneously, or by threading ghosts of the past through contemporary actions. Hare generally eschews such direct assaults, preferring not to disturb so violently the fabric of naturalism. But the ghosts and memories are no less strongly present, haunting his protagonists. Rather than making visible to the audience a past of which the characters themselves are unaware, and which remains both separate from and unable to influence the other on-stage worlds, Hare's ghosts take possession of individual characters and, in doing so, impact upon the world around them. No one is more aware of their presence than the characters themselves. Discussing his own fascination with narratives which extend and unfold gradually across time, Hare acknowledges Ibsen, Chekhov and O'Neill as his mentors. By comparison with the 'fractured techniques' which contemporary drama has absorbed from film and television, he celebrates the complexity of the four-act structure, which invites the playwright to construct 'elisions and connections between separate events'.[23] Such an approach may lack the immediately disorientating effect which comes from colliding disparate times and events in front of us, but the slow-burn may eventually be every bit as unsettling. At those moments when Hare does break the strict linearity of time – as with the 'flashback' final scene of *Plenty* – the device is sufficiently unexpected to be disruptive and disturbing.

As has been convincingly argued, it was with *Plenty* in 1978 that Hare 'found his subject' of history.[24] In an essay written in the same year, Hare defined the sort of analysis to which he was committing himself: 'what I mean by history will not be the mechanised absolving force theorists would like it to be; it will be those strange uneasy factors that make a place here and nowhere else, make a time now and no other time.'[25] In other words, it is to Lazar's 'babble of the world' that we must tune in if we wish to understand what is going on. Hare also defined what he saw as a key function for the historical playwright: 'He can put people's sufferings in a historical context; and by doing that, he can help to explain their pain.'[26] In *Performing History: Theatrical Representations of the Past in Contemporary Theatre*, Freddie Rokem quotes the powerful and evocative closing lines spoken by a character in a text by an Israeli playwright: 'If I did not know that we are living in history/I wouldn't be able to stand it.' Rokem reminds us that, although we live our lives within history, we only become aware of this 'when it becomes recapitulated, when we create some kind of discourse, like the theatre', which offers us 'an organised repetition' of history, 'situating the chaotic torrents of the past within an aesthetic frame'.[27] Without wishing to deny the value of helping people come to terms with their pain, both Hare and Rokem seem to be proposing something which sounds more like consolation and comfort rather than anything radical or assertive. Certainly, Carol Homden has argued that 'Hare's use of history can be seen as an evasion and the disguise of a deep nostalgia.'[28] Though, as she acknowledges, any nostalgia is not for a world which has actually existed but for 'a time when change seemed possible'.[29] In *Plenty*, for example, Susan Traherne is seen desperately trying to hang on to her belief that 'England can't be like this for ever.'[30] Perhaps the most crucial lesson which Hare reveals through his use of historical perspective is that things have not always been as they are now, and that they do change. By turning to the past, Hare is able to demonstrate that the world we live in is as it is for particular reasons, and has arisen from a chain of events which was not pre-ordained or inevitable. As William tells us at the start of *Dreams of Leaving*, before the narrative flashes back to the past, 'Time of course has cemented things over, so this now seems like the inevitable course.'[31] The writing of history can crack open the cement, and show us that as the past could have been different, so the future is not fixed.

There is a well-known rehearsal exercise, generally attributed to Brecht, in which actors are required to find a way to express what their character does *not* say or do as well as what is actually scripted. This is not about playing a character's subtext, but their non-text; rather than hearing and seeing what is said and done as normal and inevitable, the actor (and the audience) are encouraged to become conscious that alternatives always exist and that there is nothing inevitable about how the character *chooses* to behave. Much of Hare's writing about the past consciously aspires to a similar juxtaposition of what has occurred with what has not. He again cites Chekhov as a mentor here, even though Chekhov's plays are set firmly in rooms – a limitation which Hare generally sees to be politically confining:

> If you don't believe in change, then you can write about rooms. If you believe that what happens in rooms is important, then you don't need to show history . . . But once you decide, 'My subject is how things were, how things are, and how things might be', then that's history, and you've got to show the sweep of things.[32]

But what Chekhov is able to show us, argues Hare, is 'history is sweeping through the room'. Indeed, Hare identifies the power of Chekhov's plays to be rooted in the fact that they always manage to hint at 'that sense of what we might have been'.[33] And he goes on to refer with appreciation to a comment made by another playwright in relation to *Plenty*: 'Wallace Shawn said it was very unusual to see a play that contains an idea of how you might have lived as well as a description of how you actually live.'[34] When the glorious openness of the French countryside in high summer, bathed in colour and the optimism of 1944, emerges piece by piece from the squalor of faded hopes in a dingy 1960s Blackpool hotel for the final scene of that play, there is for an audience a bitter and almost unbearable irony in Susan's naïve optimism that things will change and the world will become better. Because the play has already shown us a future in grey, her confidence is almost unbearable to watch. But by capturing that moment of optimism at the climax of the play, it is preserved and recovered as a moment of positive hope. Any naïve sense of agitprop-style insistence is immediately undermined by the deadpan response of the middle-aged Frenchman who is Susan's companion:

> SUSAN: It may be . . .
> *(Pause)*
> FRENCHMAN: Huh?
> SUSAN: That things will change. We have grown up. We will improve our
> world.
> *(The Frenchman stares at Susan. Then offers gravely:)*
> FRENCHMAN: Perhaps . . . perhaps you like some soup.   (p207)

But perhaps an audience is left to pick up the same challenge as that thrown down at the end of Brecht's *Good Person of Setzuan*, when it is urged to take responsibility and 'write the happy ending to the play' which the playwright is unable to show.

The attempt to convey intimations of what might have been, of an as-yet-unborn world, is a crucial element in the way Hare writes and constructs his texts. It is no surprise, then, that in translating and adapting *Galileo* he should locate Brecht's 'genius' in his ability 'to turn the tragedy outwards and to ask how things might have been otherwise'.[35] For Hare,

> Political playwrighting doesn't make sense unless it has some sense of how things might be otherwise. If it doesn't contain possibility, then there isn't any point in political writing . . . A political playwright is someone who is defined by a sense of what might be, as well as what is; that argument between what we could be and what we are . . . which effectively means a sense of history.[36]

Underlying Hare's approach is the conviction that one of his tasks is to render history visible by revealing its passage and effects on the lives of realistically drawn individuals, especially on those who struggle to resist its comfortable and suburban patterns. Understanding where and what we come from is fundamental to the real task of understanding where and what we are now, and what we might become. When Hare explicitly states that 'The most important act of my life happened before I was born',[37] it is the strength of the phrase which is striking; a more conventional expression might have made reference to the Second World War as an important influence *on* his life, but by making it an event *of* his life the two become inseparable and conjoined.

According to Hare, the society we live in has been fundamentally shaped by a betrayal:

> In the Second World War millions of people died in defence of a belief, and the sense of squalor and disappointment of the post-war period seems to me inexorably to have stemmed from the feeling that the sacrifice they made has somehow been squandered.[38]

It is this betrayal of the past which destroys Susan Traherne, who pays the price of remembering what was and what might have been as well as what is. While her utopian vision has been created through a moment of lived experience, that of Victor in *My Zinc Bed* is derived more from a theoretical understanding, but it is the same betrayal. Insisting that 'It's the world that's changed, not me' (p19), Victor has to come to terms with the fact that the beliefs that inspired him are no longer fashionable or, perhaps, possible: 'Socialism was the present the British gave themselves for winning the war . . . Maybe we don't feel we deserve presents any more' (pp58–9). His youthful ideals have been trashed by time, and History itself is personified as a thug and a mugger:

> I had faith. But then it was stolen from me. I was the victim of a robbery. Like millions of others. History came along and clobbered us on the head . . . Just thrown out into the world and told to get on with it. Given a sharp lesson and told we could have no effect. (p106)

A former campaigning communist, but now disillusioned, Victor has managed, at least on the surface, to survive and reinvent himself rather more effectively than Susan Traherne, transforming himself into a rich and successful businessman. He fully acknowledges the road he has trodden, and speculates as to how his own history will be written by the future: 'What will they say of me? "He was a communist, then he made some money . . . He went from believing people could do everything for each other to wondering whether they could do anything"' (p123). But the ghost has not been exorcised. Confused now as to whether the political certainties and passionate campaigning of his youth represent a time of waste and misplaced arrogance or 'the only years I ever lived', Victor insists that in spite of all that has happened 'the fire is still in my bones' (p107). And despite his apparent conversion, this 'Marxist maniac of Regent's Park' (p92) retains a clear-sighted political consciousness which sits oddly with his status and position. By turning to the past, Hare seeks to demonstrate that society is not frozen:

> if you write about now, just today and nothing else, then you seem to be confronting only stasis, but if you begin to describe the undulations of history, if you write plays that cover passages of time, then you begin to find a sense of movement, of social change, if you like; and the facile hopelessness that comes from confronting the day and only the day, the room and only the room, begins to disappear and in its place the writer can offer a record of movement.[39]

He would surely have no difficulty in signing up to the position most clearly articulated by a playwright with whom he has sometimes been compared, Trevor Griffiths: 'I think the future has to be made. It has to be made by people who understand the past. That is why history is so important.'[40] For both playwrights, an examination of the past affords opportunities to challenge the versions which have come to dominate, and there are connections between their strategies:

> Griffiths understands history as a field of ideological contest, in which a politics of counternarrative and redescription must contend with official, class-bound representations of the past . . . [he] challenges the ruling accounts of history by reclaiming what has been co-opted and disowned, marking the structures of class, power, materiality, and ideology that makes history politically readable . . . Griffiths takes on history in order to historicise the present – to demonstrate that the contemporary moment is the result of past choices, that it could be different, and that it offers choices out of which the future will be born.[41]

Even in a play such as *The Judas Kiss*, the audience's presumed knowledge about a moment in history is undermined from the moment Wilde enters: '*He is solid, tall and fleshy, 6' 3", a mixture of ungainliness and elegance . . . not at all the languid pansy of legend.*'[42] We may think we know that Wilde was a solitary target and victim of homophobia. Hare's version challenges this:

> It appears that the whole of London is fleeing . . . I saw every invert in the metropolitan area packing his bags and heading for France . . . It is a veritable mass migration. I'd never imagined diaspora could be on this scale . . . The takings at certain fashionable restaurants will tonight be counted in pennies. At a single stroke opera will be stone dead as a form . . . I was astonished at who appeared on the streets. There is scarcely a *métier* which is not represented. All of the rabbits are being smoked from their holes.   (p19)

Yet there are also significant differences between the ways the two playwrights draw on history. As Hare himself says:

Trevor writes about sentient, conscious, political beings who articulate political ideologies or take part in political debate. I write in much more personal terms about people who don't have anything to do with politics, or very rarely.[43]

Another noticeable difference of focus is that Griffiths has often tended to concentrate on moments of political confrontation and crisis, when the fault lines within society seem to have come closest to cracking apart:

Such moments represent openings in the narrative of history, junctures in which the future lies open as a field of contending possibilities and the present offers itself as a site of action, will, vision, choice.[44]

By contrast, Hare seems more drawn towards moments when the gaps seem to have closed, or at least have become less visible, and when the dominant mood is more likely to be one of despair than of optimism: 'it is to that despair that as a historical writer I choose to address myself time and time again'.[45] In *Plenty*, it is not only Susan who has had her ideals crushed:

LAZAR: I don't know what I'd expected . . . What I'd hoped for, at the time I returned. Some sort of edge to the life that I lead. Some sort of feeling their death was worthwhile . . . I gave in. Always. All along the line . . . I hate, I hate this life that we lead.   (pp204–5)

Alice, too, ultimately concedes the failure of her rebellion against the moral codes of the 1950s: 'Perhaps I was simply out of my time' (p197). In *My Zinc Bed*, Victor, living in a world in which even politicians no longer believe that politics matter, might have reached the same conclusion:

We are told that managing things is a technical skill. What you manage is irrelevant. All businesses are essentially the same . . . That's what they tell us. Politicians boast of being plumbers, not architects. The word 'ideological' is never now mentioned.   (p19)

The disadvantage of focusing on what Hare calls 'the extraordinary intensity of people's personal despair',[46] and on individuals who are not necessarily politically conscious, is that it may leave an audience uncertain as to how far the inadequacies lie with the society and how far they are located in the individual depicted. In *The Secret Rapture*, Isobel's attempt to hold on to fundamental and absolutist ideals simply makes her look ridiculous to others: 'A *vow*? It's outrageous. People making *vows*. What are *vows*? Nobody's made vows since the nineteenth century.'[47] By contrast with the characterisation deployed in the plays of some of his socialist contemporaries, Hare's protagonists rarely seem designed as mere representatives of class or ideological position, or as crude narrative devices whose function is to persuade a reluctant audience to concentrate on political events. Yet Hare is equally adamant that the individual can never be the full focus of his own work:

> I believe in the social view – in other words, that who we are is not determined
> by what we are born with in our heads, but by the historical circumstances by
> which we arrive on the planet.[48]

As Victor says in *My Zinc Bed*: 'I still believe in history. A way of looking at things historically. You never lose that' (p15).

The perception that writers of history are engaged in essentially the same activity as writers of what is labelled fiction does not, in Hayden White's view, damage its value. Indeed he maintains that its fictionality 'in no way detracts from the status of historical narratives as providing a kind of knowledge'.[49] Nor does White's emphasis on the fact that a society's reading of the past is based on the ideological assumptions of the present seem to be at odds with the way Hare (and Griffiths) approach history. But, in order to be released from what he terms the 'burden of history', White demands something different from those who rewrite and challenge our assumed knowledge: not so much an alternative narrative which constructs another coherent reading, but 'a historiography in which we are confronted by the horror and chaos of the past'.[50] The conventional process of ordering the past in order to understand it is seen as a way of absorbing and taming its horrors and, in effect, as a counter-revolutionary project, designed to prevent disturbance. White claims that in collaborating with this process historians 'deprive history of the kind of meaninglessness that alone can goad living human beings to make their lives different for themselves and their children'.[51] Neither Hare nor Griffiths is willing to abandon the possibility of constructing an alternative narrative through history. As Victor says in *My Zinc Bed*:

> If you don't believe that the rich spend their time on this earth effectively
> fucking over the poor, then I don't see how you make any sense of what goes
> on in the world at all. (p17)

Stanton Garner argues that, by grounding his plays in the specific, 'Griffiths resists a more radically postmodern textualising of history' in which the past is stripped of identity and substance. 'History may be knowable only through its traces, but the historical field . . . retains its integrity, its ability to testify.'[52] The comment could equally well be applied to Hare.

Part of White's criticism of traditional history writing is rooted in his perception that the historian is traditionally bound to the principle of objective understanding: historical reflection is disciplined to analyse and understand the past in such a way that it tends to practise a kind of 'disinterested interest'. As a result, 'it is removed from any connection with a visionary politics and consigned to a service that will always be anti-utopian in nature'.[53] Such disciplined detachment may not necessarily be expected of the artist, though Hare has sometimes been attacked for seeming too sympathetic towards 'the enemy' and secretly wanting the wrong side to win: 'There's giving the devil the best lines, and there's wiping the floor with the opposition. The two things are distinct.'[54] White's argument echoes Brecht's hostility towards a theatre tradition which tended to present the abhorrent and unacceptable as though it was natural and inevitable, encouraging empathy for those who deserve only condemnation; Brecht called instead for a practice which would 'make strange' that which no longer shocks, encouraging audiences to see that what habitually takes place may nonetheless be intolerable ('We ask you expressly to discover/That what happens all the time is not natural/ For to say that something is natural/ . . . is to/Regard it as unchangeable').[55] Without in any way echoing Brecht's didacticism, and certainly without recommending a model for change, the effect of Hare's strategy is to invite us to consider how we might begin to construct a future which the past has been unable to make – or has been prevented from making.

One of Brecht's basic tactics was to take his audiences into a relatively remote past, in order to allow them the space to re-examine the familiar. As we have seen, the past to which Hare travels is generally much closer (and more directly linked) to the present. But an exception to this practice is found in his commitment to translating and adapting historical texts, and this site of excavation also demands consideration. Inevitably, Hare discovers in these texts some of the same concerns which lie near the centre of his own plays. In June 2006, Hare's version of *The Life of Galileo* was revived at London's National Theatre. He had first translated Brecht's text a decade or so earlier, but commenting on its importance now, Hare described it as 'a work which seeks to define the consequences of that moment at which western man realises that the universe is not as he thought it was'.[56] In showing Galileo denying his own scientific discoveries and yielding to the pressures imposed by institutionalised religion, Brecht has, in Hare's view, succeeded in creating 'one of the greatest dramas of intellectual betrayal ever written'. It is hard to think of a play by Hare which is not constructed partly on the bedrock of 'betrayal' of one kind or another. He describes Brecht's Galileo as 'a man who meets a test and fails'; but, perhaps like Victor, Susan Traherne, Kyra and other Hare protagonists who are forced to accommodate themselves to an ideology which has apparently silenced its challengers, Galileo is 'able to understand the meaning of that failure better than anyone'. Just as significantly, and by comparison with *Mother Courage*, Hare identifies *Galileo* as 'a play in which one individual can make a difference'.

Another reason for Hare's eagerness to exhume the text was that Brecht himself was in danger of being consigned to the dustbin of history:

> At the end of the 1980s, the fall of the Berlin wall was the chance for many of his long-standing enemies to declare his plays redundant. The dream of communism was over. What need was there to go on performing plays driven by that dream? But the reaction of more thoughtful actors and directors was to ask more interesting questions. How, after 50 years, could his mid-life masterpieces be released and rediscovered? And how could his most complex plays, *all of which address questions of survival in a fallen world*, be made fresh and urgent for the present day?   [my italics]

For Hare, *Galileo* needed to be disinterred not so much from the path followed by history, but from academic translations and the tendency to preserve it in the embalming formaldehyde of Brecht's company: 'my ambition was to release the play from the memory of the Ensemble'.

In his 1975 Joint Stock play, *Fanshen*, Hare had for once taken the opportunity to escape from British society and history to write about the Chinese revolution. The result was one of his most optimistic works, which seemed to demonstrate the possibility not only that a culture could change but that it could transform itself from within.

> The excitement of *Fanshen* was to write about a society and to cover a period of time in which one felt that people's lives were being materially and spiritually improved . . . to write a positive work using positive material.[57]

For obvious reasons, any revolutionary energy or positive impulse behind the emergence of the Soviet Union was harder to recover:

> When someone suggested we do a similar show about the Russian Revolution I pointed out that it was quite hard, in view of what we all knew happened later, to bring the same relish to describing the heady days of 1918. It would be dishonest.[58]

Working on Chekhov's texts has perhaps allowed Hare to edge his way towards exploring the origins of that revolution, but in 2006 his version of Maxim Gorky's *Enemies* opened the door further.[59] Gorky's play, which had enjoyed what Hare called 'the distinction' of being banned both in pre- and post-revolutionary Russia, focuses on a strike in a factory, and it partly foreshadows the coming revolution and violent class conflict. But, for Hare, much of the play's strength lies in its refusal to take sides, and its balanced depiction of a range of individuals, all of whom are trapped in a historical moment with which they have no way of dealing:

Here, rarely, is a playwright willing to take on the portrayal not just of one section of society, but of its whole, all in the service of the idea – his true theme, this – that we are, every one of us, more or less condemned to believe what our class and our social circumstances lead us to believe.[60]

Enemies, says Hare, is

A play about ideology and violence, about the wisdom of the poor and the limitations of the rich, in which revolutionaries, industrial workers, artists and landowners are all realised with the same measure of skill, humour and vitality.

Moreover, the issues and questions raised by Gorky's text are precisely those 'which have been ringing around the first five years of the 21st century, just as they rang around the first five years of the 20th'. Specifically, 'How do we begin to develop the imagination to cross the line into other people's experience?' Hare has no doubt, then, that 'Gorky ought to be ours.' He insists that, 'If devastating, paranoid change is the keynote of our times, then so it was of his', and discloses the fact that Gorky's text is 'Exactly the kind of play you dream of coming upon: true to its historical moment but also speaking to concerns of our own'. In this it is perhaps an ideal to which Hare himself aspires in documenting his own society.

Taken on its own, Gilbert's assertion in Wilde's 'The Critic as Artist' that our primary duty to history is to rewrite it is ambiguous. Does he mean that we should rewrite our understanding of a past which has already occurred, or that we should seek to ensure that it does not repeat itself? Gilbert goes on to indicate why we need to be constantly, almost obsessively engaged with the past:

When we have fully discovered the scientific laws that govern life, we shall realise that the one person who has more illusions than the dreamer is the man of action. He, indeed, knows neither the origin of his deeds nor their results. From the field in which he thought that he had sown thorns, we have gathered our vintage, and the fig-tree that he planted for our pleasure is as barren as the thistle, and more bitter. It is because Humanity has never known where it was going that it has been able to find its way.[61]

History, then, is created in reflection and analysis. The meaning of what happens can only be assessed and understood when we look back at it. Hare makes a revealing observation in the introduction to his version of *The Blue Room* (1998) when he suggests of its author, Arthur Schnitzler, that 'His essential subject is the gulf between what we imagine, what we remember and what we actually experience.'[62] Irrespective of its validity in relation to Schnitzler, this reflection hints at an interesting frame through which Hare's own plays might usefully be examined.

Near the end of David Hare's television film of the early 1990s, *Heading Home*, there is a moment which is in some respects a mirror image of the final scene of *Plenty*. The screen fades out from a glorious sunset on a deserted beach and sand dunes of the south coast of England in the late 1940s, and then, after a moment of darkness, back in on the same location forty years later. While Janetta and the camera look out at the scene from a speeding vehicle, she speaks to us in a voice-over:

> *The whole beach has been built over. We are no longer looking at dunes, but at rows of bungalows and semi-detached houses in the regular post-war style.*
>
> JANETTA: (*voice over*) These places are gone now. Last year I went down to the sea. It was bricked over. The bay has gone. England's bricked over.[63]

The camera travels rapidly 'along the endless rows of Acacia Avenues' (p272), and Janetta remembers the spaces and the countryside which no longer exist, informing us that now 'the South Coast of England is one long stretch of bricked-in dormitory town' (p272). As the bungalows flash past 'faster and faster, in endless, identical fashion' (p274), it is an effective and affecting moment, and the image is clearly intended to communicate a metaphorical as well as a literal sense of how freedom and possibility have become blocked in during the intervening decades. It is also a moment on the verge – some might say beyond the verge – of toppling over into sentimentalism, and a simple expression of nostalgia for the vanished England of Hare's childhood. The closing lines of *Heading Home* acknowledge the limitations of memory, but also, perhaps, the need to speak what and when we can.

> JANETTA: (*voice over*) These events, I suppose, detain me and me only. No one else remembers them, or if they do, then quite differently. To them, they yield a different meaning ... I remember them as if they were yesterday ... But of course I shall not remember them for long.

Fade to black.

Maps of the world must be drawn after we have travelled, and not before. But unless someone is able to chart what occurs, it may survive only in a remote and perhaps inaccessible corner of the universe. As Bosie asks Wilde in *The Judas Kiss*: 'How will England be changed unless we speak?' (p73).

NOTES

1. David Hare, 'The Play Is in the Air'. Reprinted in Hare, *Obedience, Struggle and Revolt: Lectures on Theatre* (London: Faber, 2005), p125.
2. See Michael Billington, 'The *Guardian* Profile: Sir David Hare', *Guardian*, 13 February 2004, p15. Blake Morrison, 'Profile: David Hare: He Only Does It To Annoy', *Independent*, 30 April 1995, p25.

3. 'A Defence of the New'. Reprinted in Hare, *Obedience*, p104.
4. Richard Boon, *About Hare: The Playwright and the Work* (London: Faber, 2003), p126.
5. *Obedience*, p31.
6. Boon, *About Hare*, p125.
7. Matthew H. Wikander, *The Play of Truth and State: Historical Drama from Shakespeare to Brecht* (London: Johns Hopkins University Press, 1986), p238.
8. *Obedience*, p31.
9. Colin Teevan talking about his play *How Many Miles to Basra?* in an interview published in *Metrolife*, 19 September 2006, p25.
10. David Hare, quoted in *Faber Playwrights at the National Theatre* (London: Faber, 2005), p20.
11. David Hare, *My Zinc Bed* (London: Faber, 2000), p3. All subsequent quotations are taken from this edition.
12. Hayden White, *Tropics of Discourse* (London: Johns Hopkins University Press, 1978), pp82–5.
13. Georg Büchner, *The Complete Plays*, ed. and intro. Michael Patterson (London: Methuen, 1987), p294.
14. Wikander, *The Play of Truth and State*, pp1–8.
15. Carol Homden, *The Plays of David Hare* (Cambridge: Cambridge University Press, 1995), pp62–7.
16. *Obedience*, p121.
17. Boon, *About Hare*, p98.
18. *Obedience*, p23.
19. Boon, *About Hare*, p97.
20. *Obedience*, p121.
21. Boon, *About Hare*, p97.
22. *Ibid.*
23. *Ibid.*, p144.
24. *Ibid.*, p32.
25. *Obedience*, p124.
26. *Ibid.*, p124.
27. Freddie Rokem, *Performing History: Theatrical Representations of the Past in Contemporary Theatre* (Iowa City: University of Iowa Press, 2000), ppx–xi.
28. Homden, *The Plays of David Hare*, p55.
29. *Ibid.*, p70.
30. David Hare, *Plenty*, in *The History Plays* (London: Faber, 1984), p163. All subsequent quotations are taken from this edition.
31. David Hare, *Dreams of Leaving*, in *Collected Screenplays* (London: Faber, 2002), p279.
32. Boon, *About Hare*, p97.
33. *Faber Playwrights at the National Theatre*, pp25–6.
34. *Ibid.*
35. David Hare, 'Universal Quality', *Guardian*, 24 June 2006, p14.
36. *Faber Playwrights at the National Theatre*, pp25–6.
37. *Obedience*, p243.
38. *Ibid.*, pp243–4.
39. *Ibid.*, p121.

40. Cited in Stanton B. Garner Jr, *Trevor Griffiths: Politics, Drama, History* (Michigan: University of Michigan Press, 1999), p11.
41. *Ibid.*, pp9–11.
42. David Hare, *The Judas Kiss* (London: Faber, 1998), p17. All subsequent quotations are taken from this edition.
43. Boon, *About Hare*, p91.
44. Stanton B. Garner Jr, *Trevor Griffiths*, p11.
45. Cited in John Bull, *New British Political Dramatists* (London: Macmillan, 1984), p70.
46. *Obedience*, p122.
47. David Hare, *The Secret Rapture* (London: Faber, 1988), p64. All subsequent quotations are taken from this edition.
48. Boon, *About Hare*, pp172–3.
49. Hayden White, *Tropics of Discourse*, p85.
50. Marnie Hughes-Warrington, 'Hayden White', in *Fifty Key Thinkers on History* (London: Routledge, 2001), pp350–7.
51. *Ibid.*
52. Stanton B. Garner Jr, *Trevor Griffiths*, p261.
53. Hayden White, 'The Politics of Historical Interpretation', cited in Hughes-Warrington, *Fifty Key Thinkers*, p72.
54. Dominic Dromgoole, *The Full Room: An A–Z of Contemporary Playwriting* (London: Methuen, 2002), p131.
55. Bertolt Brecht, *The Exception and the Rule*, in *'The Measures Taken' and Other Lehrstücke* (London: Methuen, 1977), p37.
56. David Hare, 'Universal Quality'. All subsequent comments by Hare on *Galileo* are taken from this source.
57. Boon, *About Hare*, p82.
58. *Ibid.*, p83.
59. Published as Maxim Gorky, *Enemies*, in a new English version by David Hare (London: Faber, 2006).
60. David Hare, 'On *Enemies*', programme for Almeida production of *Enemies*, June 2006. All subsequent comments by Hare on *Enemies* are taken from this source.
61. Oscar Wilde, 'The Critic as Artist', in *The Complete Works of Oscar Wilde* (London: Collins, 1990), p1023.
62. David Hare, 'Introduction', *The Blue Room* (London: Faber, 1998).
63. David Hare *Heading Home*, in *Collected Screenplays*, vol. I (London: Faber, 2002), p272.

13

JANELLE REINELT

Performing histories

Plenty and *A Map of the World*

Writing about two of David Hare's epic plays from 1978 and 1982, I encounter history in syncopated time. *Plenty*, overtly historical, moves from 1943 to 1962 while *A Map of the World*, not marked by year in the text, was produced in 1982 and 1983, when preparations were already underway for an observation of 1985 as the 'Year of the United Nations'. *A Map of the World* can be linked productively to debates about the role of the United Nations at that time, while *Plenty* will benefit from attention both to the history of the years represented within the play, and also to concerns and events at the time of its first production. Then there is the third dimension of time, the time of this writing – when this chapter is intended to speak to contemporary readers who may not even have been born until after both of these other periods. David Hare and I were born in the same year, and the second time stratum examined here, the decade from 1975 to 1985, found both of us living and working as thirty-something contemporaries. 'Contemporary History' can seem like an oxymoron, but the important question of when experience is past enough to be viewed as history – perceived, analysed and treated as historical – is a valid and perplexing one for those of us engaged in the pursuit of a glimpse of the newly historical past.

In his prize-winning study *Performing History: Theatrical Representations of the Past in Contemporary Theatre*, Freddie Rokem develops an idea about actors as 'hyper-historians', seeing that they link 'the historical past with the "fictional" performed *here* and *now* of the theatrical event', enabling audiences to recognise that the actor is repeating with a difference something critical about the past.[1] For Rokem, this is a kind of witnessing that both creates an account of the past and represents it, where the actors' body is the site of the articulation of this hyper-history. Living writers seem to me to partake in the role of hyper-historians, as well, especially someone such as David Hare, who engages in ongoing dialogues about his work and its interpretation, and maintains a visible presence before the public. Thus in looking back at plays written during a decade that has only recently emerged as a topic for history, I want to pay attention not only to the history-making creativity of the author, but also to his time of writing as a historical site of inquiry and reflection, seen from our present vantage point in the 'new century'.

Approaching the plays today, the intellectual history of the time of their writing is different enough from this moment to merit remembering (for those of us who lived it) and identifying (for those younger readers for whom it can only be 'history'). Second wave feminism and post-colonial theory emerged during the decades these plays were written; both made substantial impacts on educated elites, and feminism, at least, also circulated as a set of ideas in popular culture. *Orientalism* by Edward Said appeared in 1978,[2] the same year *Plenty* premièred at the National's Lyttelton. Homi Bhabha published his first essays on colonial mimeticism in 1983 and 1984, as *A Map of the World* moved from the Adelaide Festival, for which it was commissioned, to London (also to the Lyttelton). Gayatri Spivak, having established herself as Derrida's main translator, was beginning to write about India and the Third World, publishing her influential 'Can the Subaltern Speak?' in 1985.[3] These seminal texts of post-colonial theory stimulated three decades of reflection and debate about post-colonial literature, culture and politics. By the late 1970s, V. S. Naipaul and Chinua Achebe were well-known writers on post-colonial themes (different as they are from each other), and Doris Lessing's novels also featured strongly with her (post-)colonial perspective on South Africa and her early articulation of themes taken up by second wave feminism.

In the case of feminism, there are a number of key texts published during these years; in fact, it is more difficult to single out two or three for special attention. Jane Gallop argues in *Around 1981* that in the early 1980s feminist theory and criticism became institutionalised in American universities.[4] Germaine Greer, Gloria Steinem and Jane Fonda were all well-known names in popular culture on both sides of the Atlantic by the mid-1970s. British feminism had such scholarly markers as Juliet Mitchell's *Psychoanalysis and Feminism* (1974),[5] while socialist feminist Sheila Rowbotham published *Woman's Consciousness, Man's World* (1973).[6] Kate Millett's *Sexual Politics* and Germaine Greer's *The Female Eunuch* both date from 1970.[7]

The complexity and contradictions of both feminism and post-colonialism as intellectual ideologies were already quite visible, and it seems reasonable to assume that theatre audiences used the images and rhetoric of second wave emancipation to play off against representations on stage such as Susan and Alice (*Plenty*) or Peggy and Elaine (*Map of the World*). The 'chattering classes' who attend the theatre would have been familiar with post-colonial writers' and critics' views of First World economics and politics, and have encountered Left-leaning critiques of the United Nations in newspapers and books. A member of the educated elite himself, David Hare was certainly familiar with these ideas, whether he shared many of their assumptions or not.

What, then, is to be expected from the pen of a left-wing writer when he takes up post-colonial subjects? According to Gayatri Spivak in 1986, the year David Hare published the collection of his *Asian Plays*, what should be expected is risk. Reacting to her white male students in the United States, she tells Sneja Gunew that, when they say, 'I am only a bourgeois white male, I can't speak', she responds:

> From this position . . . you will of course not speak in the same way about the Third World material, but if you make it your task not only to learn what is going on there through language, through specific programmes of study, but also at the same time through a *historical* critique of your position as the investigating person, then you will see that you have earned the right to criticise, and you will be heard. . . . In one way you take a risk to criticise, of criticising something which is *Other* – something which you used to dominate. I say that you have to take a certain risk: to say 'I won't criticise' is salving your conscience, and allowing you not to do any homework.[8]

In the terms of Spivak's succinct formulation, David Hare took up the challenge of speaking about both sexual and post-colonial Others in *Plenty* (1978) and *A Map of the World* (1982). Both of these plays overtly deal with the demise of the British Empire and its aftermath; both consider the ethico-political roles of the former colonisers in new geopolitical situations. Writing on the very cusp of second wave feminism, Hare also risked representing heterosexual desire and female agency at a time when speaking for women was more than a little suspect. Roughly twenty-five years later (thirty years after *Plenty*), it is possible to examine the nature of those risks and evaluate their outcome.

The woman question

David Hare has a complicated relationship to questions of female representation. On one hand, he has deliberately written major roles for women in many of his plays, and states overtly: 'I have always aimed to give equal voice to women at a time when so many plays have been dealing exclusively with the concerns of men.'[9] He has also mentioned the risk he has taken in imagining them: 'I think a leap of the imagination is essential to all fiction . . . And what greater leap can any man make than to try to imagine what being a woman is like?'[10] Of course, this last comment sounds rather like a paraphrase of the classic Freudian lament 'What do women want?', even as it purports to risk some answers. And with the 'other hand' Hare expresses a kind of rejection of feminism (women, yes; but only on his terms) that is disconcerting to any sophisticated feminist scholar. In his strongest reaction against what he characterises as censorious feminist criticism, he states: 'You're damned if you do and damned if you don't.' Then follows the special pleading on grounds that even a guy who loves to write about – champions – women, cannot win: 'I find most academic feminist criticism of my work completely inane; it's never struck me as anywhere near the mark. But the only thing that annoys me is when that criticism becomes censorious, because it implicitly becomes a "you shouldn't".'[11] So either he dismisses feminist criticism as not worth taking seriously ('inane'), or he finds it censorious. This sounds terribly familiar in terms of a certain response to feminism typical of his generation of males, trying to dismiss what perturbs their judgements while remaining – well – virtuous.

However, I think this whole line of pursuit is a dead end. Let me be more precise: I think it is a dead end to engage in an effort to determine whether or not David Hare is a champion writer of women. The facts are that a large number of complex roles in his dramas are written for women as central protagonist or major figure, and that these women are often sympathetic, if not heroic.[12] The way to break this seeming impasse is to recognise that the texts and productions of Hare's work may or may not reflect his own possible ambivalence, and that, indeed, his ways of representing women may bear the mark of his generation of males as well as overriding it – this is the meaning of the 'author-function' as opposed to the author sui generis in our time. The more important question is in what ways and to what extent his characterisations of women bear the marks of the historical moment's understandings of gender: whether, to speak of the triangulation central to this chapter, the women represented in the plays are signifying something salient, provocative and 'true' about their times through the viewpoint of his, from the prism of ours. Did Hare manage to set up Susan Traherne in *Plenty*, for example, as a convincing representative of her time as seen from his moment of writing: a realistic if extraordinary woman from the 1950s seen by an educated and cultured male in the 1970s? Asked in this fashion, I think the answer is 'Yes'.

Hare became interested in the Second World War[13] and in particular the statistic that '75 per cent of the women flown behind the lines for the Special Operations Executive were subsequently divorced after the war.'[14] Showing how the postwar generation had failed the promise of plenty, he focused on the idealism and bravery of Susan as a member of the British resistance in order to portray the disappointment and despair of not being able to realise, after the war, the potentials for a better personal and national life that seemed so promising with the victory. The statistic is also, of course, about particular gender relations among this group. After the war, marriage rates rose, peaking in 1972, and divorce rates actually fell – only 7 per cent of marriages that took place in 1951 had ended in divorce twenty years later.[15] So the subset of women who had participated in Special Operations was out of step with other women of their generation in terms of their relations with men and the outcomes of their marriages. Hare's Susan is isolated, looking back to a time when she had experienced the agency of doing something critically important with trusted colleagues. After the war, she avoids marriage for some time, succumbing to it according to her husband, Brock, in a weak moment: 'We got engaged when she was still quite ill, and I have tried to help her back up.'[16]

The play unfolds in a series of twelve episodes ranging over nineteen years, taking Susan from 19 to 38. Most depict a central crisis in which Susan makes a decision. As Richard Allen Cave carefully notes, Hare establishes the surface representation of 'this passage of time with great attention to detail, recording changes of fashion in idiom as well as clothes and taste and the shift in people's lifestyles form austerity to plenty. Each scene has an accurate verisimilitude.'[17] Meanwhile, the Festival of Britain, the Suez Crisis, the failed bid for EEC membership and the Aldermaston March – these events are incorporated into the background of the narrative in order to keep the personal story of Susan and Brock threaded into the sociopolitical events of the different scenes/moments.

Susan's behaviour, and the nature of her crises, ranges from defiance and confrontation to emotional breakdown. Called and considered mad by one character, hospitalised on at least one occasion and two in the film version (also written by Hare), Susan 'acts out', shooting a gun over the head of a frightened suitor, threatening suicide to Brock's boss in order to pressure Brock's advancement in the diplomatic corps, and throwing many of their possessions out of the windows. Nevertheless, as I have argued elsewhere, 'her energy, her clear-sighted analysis of the hypocrisy and unproductiveness of her generation, her genuine longing to recover the experience of her youth – these attributes represent an almost-heroine'.[18]

That Susan Traherne was attractive and sympathetic to David Hare has been well established in a number of interviews, especially where he claims that his affection for her hurt the 'balance' of the play in London, thereby keeping spectators from identifying or appreciating the dilemmas of her husband. He describes both Kate Nelligan, the actress who played Susan in London, and himself as 'gung-ho for her'. But he had intended to create two recognisable choices – a path of dissent and a path of accommodation.

'It was meant to be a classical play offering those two balances – those two tendencies. But because we were so pro-Susan, we unbalanced the play in London.'[19]

Richard Boon has interpreted Hare as meaning that the politics of the play softened as Susan's personal tragedy dominated over the larger 'historical tragedy of many wasted lives'.[20] Because critical opinion evidenced an irritation with Susan (and also with Peggy in *Map*), I think it is more likely a problem with a strong characterisation that produced ambivalence in spectators. When Hare published *Plenty* together with *Knuckle* and *Licking Hitler* in 1984, under the title *The History Plays*, he commented on the English opposition to Susan that 'from the start Susan Traherne contains the seeds of her own destruction, and that the texture of the society in which she happens to live is nearly irrelevant, for she is bent on objecting to it, whatever its qualities'.[21] Surely this accommodates Boon's point of view, because it interferes with a political critique of the whole society, but it also reinforces my point about resistance to Susan on other grounds. Hare comments directly on reactions by men, as well:

> It's a common criticism about my work that I write about women whom I find admirable, but whom the audience dislikes. The truth is more complicated than that, but it is true that large sections of an English audience, particularly the men, are predisposed to find Susan Traherne unsympathetic, and it is also true that it is possible to play the part rather stridently, even forbiddingly, so that the audience watches and is not engaged. This was never my intention.[22]

He also reflects that 'the play fails because people leave the performance believing that the man's fate – a degraded life in insurance – isn't as frightful as going mad'.[23] Of course, women perceived to be going mad constitute a classic trope for women who do not conform to patriarchal expectation.[24] In other words, typical gender assumptions have been stimulated by the play and yet the playwright is not straightforwardly responsible for the results, for, as I have indicated, the degree of Susan's 'madness' is definitely a matter of interpretation. Susan characterises herself in language that mixes medicalisation with an emphasis on her agency: 'Listen, I have to tell you, I've not always been well. I have a weakness. I like to lose control. I've been letting it happen, well, a number of times' (p82). This way of putting it preserves a fair amount of agency . . . and sanity for the speaker.

Clearly, then, the representations of Susan may have captured the contradictions and ambivalences of the moment of production, the zeitgeist, and we should pay attention to them in a play poised at the moment of significant upheaval and change in understandings of gender (and sexuality). So an alternative way of understanding the reception of Susan in London and

New York reads as a palimpsest of postwar womanhood intermingled with an emerging second wave feminism. Perhaps what could be an ambivalent lightning rod in England in 1978 was more acceptable in New York in the context of American feminism a year later. This palimpsest character would, however, be an anachronism in relation to the historical specificity of someone like Susan Traherne, who would be more closely related to the milieu of such initial feminist texts as de Beauvoir's *The Second Sex* (first published in English in 1953) and Betty Friedan's *The Feminine Mystique* (1963), taken up in Britain by Eva Figes in *Patriarchal Attitudes* (1970), and certainly to the women characters in Doris Lessing's fictions such as *The Golden Notebook* (1962).[25]

Several scenes in *Plenty* connect rather directly with second wave feminism viewed through the later moment of the play's production rather than the postwar 1950s and early 1960s of the fiction. Germaine Greer, for example, became a highly public figure and precipitated a lot of debate about her attitudes toward women and sex, the institutions of marriage and motherhood. After publishing *The Female Eunuch*, she wrote a regular newspaper column for *The Times* of London, and was often on television. She was also for a time professor of English at Warwick University, thus quite prominent on the UK scene. Along with proclaiming women's subjection to heterosexism, she called for sexual emancipation as a way to break out of those institutions that oppress women. She recommended detaching sex from marriage and establishing independence to the point of having children without desiring an ongoing relationship.[26] In her own life, she strove to practise what she preached: in his 1983 memoir, *Difficult Women*, David Plante states that 'Germaine has made public requests for a man to give her a baby.'[27] Greer was outspoken and outrageous as well as compelling and charismatic. In collected famous quotes of Greer's on the web, this one might have been said by Susan Traherne: 'Yet if a woman never lets herself go, how will she ever know how far she might have got?'[28]

In the early scenes of *Plenty*, Susan is depicted knowing how to use her sexuality to attain her ends, and capable of separating herself from her sexual actions (in scene 3 she uses her sexual promise to ensure her dead lover will be sent home without exposing their relationship to his wife). She jokes with her friend Alice about her boss's sexual predation (scene 4). In the last (chronological and post-coital) scene, she proclaims that 'There's only one kind of dignity, that's living alone' (p83).

But it is scene 5 that most reminds me of the efforts of my generation of young women to test out some of the radical ideas of someone like Greer. Susan asks a young working-class bloke, Mick, to father a child with her, no strings attached:

I'm looking for a father. I want to have a child. (*Pause.*) Look, it really is much easier than it sounds. I mean marriage is not involved. Or even looking after it. You don't even have to see the pregnancy through. I mean conception will be the end of the job. (p40)

He questions her about whether she doesn't have friends from her own class more suitable, but she responds that these men 'have very limited ideas' and would be afraid of the unknown, and they wouldn't do as she asked if she told them she was after a child. When Mick suggests she could not tell them, she says she thought of it, but decided it would be 'dishonest'. So she picked somebody she 'barely knew' (p40).

So, although Susan is perfectly willing to lie to achieve her goals when, for example, she wants to stop seeing Brock in scene 2, this matter of the baby is a matter of principle, and not something to lie about. Furthermore, when Mick worries about a child brought up this way, with no contact with his father, Susan replies, 'The child will manage.'

MICK: How do you know?
SUSAN: Being a bastard won't always be so bad . . .
MICK: I wouldn't bet on it.
SUSAN: England can't be like this forever. (p40)

This scene, both on the page and on the screen as played by Sting and Meryl Streep, has always struck me as touching. They are both idealistic young people, sexually attracted to each other, trying to make a bargain to protect themselves from hurt. It does not work, of course, and their failure to get pregnant results in Susan dumping Mick, and Mick accusing Susan of using him. They have a terrible, predictable argument, which she says is precisely what she was trying to avoid. He calls her names, and she shoots at him.[29]

Another major narrative played itself out during the decade of the 1970s that was surely in the public consciousness in 1978. Sylvia Plath's suicide early in 1963 had been followed by a huge public interest in, and debate about, her marriage to Ted Hughes, her mental state, and the relationship between her writing and her own autobiography (*The Bell Jar* was published under a pseudonym a month before the suicide and, as is well known, seemed in many ways a record of Plath's descent into madness and suicide). During the 1970s these debates raged in literary circles but also in the newspapers and media. In 1975, *Letters Home: Correspondence 1950–1963* was edited and published by Plath's mother Aurelia, and her *Journals* were edited and published in 1982 by Hughes, who was the executor of her estate, since they were still legally married at the time of her death. The first two full-length scholarly studies of Plath appeared in 1973 and 1976.[30]

Each major publication occasioned controversy, both because Hughes was held by many, especially feminists, to be responsible for suppressing information and thereby controlling and abusing Plath beyond the grave, and also because of arguments among the family members involved and at least one legal case arising as a result of a too-transparent character identified as lesbian in *The Bell Jar*. Between her death in 1963 and 1989, her grave was desecrated four times; each time involved an attempt to remove 'Hughes' from the inscription 'Sylvia Plath Hughes'.

While I am not making the case that Sylvia Plath was in any direct way related to Susan Traherne, I am suggesting that the kind of high emotions stimulated by the extreme visibility and highly charged themes of what some have called the Plath 'myth' – because of the undecidability of the truth and the legendary status of the narrative – provided one backdrop to the production of *Plenty* and its possible reception. Susan, tottering on the edge of sanity and seeming self-destruction because she was bitterly angry at how the world was turning out, could easily stimulate the same kinds of harsh judgements, as well as strong defences, as Sylvia Plath had done. Plath was ten years younger at her death than Susan in her last scene (40 versus 30), which makes the overlap between their generations just acute enough to indicate some shared experience of the 1950s. Plath can be seen as succumbing to the role of wife and mother that Susan had hoped to avoid.

Plath aspired to some high literary ideals that make her tragedy not unlike Traherne's – the waste of a gifted life. Recently, in the title essay to his book (*Obedience, Struggle and Revolt*), David Hare brought up Sylvia Plath and Ted Hughes, and linked his own tumultuous feelings about the theatre in the 1970s to something he recalled while watching *Sylvia*, the recent film about Plath. He acknowledges that the film itself was weak and discloses that he turned down the opportunity to write the screenplay because 'I had no idea why Sylvia Plath put her head in the oven. I equally felt I had no moral right to reconstruct the dialogue and sentiments of a marriage to which I had no privileged access. *I wasn't there. I don't know*' [italics in text].[31] But what moved him to tears was a scene in the film in which Ted and Sylvia pledge to write the greatest poetry of their day. To some extent, both of them achieved at least a good part of this claim. But, for Hare, 'what made the scene overpowering, to me at least, so long after the events it described, was the sheer lunatic ambition, the awkward innocence of a time in which poets, from the unlikely base of provincial England in the late 1950s, set out not just to write the odd poem, but to change everything'.[32] Hare embarked on this excursus about his reaction to the film as a way to explain his own strong emotions about the theatre in the 1970s: 'You may, at this distance, find it hard to credit the measure of passion which moved us all . . .'.[33] Here, I think, we also see the central motif in much of his work: a utopian moment of possibility linked to youth and idealism looked at from a later time of ruined promise and disappointment; often it is also a romantic moment.

Returning to Susan through Sylvia, I am arguing for seeing the intellectual and emotional background to the original production of *Plenty* in 1978 as providing a number of associations for spectators that could provoke among educated elite men – and some women – a dislike for, or irritation with, a character such as Susan, who seems to be demanding emancipation while proving unable to handle it. Alternatively, for David Hare, myself and many others, Susan is admirable as she tries to find a different, honourable way to live in a depressing time, and her human failings are more heartbreaking than despicable.

A similar kind of antagonism could be provoked in some spectators by the character of Peggy a few years later. In *A Map of the World* (1982), a beautiful and intelligent actress enjoys her power over several interesting men and playfully offers herself as a sexual prize in the ideological battle between them. In so doing, she refuses to be merely a commodity in their traffic in women, instead controlling the conditions and nature of her exchange herself: arguably an emancipated woman having things on her own terms. However, from another point of view, she ignores the serious content of their disagreement at a UNESCO conference on poverty, and in so doing demonstrates a First World white woman's privilege – the privilege to ignore the serious issues of post-colonial nations' struggle for dignity and adequate resources, and also the tendency to objectify and exoticise the racial other – in this case, the Indian novelist Victor Mehta. In the course of this play, however, Peggy comes to see how she has behaved and makes a series of moral choices about how to live the rest of her life that might be seen to redeem this one impulsive act. Before turning to a fuller discussion of the play in terms of its post-colonial thematics, I want to pause briefly on the meaning of Peggy's wager.

In the play, Peggy is clearly an example of American feminism of the kind that tried to find a new open sexuality as a means of empowerment. While American women read *The Female Eunuch* in droves in the early 1970s, it was perhaps Erica Jong's *Fear of Flying* (1973)[34] that most kindled the imagination of young women trying to reimagine new liberated identities. In the novel, her protagonist imagines a 'zipless fuck', the equivalent of a no-strings-attached brief sexual encounter based on simple desire. The book insisted on women's experiences of lust, or desire without relationship, and the zipless fuck fantasy became a touchstone for the view that women might like to have the kind of casual encounters often attributed to men at women's expense. Peggy tries to explain to Stephen, the young journalist who is both smitten with her and defiantly opposed to his rival, Victor Mehta (with whom Peggy has slept the previous night), what her code of behaviour is, and how it came about. She ascertains that he has not been to America and then explains it as something connected to striving to be independent in a country known for freedom of choice. Then she tells him:

> I mean relationships – *why?* What's the need? You understand? (*Stephen does not react.*) They're just trouble. And . . . well . . . when I was sixteen, I made a resolution. I had a girlfriend. We were walking in the Rockies, and the view, I can tell you, was something as you came over to Boulder, Colorado. And we had a six-pack right there on top of the mountain. And she was a *good* girl, I mean a really good girl, you could trust your life to her, And we said: let's not ever mess with the bad things at all . . . I mean, we don't need it. So let's not.[35]

This description of a young person's vow to live differently, to live better (in her eyes), is the moment of idealistic promise. Peggy has been trying to follow this way of thinking, and she criticises both Stephen and Victor for their sexual jealousy in vying for her: 'That sort of behaviour, men being jealous, men fighting, it's out of date. Outdated, Stephen. Unnecessary, Stephen. I mean, drop the bad behaviour and you might get somewhere' (p44). When Stephen and Victor persist in their antagonisms, Peggy misjudges that the serious part of their disagreements can be resolved by calling them on their sexual immaturity. She proclaims that they should have a public debate, and that she will sleep with the winner. Because it doesn't matter, because it's freedom, or as Elaine, the African-American journalist who is the Alice of this play, comments, 'Putting her body where her mouth is – how can that be wrong?' (p47). It may be difficult for a generation of young people living in the present to grasp how familiar and how passionate these sorts of words were to my (and David Hare's) generation of young women. But for the decade under discussion, these were words that could lead to the folly of not taking the full measure of the situation or underestimating the consequences of the 'freedom' in question.

In this case, the case of *A Map of the World*, the blind spot is twofold. Not only does Peggy underestimate the seriousness of the disagreement between Victor and Stephen; she also underestimates the power she has to hurt them both by being cavalier. The first shortcoming would be by rights the most important, if Stephen wasn't accidentally killed in a train wreck late in the play. The finality of death makes the personal stakes suddenly much higher than originally calibrated.

But first, to the United Nations.

The United Nations, poverty and imperialism

The setting for *A Map of the World* is a UNESCO conference on poverty in 1976, being held in a posh hotel in India. The initial contradiction, of discussing Third World poverty while complaining because the Indian waiters are slow and the champagne is not good, is obvious and amusing. But the heart of the matter is the struggle over ways of viewing the international situation, which is also the present time of production. Hare triangulates viewpoints to capture the dynamics of the UN in the early 1980s. Victor Mehta, famous Indian novelist, has been invited to address the conference. He is an arch-conservative who believes 'All old civilisations are superior to younger ones. That is why I have been happiest in Shropshire. They are less subject to crazes. In younger countries there is no culture. The civilisation is shallow. Nothing takes root' (p18). Stephen Andrews is a reporter on a small British left-wing magazine, and he views Mehta as a fraud, an Indian in drag as an English gentleman who cares nothing for the plight of the poor and only desires self-aggrandisement by holding himself aloof from any meaningful effort to improve the world. M'Bengue is the third voice – the delegate from Senegal who is trying to negotiate an aid package for his own country, and who has helped draft a statement for Mehta to deliver to the conference to placate a number of Marxist countries who are offended by Mehta's fiction. Martinson, the Swedish diplomat running the conference, tells Mehta: 'There's a phrase where you call Marxism "dictatorship's fashionable dress". Well, they do find that peculiarly insulting' (p33). Mehta, of course, refuses to back down, and all three of the main voices are given lengthy expressions of their viewpoints during the ensuing two acts.

To get a picture of the United Nations as it appeared in the early 1980s, I turn to a book of essays published as a result of the decision of the Seventh Non-Aligned Summit to celebrate 1985 as the 'Year of the United Nations'. This meeting was held, ironically, in New Delhi in March 1983 (between the two first productions of *A Map of the World*) and the volume published several years later included contributions from a variety of scholars and diplomats from the so-called non-aligned nations, plus a few sympathetic First-Worlders. The Non-Aligned Movement (NAM) dates from 1955 when twenty-nine Asian and African heads of state met in Indonesia to combine their efforts as Third World countries not to become involved in the ideological struggles of the cold war.[36] The membership expanded rapidly, and today stands at around 115. The purpose of the organisation, formalised at the Havana Summit in 1979, is to ensure 'the national independence, sovereignty, territorial integrity and security of non-aligned countries in their struggle against imperialism, colonialism, neo-colonialism, apartheid, racism, including Zionism, and all forms of foreign aggression, occupation, domination, interference or hegemony as well as against great power and bloc politics'.[37] During the 1970s, and until the collapse of the Soviet Union in 1989, NAM played an important role in organising Third World opinion and representing it, often in the forums of the United Nations.

In *The Nonaligned and the United Nations*, then-Secretary General of the UN Javier Perez de Cuellar acknowledges the founding of NAM as 'one of the great acts of creative statesmanship in our time'. He worries, however, that 'The weakening of international dialogue, the accentuation of regional tensions, the remorseless arms race, the continuance, indeed, the widening, of grave disparities between the world's privileged and the world's deprived, and a general climate of fear and discontent, are the symptoms of a deep-seated global crisis.'[38] In the essays that follow, there is an expectation that the United Nations (and the NAM bloc in relation to it) will be able to address some of these crisis dimensions. On the other hand, the difficulties facing both these bodies since their founding is also apparent. Addressed most directly to developing countries (at this time both 'Third World' and 'developing countries' were the terms in use), their dilemmas are clear. As Frank Enrique Bracho wrote, 'The developing countries have to decide whether they want to continue to live with their uncertain and painstaking ties of dependency upon powerful countries – which persist in considering the Third World as a marginal economic "partner" – or whether they prefer to develop self-sustained national economies, based both nationally and in their more diversified external economic relations on greater association among weak countries with similar interests.'[39] While many articles praise the UN and the work of NAM for 'promoting self-determination for colonial peoples', there is also the criticism, often in the same article, that the bureaucracy and stasis of the world organisation is the source of its failure, that the cold war structures the major issues and occludes other important or competing topics, and that NAM itself has been split by internal dissension and inevitable involvement with First World dependencies.

In this situation, Hare demonstrates the multiple levels on which the United Nations malfunctions, while not giving up on its promise. M'Bengue has the major critique of the West:

> We take aid from the West because we are poor, and in everything we are made to feel our inferiority. The price you ask us to pay is not money but misrepresentation. The way the nations of the West make us pay is by representing us continually in their organs of publicity as bunglers and murderers and fools . . . All your terms are political, and your politics is the crude fight between your two great blocs. Is Angola pro-Russian? Is it pro-American? These are the only

questions you ever ask yourselves. As if the whole world could be seen in those terms. In your terms. In the white man's terms and through the white man's media.   (p40)

When, at the end of the conference, an aid deal is cut with Senegal, it turns out the IMF and the World Bank will put strings on the money that will effectively ruin the country and interfere with its internal policies. 'In sum', M'Bengue comments, 'the destruction of the policies which brought our government into being. You throw us a lifeline. The lifeline is in the shape of a noose' (p82).

If the play is illustrating and commenting on the plight of the non-aligned nations in the situation of United Nations operations, it also establishes a dialectical view of the proceedings. Victor Mehta is finally not the strongest voice, but his is indeed polished, pointed and pitiless. There are many reasons for thinking that he is patterned on the novelist V. S. Naipaul. Like Naipaul he has a a disdain for post-colonial cultures, an existential individuality that holds himself apart from affiliation and considers himself in permanent exile, and a comic style that lampoons what he calls 'colonials' (those living in or coming from former colonies, rather than the European colonisers as one might assume). Rob Nixon, in one of the most detailed critical scholarly appraisals of Naipaul, details the imperialist rhetoric typical of Naipaul's characterisations of the former colonies as '"barbarous", "primitive", "tribal", "simple", "irrational", "static", "without history", "futureless", "bush", "philistine", "sentimental", "parasitic", and "mimic"'.[40] Naipaul was born in Trinidad to a Brahman family who had immigrated there, and came to England on scholarship in the 1950s. He was a well-known figure in the UK by the early 1980s, having won the Booker Prize and a number of other literary honours. He produced a string of publications, especially travel and non-fiction books, almost yearly between 1977 and 1981. In addition, his opinions have always plunged him into controversy. Recently, Rachel Donadio wrote about him:

> Naipaul's cold, unsparing look at the corruption and disarray of the postcolonial world, his disdain for Marxist liberation movements and his view that Islamic society leads to tyranny are implicitly political positions, and have made him the object of much political criticism. He has been sharply criticised by, among others, Derek Walcott, the Caribbean poet and Nobel laureate, and Chinua Achebe, the Nigerian novelist, who said 'although Naipaul was writing about Africa, he was not writing for Africans'. The scholar and critic Edward Said, who died in 2003, called 'Beyond Belief' 'an intellectual catastrophe'. Naipaul, he added, thinks 'Islam is the worst disaster that ever happened to India, and the book reveals a pathology'.[41]

Hare includes certain characteristic behaviours, such as his criticism of other writers and a reputation for philandering, without providing a specific identification.[42] He gains, I would argue, a number of advantages by invoking Naipaul. First, his wit and intelligence make a perfect model for a position that must be represented as attractive, if Hare were not to be accused of setting up Mehta as a straw man. Second, Peggy's attraction to Mehta can also represent the romance of those American and English critics who have admired his work and his style. Third, by alluding to someone with a well-known reputation for provocation, the audience can be expected to fill in more detail from the exemplary celebrity – this is what Hare's playwright colleague David Edgar calls 'adjacency'.[43]

It is left to the young idealistic journalist, Stephen Andrews, to finally expose Mehta in an attack that criticises both his politics and his humanity simultaneously. Stephen has been drawn by Hare to be young and 'naff', and therefore not worthy of being taken seriously early in the play, but he grows in stature during the play, and finally speaks clearly and convincingly against Mehta:

> You will never understand any struggle unless you take part in it. How easy to condemn this organisation as absurd . . . Why do you not think that at the centre of the verbiage, often only by hazard but nevertheless at times and unpredictably, crises are averted, aid is directed? . . . Why do you not imagine that if you stopped distancing yourself, if you got rid of your wretched fastidiousness, you could not lend yourself for once not to objection but to getting something done? (p71)

Of course, in the play, there is a utopian ending: the young idealistic Stephen pulls out of the wager for Peggy's favours and announces he is leaving the conference, taking the train for Jaipur, after finally standing up for his beliefs without apologising for them. When he is killed in a train wreck, Mehta has a change of heart (toward Stephen, if not the conference). He leaves and drives with Peggy to the accident site, and later the two of them marry. Mehta writes a book about what happened as a tribute to Stephen. He summarises the denouement succinctly: 'Each of the characters is forced to examine the values of his or her life . . . The novelist is accused of dalliance and asked to put a value on what he has seen as a passing affair. The actress questions her easy promiscuity and is made to realise adulthood will involve choice. And the journalist assumes the confidence of his own beliefs' (p75). This resolves the ethical problems of the protagonists (even if it leaves Stephen confident but dead), but it does not resolve the political problems which have been clearly highlighted. Hare has perhaps softened Mehta beyond any imaginable comparable sentiment possible from Naipaul, and he has given Peggy the insight and character to make a serious commitment to her life with Mehta. This can be seen as Romance rather than realism. But it gestures back to the epigram from Oscar Wilde which begins the play, 'A map of the world that does not include Utopia is not worth even glancing at . . . ' (np).

The metatheatrical structure of the play, the embedded narrative inside a film being made based on a fictional book, confused the original critics, but seems exactly appropriate to the questions of memory and interpretation that inevitably encircle the play. The narrative can easily be made into a cheap Hollywood film in which the African-American journalist/actress is forced to bare her breasts without justification. It can also be seen as a memoir in which guilt and regret are expiated, or as a dramatic parable that comments on contemporary attitudes toward the Third World, the United Nations and gender relations. Seen from our perspective in the new century, reconsidering the play now can remind us of a time when utopian possibility was still viable on all counts, something I am not sure persists today with respect to its three main themes.

The imperial dinner party

Returning to Gayatri Spivak's challenge to take the risk of representing the cultural other, David Hare's solution has been to ground his representations in the governmental and diplomatic elites who react to the break-up of the empire in *Plenty*, or in the efforts of new leaders of Third World countries to achieve workable international solutions to chronic problems of development in *A Map of the World*. Hare, seeming to respond to Spivak, comments, 'The wretched of the earth are, for some reason, rarely thought to be a suitable subject for the arts. I was ambivalent about being able to represent the poor themselves. But I did feel qualified to write about our attitudes to them.'[44] In addition, both plays also risk depicting native figures in negative lights. While Mehta is the exiled Indian who out-Englishes the English, the Wongs in the dinner scene of *Plenty* represent the comprador class in Burma, newly come to power after independence, seen jockeying to establish their place in Western culture and society. Darwin also comes across in a harsh light with his racial slur ('that appalling wog') and his condescension to both Wong and his wife, correcting Wong's use of English and Madame Wong's mischaracterisation of Ingmar Bergman as Norwegian. The scene is marked by black humour, as Wong himself later tells Darwin, referring to Nasser and the Egyptians, 'These gyps need whipping and you are the man to do it' (p56).

The portrait of Darwin is particularly accomplished. We first see him in Brussels, where he is involved in the clean-up at the close of the war in 1947, and he says his former posting was Djakarta. Based on the dinner-party scene, he apparently came to that posting after serving as the top British colonial official in Burma before independence (gained along with India and Sri Lanka in 1948). Thus his meeting up with Wong is especially ironic – Wong is now the First Secretary at the Burmese embassy, but he was clearly in a subaltern position before independence. Darwin is the last of the old colonial administrators, and the Suez Crisis breaks him. The party takes place just as the situation becomes clear: the English claimed to be a neutral party intervening in the dispute over the canal between Egypt and Israel, but actually there was a secret plan with the Israelis and the French to seize the canal. Darwin is extremely upset about this because he was not told about it. 'The government lied to me . . . They are not in good faith' (p53). When Brock counters that he was always against the policy from the start, Darwin claims that he would have defended it 'if it had been honestly done'. He is the last of the old guard, and, when he resigns and then dies shortly after Suez, his death is symbolic of the change at the end of empire. Brock, however, as representative of the new generation, lacks Darwin's principles: Brock cannot see what difference it makes whether or not the thing was done 'honestly'. Susan, acting out, uses sarcasm to underline the fiasco:

> The words 'Suez Canal' will not be spoken . . . They are banned. You will not hear them . . . Nasser, nobody will mention his name . . . Nobody will say blunder or folly or fiasco. No one will say 'international laughing stock' . . . Nobody will say 'death-rattle of the ruling class'. (pp50–1)

The play comments briefly on Brock's posting to Iran (Jordan in the film version). The separation of the diplomats from the life of the country is clear. 'The people are fine', he tells Alice. 'Insofar as one's seen them, you know. It's only occasionally that you manage to get out' (p65).

Although this aspect of *Plenty* may seem to stay contained within its historical fictional frame, here too the marks of a more contemporary moment of production can be seen. Hare, perhaps thinking about younger audience members, has Dorcas ask about Suez. This pregnant teenager, whom Alice brings to Darwin's funeral and who subsequently takes abortion money from Susan, knows next to nothing about the history of Suez, although the scene takes place only four years later. Perhaps the short recitation – 'It's a historical incident four years ago; caused a minor kind of stir at the time' (p62) – marks the fragility of history for audiences looking back from the 1970s, and certainly from this moment as well, when Vietnam and the first Gulf War can seem similarly lost in time. For British adults viewing the play in

1978, however, Suez marked the end of Britain's international influence, and they would remember that in early 1963 France thwarted Britain's desire to join the EEC.

Both of these plays, then, create history through today's looking glass. The current diminution of the credibility of the United Nations, the inability to intervene positively in Iraq and Somalia, the charges of corruption and bureaucratic mismanagement all render the world of 1982 an almost nostalgic other time of possibilities which are now seemingly lost. From 2006, both the time of the immediate postwar era and the decade 1975–85 are equally remote. In terms of evaluating the risks taken in these two plays, their value seems clear: Hare's use of history sharpens our own understanding of the periods in question, historicising himself and his perspective as well as his subjects. David Hare's elegiac criticism and lament for these moments can help explain the past and provoke the future. As Walter Benjamin puts it:

> To articulate the past historically does not mean to recognise it 'the way it really was' (Ranke). It means to seize hold of a memory as it flashes up at a moment of danger.[45]

NOTES

Thanks to Gerald Hewitt for his careful reading and commentary on this chapter.

1. Freddie Rokem, *Performing History: Theatrical Representations of the Past in Contemporary Theatre* (Iowa City: University of Iowa Press, 2000), p13.
2. Edward Said, *Orientalism* (New York: Pantheon, 1978).
3. Gayatri Spivak, 'Can the Subaltern Speak?', in Cary Nelson and Larry Grossberg (eds.), *Marxism and the Interpretation of Culture* (Chicago: University of Chicago Press, 1988), pp271–313.
4. Jane Gallop, 'Introduction', in *Around 1981: Academic Feminist Literary Theory* (London and New York: Routledge, 1992), pp1–10.
5. Juliet Mitchell, *Psychoanalysis and Feminism* (New York: Pantheon, 1974).
6. Sheila Rowbotham, *Woman's Consciousness, Man's World* (Harmondsworth: Penguin, 1973).
7. Kate Millett, *Sexual Politics* (New York: Doubleday, 1970); Germaine Greer, *The Female Eunuch* (London: MacGibbon and Key, 1970).
8. Sarah Harasym (ed.), *The Post-Colonial Critic: Interviews, Strategies, Dialogues* (London: Routledge, 1990), pp62–3.
9. Richard Boon, *About Hare: The Playwright and the Work* (London: Faber, 2003), p145.
10. *Ibid.*, p90.
11. Hersh Zeifman, 'An Interview with David Hare', in Hersh Zeifman (ed.), *David Hare: A Casebook* (New York: Garland, 1994), p9.
12. For a balanced evaluation, see Ruby Cohn, 'Rare Hare, Liking Women', in Zeifman (ed.), *David Hare: A Casebook*, pp23–44.

13. 'Once you decide, "My subject is how things were, how things are, and how things might be", then that's history, and you've got to show the sweep of things'; Hare quoted in Boon, *About Hare*, p97.

14. David Hare, 'Now Think This Time: An Introduction to the History Plays', *Writing Left-Handed* (London: Faber, 1991), p81.

15. Edward Royle, 'Trends in Post-War British Social History', in *Understanding Post-War British Society*, ed. J. Obelkevich and P. Catterall (London: Routledge, 1994), p23.

16. David Hare, *Plenty* (London: Faber, 1978), p51. See Susan's own statement about this 'weakness', p55. All subsequent quotations are taken from this edition.

17. Richard Allen Cave, *New British Drama on the London Stage: 1970–1983* (Gerrards Cross: Colin Smythe, 1989), p197.

18. In *After Brecht: British Epic Theatre* (Ann Arbor: University of Michigan Press, 1994), p131.

19. Quoted in Boon, *About Hare*, p92.

20. *Ibid.*, p31.

21. Hare, *Writing Left-Handed*, p81.

22. *Ibid.*, p82. This passage is also included in the 1978 edition of the play as 'A Note on Performance'.

23. Quoted in Boon, *About Hare*, p91.

24. Darwin tells Brock he assumes Susan is 'barking' like other diplomats' wives, even though Brock demurs from being complicit in that judgement. Surely Hare is marking the history of the reception of 'rebel' or, even less theatrically, 'resistant' women, by placing these words in the mouth of the 'old guard' – but sometimes sympathetic – character, Darwin.

25. Simone de Beauvoir, *The Second Sex* (New York: Knopf, 1963); Betty Friedan, *The Feminine Mystique* (New York: Dell, 1963); Eva Figes, *Patriarchal Attitudes* (London: Faber, 1970); Doris Lessing, *The Golden Notebook* (New York: Ballantine, 1962).

26. For example, 'If women are to effect a significant amelioration in their condition, it seems obvious they must refuse to marry' (Greer, *The Female Eunuch*, p319).

27. David Plante, *Difficult Women* (London: Victor Gollancz Ltd, 1983), p155.

28. www.brainyquote.com/quotes/authors/g/germaine_greer.html (accessed 16 April 2006).

29. We later learn he was actually wounded, but in the scene itself the stage directions say she fires once over his head, then fires three more times. It does not say he is hit. Since she is a trained shot, it seems surprising in the later scene when she tells Lazar that she shot someone, clearly Mick. In the film version, she shoots three times but is not shown hitting him. See Hare, *Plenty*, p82.

30. Eileen M. Aird, *Sylvia Plath* (Edinburgh: Oliver and Boyd, 1973) and David Holbrook, *Sylvia Plath: Poetry and Existence* (London: Athlone, 1976). Sylvia Plath, *The Bell Jar* (London: Faber, 1963) and *Letters Home: Correspondence 1950–1963* (New York: Harper and Row, 1975); Ted Hughes and Frances McCullough (eds.), *The Journals of Sylvia Plath* (New York: Ballantine, 1982).

31. Hare, *Obedience*, p14.

32. *Ibid.*, p15.

33. *Ibid.*, p13.

34. Erica Jong, *Fear of Flying* (New York: New American Library, 1973).

35. David Hare, *A Map of the World* (London: Faber, 1982), p43. All subsequent quotations are taken from this edition.
36. http://news.bbc.co.uk/2/hi/2798187.stm (accessed 7 February 2007).
37. http://en.wikipedia.org/wiki/Non-Aligned_Movement (accessed 7 February 2007).
38. M. S. Rajan, V. S. Mani and C. S. R. Murthy, *The Nonaligned and the United Nations* (New Delhi: South Asian Publishers, 1987), pv.
39. Frank Enrique Bracho, 'Utopia and the Reality of Economic Co-operation among Developing Countries: Lessons from the Implementation of the Caracas Programme of Action', in Rajan et al., *The Nonaligned and the United Nations*, p117.
40. Rob Nixon, *London Calling: V. S. Naipaul, Postcolonial Mandarin* (Oxford: Oxford University Press, 1992), p6. Nixon went to Colombia University and is associated with Edward Said in his critique of imperialism and decolonisation.
41. Rachel Donadio, 'The Irascible Prophet: V. S. Naipaul at Home', *New York Times*, 7 August 2005, http://www.nytimes.com/2005/08/07/books/review/07DONADIO.html (accessed 7 February 2007).
42. Nixon notes in passing that Naipaul 'served as a direct model for the intellectual style of the play's conservative character', but offers no support for the assertion. Likewise, I have no evidence except an uncanny likeness and a strong guess. *London Calling*, pp2–3.
43. David Edgar, 'Reality Time'. Unpublished manuscript of keynote speech, 'Reality Time: A Conference about Factual Drama on Stage and Screen', Birmingham University, 1996.
44. David Hare, 'Introduction', *Plays: Two* (London: Faber, 1997), px.
45. Quoted in Rokem, *Performing History*, p209.

14

MICHAEL MANGAN

'Marbled with doubt'

Satire, reality and the alpha male in the plays of David Hare

Critics have always been interested in the gender politics of David Hare's work. In general this interest has resulted in a focus of attention on his female characters – understandably, since Hare, more than most male playwrights of his generation, has tended to write plays with large central parts for women. Hare has talked, too, of his ambition to write plays in which women would be 'represented as I thought more roundly and comprehensively than was then usual'.[1] He has also attributed certain kinds of values to his female characters. 'Women', he has said, 'are characteristically the conscience of my plays. They often stand outside a man's world and so can see it much more clearly.'[2] In *Changing Stages* Richard Eyre and Nicholas Wright put it in these terms:

> Pervading all these resonant places is a sense of something lost. Just what's been lost appears from time to time in the form of a woman. She may be a woman of startling goodness, or impossible integrity, or she may be simply kind and loving, but she's always a beacon of light.[3]

Thus in *Teeth 'n' Smiles* (1975) Maggie seeks to transcend the grubbiness of 1970s England through martyrdom; in *Plenty* (1978) Susan Traherne strives to stay in touch with the idealistic vision which she had found during her undercover military service in France during the war; in *The Secret Rapture* (1988), Isobel has been seen by some as a kind of modern saint – although Hare describes her more simply as 'lumbered with being good . . . that's her fatal flaw';[4] in *Skylight* (1995) Kyra's idealism is contrasted with Tom's pragmatism. Repeatedly, central female characters such as these carry the moral weight of the play.

It is a trope which has led to Hare being criticised for having an over-schematic view of women: Michelene Wandor's critique of *Teeth 'n' Smiles* is not untypical.

Certainly the major central female role is a real challenge for an actress, but it is used in a pre-censorship context to reassert pre-feminist images about the relative male sphere of the creator, and the female sphere of the interpreter. With an additional bitter twist: where the romantic image leaves the female muse pure and undefiled, in the 1970s, the independent woman is a danger, and must be imaginatively destroyed for art (i.e. male creativity) to survive.[5]

Wandor is clear on the matter: Hare might write good parts for women but he does not write the woman-as-subject (unlike, for example, Mary O'Malley, Pam Gems and Nell Dunn, who 'introduce woman as individual . . . women as a subject of the drama and mistresses of their own destinies').[6] Hare, unsurprisingly, has reacted irritably to this line of criticism:

The thing is that you're damned if you do and damned if you don't . . . you're criticised either because the women are too good or because they're villainesses. If they're villainesses you're called misogynistic, and if they're not villainesses – if they're good – you're told you're stereotyping. So frankly I find most academic feminist criticism of my work completely inane; it's never struck me as anywhere near the mark.[7]

In fact, not all feminist criticism has dealt as clumsily with Hare's work as he suggests. But the issue is obscured if it is assumed that female subjectivity has typically been his subject matter, in the way that it was the subject matter of the generation of women playwrights with whom Hare shared the radical theatres of the 1970s and 1980s. For Hare's most frequent subject matter is not women but men. (This is, of course, implicit in Hare's own description, quoted above, of the function of the good women in his plays being to provide a perspective, from the outside, on the world of the men.) One of Hare's key themes throughout his writing career has been the various contradictions which lie at the heart of British society – a society which is insistently male-dominated and 'masculine' in its structures of power and its structures of feeling; he has consistently written about these men and their institutions in satirical tones.

To claim that Hare writes satires about men and their institutions would not seem particularly contentious. Yet Hare himself is dubious about both these terms: 'I don't normally write plays about men in grey suits in offices', he said in an interview with Georg Gaston in 1993. 'I don't normally write about men. I don't write plays whose subject is primarily power.'[8] He attributes that theme, rather, to the fictional 'Howard Hare' – the mysterious 'third man' that emerges whenever he and Howard Brenton collaborate on a play. But even a quick survey of Hare's own plays reveals that Hare himself finds the power structures of the masculine world an irresistible theme: his plays are set in male-dominated environments such as Cambridge colleges and Whitehall offices, at UNESCO conferences and political rallies, in bishops' palaces and Crown courts, in Downing Street and the White House. And in these environments Hare regularly returns to one particular stereotype of masculinity: the figure of the 'alpha male'. The term, derived from post-Darwinian biology, refers to the highest-status male in a group of social animals, the leader to whom the others defer. In (human) gender studies it has become a useful shorthand for a certain kind of dominant and dominating masculine behaviour and personality type: the powerful figure of hegemonic masculinity who wields a power which is often as much to do with gender, class, money and privilege as it is with physical strength. The alpha male in Hare's plays is often the figure who most clearly represents the relevant power elite and its values, whether that power is seen in financial, political or cultural terms; he is also characterised, as is the typical alpha male in real life, by a high degree of self-confidence. We see him in central dramatis personae such as Patrick Delafield in *Knuckle* (1974), Alfred (and later Sidney) Bagley in *Brassneck* (1973), Victor Mehta in *A Map of the World* (1982), Lambert Le Roux in *Pravda* (1985), George Jones in *The Absence of War* (1993), Tom Sergeant in *Skylight* (1995), and Victor Quinn in *My Zinc Bed* (2000). And, while Hare's developing interest in verbatim and documentary-style dramas has meant that the mode of presentation has changed, there is a continuing fascination with the figure of the powerful masculine leader: the political leaders on both sides of the Israeli/Palestinian conflict in *Via Dolorosa* (1998); the politicians, senior civil servants and rail executives who deal so shoddily with the grief of the bereaved in *The Permanent Way* (2003); and, in *Stuff Happens* (2004), the alpha male of all alpha males, the leader of the one remaining superpower, the President of the United States.

Hare, then, *does* 'write plays about men', and with great frequency about a certain type of man. One reason for this might be seen in a statement made by Hare in an interview with John Tusa in 2005:

> [A]s you get older, I can see that an awful lot of my feeling in life has been to do with fatherlessness. My father was a sailor, and he was away ten or eleven months of the year, and when he came back he would sort of flood money and excitement into our lives, very very briefly, and then give the impression he was bored. And I do think that that left a certain anomie in me, and a certain feeling that I wanted . . . I grew up wanting my life to be more interesting than I felt it could be when I was a child.[9]

When Tusa seized on this point and suggested that this absence of the father might have led to his writing strong and vivid parts for women as 'a kind of belated tribute to your mother', Hare rejected the notion. But it is possible to propose an alternative reading of the implications of this sense of fatherlessness for Hare's work – and again this has more to do with the way in which he writes about men rather than about women. There is in many of Hare's plays a recurring pattern: a confrontation between an older man – the dominant and sometimes tyrannical 'alpha male' – and a younger man. Frequently, there is some bond – of affection, of blood, of fascination, even of love – between the two. Typically the older man is challenged by the younger. Often, too, the two men represent opposing ideological positions and the battle between them has political and moral implications. And, while Hare's dramaturgy is always sophisticated enough to avoid any simple identification with any one of his characters, it is usually the case that the younger of these opponents takes the position of the protagonist ('hero' is seldom quite the word in a Hare play), so that the audience is invited, initially at least, to look at the world of the play through his eyes. I do not intend to take Hare's remarks as a cue for a reductive psychoanalytic criticism: it is pointless to attempt to explain away all the complexity of an oeuvre in terms of a displaced Oedipal need to enact in the realm of the imaginary all those psychic conflicts with the father which could not be worked through in the reality of childhood and adolescence. Nonetheless, Hare's remarks about his sense of fatherlessness suggest that it may be an important context for the way in which structure and meaning are interwoven in his work.

More often than not the alpha male is presented, to some degree, satirically. Hare, however, is uncomfortable with the term 'satire', and from very early on in his career has sought to distance himself from the label of satirist; although he acknowledges the satirical elements in the plays of 'Howard Hare', he tends to attribute this to Brenton rather than to himself. From his own perspective, Hare seems to regard satire as a very limited mode of writing: 'Satire, essentially, doesn't stretch you very far towards working out what you believe or what you are trying to do. It's more instinctive', he told Gaston.[10] At a lecture given at King's College, Cambridge, in 1978, he takes the point further:

> [T]he satirist can rail, 'If only you knew that Eden was on Benzedrine throughout the Suez crisis, stoned out of his head and fancy-free; if only you knew that the crippled, stroke-raddled Churchill dribbled and farted in Cabinet for two years after a debilitating stroke, and nobody dared remove him; if only you knew that Cabinet Ministers sleep with tarts, that Tory MPs liaise with crooked architects and bent off-shore bankers: if only you knew'. But finally after this railing, the satirist may find that the audience replies, 'Well we do know now; and we don't believe it will ever change. And knowing may well not affect what we think.'[11]

There are two aspects to Hare's rejection of satire. One of these – that satire comes from an impulse to rail which is largely instinctive, which has no room for doubt, and which does not take into account the need for positive values – is comparatively easily answered: this may be generally true of much popular contemporary satire of the kind represented by *Private Eye* or *Have I Got News for You*, but not of the broader tradition of literary satire to which Hare (along with the likes of Juvenal, Horace, Swift, Fielding, Shelley, Dickens, Wilde, Bulgakov and Orwell) belongs. Hare's second point, however, the argument from his 1978 Cambridge address, which seems more deep-rooted, is harder to answer: in a way there *is* no answer to it. If Hare is right in his assertion that knowledge of the world's corruption is unlikely to affect the way in which people think – or act, or vote – then satire is indeed a feeble kind of weapon. Yet such a position is a contradictory one for a socialist democrat such as Hare: raising consciousness of injustice may not be enough in itself to bring about change in the system, but that it is important to do so is an essential article of faith for anyone who believes, as Hare clearly does, in the possibility of social change. Because of this, the satirical impulse remains a potent – although increasingly complex – weapon in the armoury of David (as well as of 'Howard') Hare.

Thus, in *Knuckle* (1974) we encounter an early version of the alpha male in Patrick, the father of the play's hero, Curly. A powerful, ruthless and corrupt financial operator in the City, Patrick's power is symbolised by all the trappings of high culture: classical allusions, the study of the novels of Henry James, the music of Rimsky-Korsakov, which he reads to himself and plays on the piano. Patrick's Guildford home represents not just money but, in Bourdieu's phrase, cultural capital.[12] Mrs Dunning, his housekeeper (and, we discover, his lover, or at least sexual servant), sings his praises in an encomium which is continually punctured by ironic comments from Curly:

> MRS DUNNING: A wonderful man. He's undertaken an intensive study of Anglo-American literature . . .
> CURLY: Mickey Spillane.
> MRS DUNNING. He's on *The Golden Bowl*. He knows an incredible amount.
> CURLY: For a merchant banker.
> MRS DUNNING: He's a cultured man . . .
> CURLY: Sure he's cultured. What good does that do?
> MRS DUNNING: His culture enlarges his . . .
> CURLY: Mrs Dunning. Who ran Auschwitz? A pack of bloody intellectuals.[13]

To Curly, Anglo-American literature means Mickey Spillane not Henry James, and the play as a whole supports this perspective: Curly's quest is presented as a kind of noir thriller, although (as critics and audiences at the time quickly realised) it is a thriller more in the mode of Raymond Chandler than of Spillane. Much of the play's meaning resides in the audience's ability to read intertextually between the norms of that genre and the particular uses Hare makes of it in *Knuckle*.

If Patrick represents the corrupt status quo of the City and the stockbroker belt, Curly is the investigator who seeks to uncover the truth about it. Like the cowboy movie, and the action adventure film, film noir is a classic site of masculine representation. The Chandleresque world of the private eye movie, especially in its classic 1940s and 1950s period, both explores and affirms masculine identity in the problematic postwar era. It was the actor John Houseman, in his influential 1947 essay 'Today's Hero: A Review', who first characterised the tough hero of the typical crime thriller of the period as a man whose alienation and apparent cynicism articulate a rejection of the idealised values represented by more conventional male hero figures.[14] When Hare transposes the hard-boiled hero from Los Angeles to Surrey, he does so in order to cast Curly in the role of the morally ambivalent private eye, prowling the mean streets of Guildford, in search of answers to the mystery of his sister Sarah's disappearance and apparent death. Sarah is another of Hare's fiercely idealistic women; her motto is that everyone should know everything, whatever the cost. 'She told the Bishop of Guildford that his son was known as Mabel and was the toast of the Earls Court Road', recalls Patrick ruefully (p9). And, as Curly unpeels layer after layer of evil – most of it involving Patrick – he discovers just how dangerous Sarah's insistence on the absolute truth must have been. We discover at the end that Sarah has not been killed, but has faked her own suicide in order to escape the world which her father seems so successfully to control. Like Maggie in *Teeth 'n' Smiles*, she can be seen as a figure shot through with tortured idealism, a martyr-victim who has to 'die' in order to escape the corruption which surrounds her. But in the experience of the play her function is not to become another of the iconic 'beacons of light' that Eyre and Wright describe; it is to act as the focus for the narrative interest which lies in the unravelling of the reasons for her disappearance – and therefore the truth about the nature of Patrick's world. The central emotional and ideological conflict of the play is between Curly and Patrick. Curly has rejected his father's world and all its values – as had Sarah. But his is a thoroughly compromised kind of rejection. Patrick lives a life of quiet and apparently respectable affluence in his Guildford home; Sarah, the idealist, has worked as a nurse in a local psychiatric hospital; Curly, on the other hand, is an arms dealer, mired in the bloody trade of selling guns to dictators and guerrillas alike. His justification of this is articulated in terms of his rejection of his father:

Have you ever met my father? . . . Have you seen inside the City of London? Inside the banks and the counting houses? It's perfect. Men with silver hair and suits with velvet pockets. Oiling down padded corridors . . . My father moved as silkily as anyone. A clear leather desk in a book-lined room. A golden inkwell. That was all. That and the sound of money gathering like moss on the side of a west building. When he got home at night out with the cello and the Thackeray. He made his money with silent indolence . . . So I chose guns. The noisiest profession I could find. (p23)

In Hare's noir thriller the twist is that the relationship between the hero and villain is that of father and son. Recent approaches to masculinity in film noir have taken Freud as their starting point, and certainly the relationship between Curly and Patrick seems redolent of Oedipal tensions. And, of course – as the play later makes clear – the similarities between father and son are as significant as the differences: Patrick's world, the City of London, with its 'casual cruelty of each day; take-over bids, redundancies, men ruined overnight, jobs lost, trusts betrayed, reputations smashed' (p48), is as cruel and corrupt as Curly's, and Curly has rejected the superficialities of his father's lifestyle and value system, but not the moral ambiguities which haunt them both. On one level, Curly's is the more honest choice of the two: at least he is upfront about the immorality of the trade in which he is engaged, and the literary and filmic stereotype of the honest rogue seems to fit him well. Sarah represents one pole, Patrick the other, while Curly tries to reconstruct the narrative that links them. The story is told through his eyes, and he looks set to become a Bogart-like figure (like Sam Spade, or Rick in *Casablanca*) – a tough guy with a streak of decency, a man who can walk the mean streets but who is not himself mean. But the volte-face at the end of the play is a double one: not only is Sarah not dead, but Curly's final confrontation with Patrick, the classic scene from the end of a crime movie in which the detective confronts the criminal with the knowledge of his crimes, turns out to be a damp squib. Patrick walks away from it more or less unscathed:

> CURLY: I possess a lethal combination of facts. Suppose I go to the press? The old woman, the dog, abandoning your daughter on the beach . . .
> PATRICK: . . . You let it out. You ruin me. He left his daughter to kill herself. A despicable thing to do. Bad publicity. I leave my job. What happens? Someone else pops up in my place. Life covers up pretty fast. Only the people bleed . . . You wanted me to say I was degraded. Well . . . *(Pause)* I am. OK? So now can I please go back to work?. (p49)

Curly's final choice is not to defy the success and corruption of the dominant class, but to embrace it: he ends up assimilated by the world he appeared to have rejected. He is, after all, no hard-bitten moralist in the Bogart mould. He turns out to be more like a malcontent from a Jacobean revenge tragedy: a cynical commentator, increasingly complicit in the very corruption he denounces. Unlike the typical malcontent, however, he is not granted the dignity – perhaps the false dignity – of a heroic death. For Curly to make his knowledge public would, he realises, change little in the long run. Someone else pops up to fulfil the same function, and none of the victims is saved from destruction. Curly does nothing with his knowledge, and goes back to making money. Patrick, too, goes back to work; and when another character, Jenny, does go to the newspapers with the story, she is not believed. *Knuckle* asks the same question that Hare repeats more explicitly in his Cambridge lecture: the value of raising consciousness about injustice. The play, however, answers that question in more ambivalent terms than the lecture might suggest. Curly's decision to do nothing looks, on one level, like an endorsement of a doctrine of pessimistic quiescence, but the journey on which the audience has been taken in order to reach that point suggests a rather different attitude towards the need to speak out.

In *A Map of the World* (1982), the question of speaking out arises in a rather different way. In this play another version of the alpha male appears – and once more there is a sharp-talking young man to challenge him. The conflict between the intellectual novelist Victor (the name is significant) Mehta and the journalist Stephen Andrews certainly has some similarities to that between Curly and Patrick. Stephen's attack on Victor's character could almost have been spoken by Curly about Patrick:

> You speak all the time as if you, Victor Mehta, are a finished human being, and beneath you lies the world with all its intolerable imperfections. As if you were objective and had no part in its emotions.[15]

Here, however, the diagram is rather more complicated than it was in *Knuckle*. The setting of this confrontation is a hotel in Bombay/Mumbai where a UNESCO conference on world poverty is taking place. Like Patrick, Victor – though Indian-born – is a man whose mastery of the codes of Western culture is, in part at least, a display of his sense of his own power: arriving at the hotel for the conference, Victor calls for Pouilly Fuissé – and is dismissive when the hotel can only supply Pouilly Fumé. English-educated and now more English than the English, this Indian writer of genteel comic novels, living in Shropshire, is himself a right-wing satirist of sorts, given to making mandarin public pronouncements about the failings and corruptions of Third World countries and cultures. These pronouncements are so offensive to the sensibilities of many of the Third World delegates that they threaten to walk out unless Victor prefaces his address with a statement about the

nature of fiction, acknowledging that 'all fiction is lies' (p34). The conference, and whatever good it might possibly achieve in the real world in terms
of stimulating aid, is threatened because of Victor's presence.

Victor is a witty and articulate spokesman for a certain kind of right-wing
global pessimism, and much of the play is structured around the developing
argument (which eventually becomes a formal debating contest) between
his 'map of the world' and Stephen's left-liberal one. But, while this is very
much a play about ideas, there is also a strongly atavistic element to the
encounter between these two combative males. The political debate between
them has underneath it something much more primitive: they are essentially
fighting not only over ideology and belief, but also over a woman. Peggy
is a young and rather naive American actress, who – in an ironic move
which comments satirically on these masculine displays of aggression – has
agreed to sleep with the winner of the debate; has become the prize in their
competition. In a bathetic move typical of the satirist we are led to see that
the highly sophisticated, civilised political and philosophical debate between
two highly educated individuals – a debate upon which the success of the
whole conference depends – has an underbelly which amounts to little more
than two male pack animals fighting over a female.

Knuckle was a satire that questioned the efficacy of satire, on the grounds
that to expose injustice brings with it no guarantee of remedy. *A Map of the
World* explores the effectiveness of art in a different way, questioning the very
relationship between art and reality. The satirical mode is still in evidence –
the play contains satires against Hollywood films, against a certain kind of
cultural arrogance, against the aid industry itself. Victor himself is not only
a satirist but also the object of satire. His race gives him – for Hare's implied
audience, as well as for Stephen – a kind of authority in this context. Spoken
by a figure like Patrick, his reactionary opinions would be comparatively
easy for a liberal spectator to 'place' and dismiss; wittily articulated by the
Indian intellectual, however, they prove more problematic. The audience is
invited to laugh at Victor's attacks on Stephen, but also, as Richard Allen
Cave observes, 'as the play develops Hare makes the audience suspicious of
Mehta's wit and indeed embarrassed at their own tendency to laugh at it. In
the context of the conference it seems undeniably cheap.'[16]

Victor's ambiguous authority is complicated even further by the fact that
he seems – in part, at least – to represent a contemporary real-life person.
A public figure, a writer whose pronouncements on the Third World have
already given him a great degree of fame/notoriety, it was hard for a contemporary audience not to draw comparisons between Victor and the Nobel
Prize-winner V. S. Naipaul. But if the real world seems to encroach on the
play in one way, in another way it is problematised. The play's structure

and dramaturgy is intensely metafictional, questioning almost obsessively the relationship between art and reality. No sooner has the conflict between Stephen and Victor been established than the theatrical style shifts, and we find ourselves in a film studio, watching the filming of the very action that we have just been watching. The apparent realism of the play is exploded, and the theatrical experience becomes not only a battle between the two world-views of Stephen and Victor, but also a reflection on fictional and dramatic representation, and a meditation on the various distortions of art. Victor, we discover, later wrote a novel, 'a moral story' as he calls it, about the events in the conference (which had culminated in Stephen's death in a railway accident). Now, in another dramatic 'present tense', a film is being made of the novel, and Peggy and Victor are visiting the film set – Victor specifically in order to express his dislike of the travesty which the film is making of his writing. The relationships between the various fictional levels of the play are complex and not always clearly delineated: the actors who play Stephen and Peggy in one scene play the film actors who are representing them in another. The audience is not always entirely sure whether they are watching the film, the 'reality' which the play itself depicts, or a version of Victor's novel.

Hare himself has spoken critically about the dramaturgy of A Map of the World, calling it 'a mess' and 'clumsy and disparate'.[17] It is certainly true that there sometimes seems to be too much for the play to deal with: the ideological confrontation between Victor and Stephen, the political analysis of Third World debt, the metatheatrical disquisitions on the nature of fiction and its relationship to reality – all struggle against each other for artistic and intellectual headroom. But these same devices serve the gender politics of the play well: the play offers the audience a viewpoint which is constantly shifting. Victor's urbane wit pulls it in one direction; Stephen's passionate egalitarianism pulls it in another. ('In an ideal production of the play', Hare suggests, 'you find yourself agreeing with whoever has last spoken'.)[18] The shifting ground between the various discourses – realist drama, Hollywood biopic, Victor's novel – and the time frame which allows characters to comment on their past selves undermines still further the audience's confidence in their own perspective, and creates a greater complexity of tone than Hare had achieved before. The ending of the play replays but then reverses Curly's capitulation to Patrick. In A Map of the World, Stephen retires from the contest, leaving the field to Victor. But Victor also capitulates in his own way. His 'map of the world' has been affected by Stephen's, in memory of whom he quits the conference, enabling it to go ahead, and the various aid deals to be negotiated.

A much less complex and sophisticated version of the late twentieth-century British alpha male is the larger-than-life Lambert Le Roux of the

Hare/Brenton collaboration *Pravda* (1985). Le Roux is a media mogul, whose takeover of *The Daily Victory* lies at the centre of the play. The *Victory* is the 'one small part of your country that you all say will never be for sale. An Everest of probity. . . . An institution, like Buckingham Palace, the Tower of London'.[19] Again, there is a clear real-life correlative for the figure: audiences rapidly made the connection between Le Roux and Rupert Murdoch, who, in 1981, had acquired both *The Times* and *The Sunday Times*, and was in the process of forging a media empire in which the distinction between broadsheets and tabloids was increasingly eroded. At the end of *Pravda*, Le Roux shuffles his editorial team, sacks half his workforce and announces, 'I've decided to combine the two newsrooms. I'll cut both papers in half. Up market, down market, it's all the same stuff . . . Welcome to the foundry of lies' (p113). It is a prescient image of what happened in real life: soon afterwards, with the loss of over 5,000 jobs, Murdoch's News International group moved production from Fleet Street to his new headquarters in Wapping, surviving months of high-profile picketing in what turned out to be a landmark defeat for trade unions.

Once more, too, there is a younger male journalist whose part-antagonistic, part-fascinated relationship with the powerful older man forms the narrative spine of the play. The young man is Andrew May, whom Le Roux appoints as editor, first of all on a small local paper and then on the *Victory*. Le Roux takes on the inexperienced Andrew as his protégé, but if he is in one sense a kind of father figure to Andrew, he is a destructive one. Andrew ends up in the classic position of the liberal: in this case caught, as Le Roux puts it, between a left-wing wife (Rebecca – another female moral touchstone) and a right-wing proprietor. He resists, rebels, challenges, is beaten, and eventually returns to the fold to be re-employed as the editor of the tabloid *Tide*. Like Curly, he ends up assimilated by the values of the dominant male; Andrew, however, is comprehensively defeated before he is accepted back. He, along with the rest of the ineffective liberal journalists who represent the only resistance to Le Roux, is outmanoeuvred and totally humiliated: he ends up physically on his knees before Le Roux, begging for a job. The price of employment is betrayal: in order to return to Le Roux, he betrays his principles, his wife and his friends. We are left in no doubt at the end of *Pravda* that Andrew, and all he represents, is no match for Le Roux.

Perhaps because this is a 'Howard Hare' play, the satirical streak is much more obvious: even the names of some of the characters (Elliott Fruit-Norton, Cliveden Whicker-Baskett, Ian Ape-Warden) suggest a tradition of satirical typology reaching back to Ben Jonson. Moreover, Lambert Le Roux is a much broader kind of masculine stereotype than Patrick or Victor: while they expressed their power and privilege in terms of culturally elite and intellectual pursuits, these are values which, in *Pravda*, are consigned to the old guard – the defeated right-wing liberals such as Fruit-Norton, the ousted, literate editor of the *Victory*. Le Roux represents a new kind of dominant figure – but one which is also very traditional. '*Heavily built and muscular*', as the stage directions describe him, Le Roux emanates an aura of male physicality. When we see him outside the workplace, he is engaged in typically male pastimes of fighting and hunting: he practises martial arts and shoots birds. Equally brutal in his business practices, he exemplifies a macho masculinity – which in the plays is associated with a political and ideological position. The key to Le Roux's success can be seen in his contemptuous dismissal of Andrew and his liberal allies: 'You are all weak because you do not know what you believe' (p104). In this powerful caricature of the alpha male of the business world, Brenton and Hare created a figure which embodied their developing analysis of how Thatcher's Britain had come to be the way it was:

> I didn't get together a play about the way England had changed until Howard Brenton and I wrote *Pravda* . . . it's the play in which we formulate this idea that the man who believes in nothing but who *knows* what he believes in – even if it's nothing – will always conquer people who don't know what they believe. So the journalists who saw the play quite rightly intuited that the villain of the play is not Lambert Le Roux: the villains of the play are the journalists, because the journalists don't organise, the journalists don't fight . . . [That analysis] was about how, when Thatcherism arrived, nobody knew how to respond to it – because liberals actually thought they had values in common and found, in the event, that they didn't.[20]

With Lambert Le Roux the alpha male becomes a political icon. His stereotypical male assurance and confidence, his knowledge of what he himself believes in, was an analysis of how liberal England lost the battle for its soul.

In *My Zinc Bed* (2000), Hare re-stages the confrontation – once more with a woman as a prize – between an elderly alpha male called Victor and a younger writer. In this play (the title of which, like that of *The Secret Rapture*, refers to an image of death) the older man is software mogul Victor Quinn, while the young writer, Paul Peplow, is a recovering alcoholic. Critics have occasionally compared Hare's technique of combining vivid characterisation with debate about moral and political issues to that of George Bernard Shaw,[21] and Hare himself has both directed and written brilliantly about Shaw.[22] Certainly, the situation in *My Zinc Bed* is very reminiscent of Shaw's *Candida*. In both, a successful, attractive and powerful older man invites a weaker, more vulnerable younger one into his home. Like Shaw's Marchbanks, Paul Peplow is a poet; and, like him, he had hit rock bottom soon before being taken in: the aristocratic Marchbanks had been sleeping rough on the Embankment while Peplow was picked up naked and raving drunk on the M4. Both of them recognise the older man as their saviour, and both also fall in love with – and almost win – the older man's younger wife. Like *Candida*, too, the Shavian debates in *My Zinc Bed* are focused not so much on the political as on the personal: much of the play is taken up with debates about addiction and the effectiveness or otherwise of Alcoholics Anonymous.

The first meeting between Paul and Victor is, on one level, a status battle: Paul has come to interview Victor for a newspaper, but it is Victor who sets the agenda, continually takes Paul off guard, quizzing him about his addiction. Paul is unnerved:

> I've noticed you use certain techniques. Which, rightly or wrongly I associate with the rich. Or at least with the powerful . . . is it a manner? Is it a game? You read my poetry before the meeting. You put yourself instantly at an advantage . . . If the purpose was to unsettle me, then I'm afraid you've succeeded. I've been uncomfortable ever since you arrived.[23]

It turns out that it is Paul who is really being interviewed – for a job. Victor befriends the impoverished poet, employs him, and introduces him to his attractive young wife, Elsa. In this replay of the sexual triangle from *A Map of the World*, it is, on the surface, the younger man who wins – at least, in the sense that he wins Elsa's love. It is a bittersweet victory, short-lived and fraught with ambivalence. Eventually Paul walks away from the relationship, while Victor – whose internet company is in collapse at the end of the play – dies soon afterwards in a car crash that is an odd mirror image of Stephen's train-crash death in *A Map of the World*.

Paul describes the beginning of his affair with Elsa in these terms:

> What did I think? What did I think at that moment? That I could be solid in the way Victor was solid? Never. I knew I could never replace him. But I felt the power of her and her warmth. The alcohol drained out of me and her warmth filled me. I vanished into her warmth and was consumed.
> *Victor appears a long way away, reading a file. He stands, quite still.*
> The hour that followed was the happiest of my life.   (p98)

Victor's appearance in the background at the moment of Paul's greatest happiness is significant, since his presence dominates their relationship: even as he talks about his happiness with Elsa, he is thinking about the comparison between his own frailty and Paul's 'solidity'. The play is not only about the love between Paul and Elsa, but also about that between Paul and Victor – a love which is never sexual, nor even quite ever on the level of father/son; but which Elsa sees and mistrusts. She warns Paul, 'you are not the first person to become obsessed with my husband . . . I won't be a channel to Victor' (pp90–1). A line from Jung haunts Paul:

> I thought of Jung when Victor died. When we love another person the temptation is to love only what we lack in ourselves. But the search to complete ourselves with another person can never succeed. (p128)

Issues of completeness and completion lie at the heart of *My Zinc Bed*. In the opening scene Paul and Victor discuss fiction. Victor quotes one of Paul's own lines: 'Many are the stories with interesting beginnings, but harder to find are the stories which end well' (p3), and asks whether 'well' means happily for the subject or in a way which satisfies the reader – or both. The line reappears at the end of the play, and it reflects back self-referentially on the play itself, for the ending of *My Zinc Bed* comes to few conclusions: the final scene recycles earlier moments from the play.

An open-ended text such as *My Zinc Bed* is usually a refusal of certainty, a refusal on the part of the author to make pronouncements about meaning. In the case of David Hare, this seems to link with his earlier concerns about the efficacy of satire. Most of Hare's plays reflect on their own artistic dimensions, or explore the relationship between the real world and its representation in words and images. *Knuckle* press-gangs a literary mode, the noir thriller – which implies that crimes may be 'solved' – into the service of a narrative which denies the efficacy of solutions. In *A Map of the World* the central story asks disturbing questions about the effect of the writer's presence on the political realities of the UNESCO conference, while the metatheatrical structure simultaneously calls into question basic assumptions about the way in which art distorts everyday reality. The notion of distortion is taken further in *Pravda*, where the 'foundry of lies' over which Le Roux presides testifies to a complete breakdown of meaning: in this world, that which is written need bear no relation at all to that which happens. The theme of the relationship between art and reality is a constant one in Hare's writing – not only in the plays we have looked at in detail here, but also elsewhere in his oeuvre: thus, for example, in *Via Dolorosa*, in *The Permanent Way* and in *Stuff Happens*, Hare reverses earlier-career rejections of documentary-style theatre, producing complex plays which are rooted in the words and actions of real-life people but which also raise questions about presenting these people, these words and actions, in theatrical form.

It is perhaps not surprising that Hare comes to no conclusions in this exploration of the limits of theatre. On the contrary, Hare's position seems to be one which deliberately avoids conclusions and pronouncements. If Hare and Brenton formulated in *Pravda* the 'idea that the man who believes in nothing but who *knows* what he believes in – even if it's nothing – will always conquer people who don't know what they believe',[24] one of the paradoxes about David Hare is that this kind of uncertainty seems to be rather closer to his own characteristic position. It is in this light that we may make sense of Hare's rejection of satire. 'Howard Hare', he says, 'writes in a tone of caustic, abrasive, satirical confidence, a tone without doubt, if you like. Whereas when I'm writing as myself, my work is marbled with doubt.'[25] And if the satirist is characterised – as Hare believes he is – by a tone without doubt, the contradiction becomes clearer: Hare is alienated from the position of the satirist because that kind of confidence is a mark of the alpha males he portrays. Patrick Delafield, Victor Mehta, Victor Quinn, Lambert Le Roux all speak with certainty, knowing what they believe. Hare's observers are consistently in the position of Paul Peplow, haunted by the sense that they will never be as 'solid' as their antagonists. And in the self-consciousness which Hare shows about dramatic and theatrical form there is an echo, and also perhaps a sympathetic vindication, of their uncertainty.

NOTES

1. Richard Boon, *About Hare: The Playwright and the Work* (London: Faber, 2003), p65.
2. Interview with Benedict Nightingale, 'An Angry Young Man of the Eighties', *New York Times*, 17 October 1982, section 2, p6. Reprinted in Malcolm Page (comp.), *File on Hare* (London: Methuen, 1990), p83.
3. Richard Eyre and Nicholas Wright, *Changing Stages: A View of British Theatre in the Twentieth Century* (London: Bloomsbury, 2000), p289.
4. Quoted in Boon, *About Hare*, p121.
5. Michelene Wandor, *Drama Today: A Critical Guide to British Drama 1970–1990* (London: Longman, 1993), p46.
6. Michelene Wandor, *Look Back in Gender: Sexuality and the Family in Post-War British Drama* (London: Methuen, 1987), p150.
7. Interview with Morris Zeifman, in Boon, *About Hare*, p130.
8. Georg Gaston, 'Interview: David Hare', *Theatre Journal* 45, 2 (May, 1993), p224.
9. Interview with John Tusa. Broadcast on Radio 3, 27 July 2005, www.bbc.co.uk/radio3/johntusainterview/hare_transcript.shtml (accessed 17 August 2006).
10. Gaston, 'Interview: David Hare', p215.
11. Reprinted in David Hare, *Writing Left-Handed* (London: Faber, 1991), p27.
12. Pierre Bourdieu, *Distinction: A Social Critique of the Judgement of Taste*, trans. Richard Nice (London: Routledge, 1984), pp128–9.
13. David Hare, *Knuckle* (London: Faber, 1974), p12. All subsequent quotations are taken from this edition.
14. John Houseman, 'Today's Hero: A Review', *Hollywood Quarterly* 2, 2 (1947), pp161–3.
15. David Hare, *A Map of the World* (London: Faber, 1982), p65. All subsequent quotations are taken from this edition.

16. Richard Allen Cave, *New British Drama on the London Stage 1970–1985* (Gerrards Cross: Colin Smythe, 1989), p207.
17. David Hare, *The Asian Plays* (London: Faber, 1986), pxiii.
18. *Ibid.*, pxiv.
19. Howard Brenton and David Hare, *Pravda: A Fleet Street Comedy* (London: Methuen, 1985), p34. All subsequent quotations are from this edition.
20. Duncan Wu, *Making Plays: Interviews with Contemporary British Dramatists and Directors* (London: Macmillan, 2000), p172.
21. See, for example, Elyse Sommer's review of *Skylight*, http://www.curtainup.com/skylight.html (accessed 13 January 2007).
22. Hare directed *Heartbreak House* at the Almeida Theatre in 1997. His programme notes for the production are reprinted in Wu, *Making Plays*.
23. David Hare, *My Zinc Bed* (London: Faber, 2000), p18. All subsequent quotations are taken from this edition.
24. Wu, *Making Plays*, p172.
25. Gaston, 'Interview: David Hare', p224.

15

CHRIS MEGSON AND DAN REBELLATO

'Theatre and anti-theatre'

David Hare and public speaking

> It's always the content of the work that determines everything – which I say
> over and over again, and I know you don't believe me, but it's true![1]

Over the past four decades, David Hare has accompanied his work in theatre with a broad spectrum of other kinds of public intervention. These
include his early reviews for the theatre magazine *Plays and Players* in the
late 1960s, his plethora of articles and interviews, his contribution to platform discussions, the prefaces to his published plays, his diary on acting and,
most distinctively, the virtuoso lectures and speeches that he has given with
increasing frequency, in a variety of speaking contexts, since the late 1970s.
Without doubt, Hare's public speaking has functioned time and again to
reiterate and elaborate his sense of the purpose and ethical value of theatre
in changing political contexts; this, in turn, has helped to fashion his stature
as public figure and latter-day 'man of letters' in the tradition of Bernard
Shaw and John Osborne.

This essay attempts to fathom the relationship between Hare's playwrighting and his non-theatrical work, exploring how the latter has expressed a
unified set of preoccupations about the nature of his theatre's engagement
with historical and contemporary political realities. Our aim is to examine
that which is both notable and intriguing about Hare's numerous commen-
taries on performance: namely, the sharply anti-theatrical rhetoric that permeates many of his speech acts. Our hypothesis is that Hare's long-standing
commitment to the pure, transparent and direct communication of subject
matter in performance has led to his increasing discomfiture with the mediating discourses of theatre and, consequently, to his reification of the lecture
format as the preferred mode of public address both on and off the stage.

'The curse of theatre'

Hare's unease with the inherent artifice of theatre can be traced back to his
earliest public statements. These describe how his working methods have variously sought to counter the perceived falsity that indelibly suffuses theatrical representation. In a 1975 interview, for example, reflecting on his work

with Portable Theatre, he recounts how the company strove to promulgate a 'deliberately and apparently shambolic style of presentation where people simply lurched onto the stage and lurched off again, and it was impossible to make patterns . . . we worked on a theatrical principle of forbidding any aesthetic at all'.[2] This unequivocal attempt to stonewall the incubation of any distracting aesthetics in Portable's productions exemplifies Hare's emergent distrust of theatrical contrivance, his aspiration for unmediated and unalloyed modes of address within the theatre event (although his use of the word 'apparently', and his reference to 'principle', suggest that the 'shambolic' was itself systematised carefully as part of Portable's visual aesthetic). Indeed, the endeavour to emancipate theatre from distorting aesthetics so as to offer the audience a more direct and clear-eyed engagement with subject matter has remained a consistent trope in Hare's accounts of his early work. He returned to a similar theme in an interview published in 1993:

> So, we wanted to bundle into a van and go round the country performing short, nasty little plays . . . And by doing so we hoped to push aside the problem of aesthetics, which we took to be the curse of [the] theatre. People were more interested in comparing the aesthetics of particular performances than they were in listening to the subject matter of plays. And we thought that if you pushed aesthetics out of the way by performing plays as crudely as possible, and in work places, or places where people lived, you could get a response to what you were actually saying.[3]

In this respect, Portable's deliberately crude and 'shambolic' approach to production, combined with its mission to perform in non-traditional theatre venues, cohere as part of a broader strategy to reconstitute the terms of an audience's engagement with live performance by placing its focus squarely and viscerally on content: 'It was resilient drama', Hare argues, 'designed to grab people by the throats at once'.[4] His repeated insistence on the adverse potential of style to thwart an audience's engagement with throat-grabbing content surfaces again in a discussion of *Fanshen* (1975), produced by the Joint Stock ensemble. After identifying the working processes of the company, Hare's conclusion is studiously understated but nonetheless emphatic: 'I don't think we have an "acting style".'[5]

In the 1970s and 1980s, Hare's work with Joint Stock and his occasional forays into collective writing can be construed as further attempts to extirpate – this time through processes of collaboration – the diversionary effects that might issue from individually authored dramaturgy. Further, his reflections on his experiences of collective composition reveal the extent of his commitment to effacing the mediating presence of the author altogether. His comments on the group-written *Lay By* (1971) and *England's Ireland* (1972) are particularly illuminating:

> As a writer, I know that most of the time people will say to you: 'Oh, I see, this is funnier than your last work. Oh, you're developing that point. Oh. It's more serious in tone. Oh, it's in that familiar David Hare way.' Now, to put seven names on a play is to put, in a way, no name on the play. Nobody can work out whose voice it is. And so the idea was that if you did that, then you would be forced to concentrate on the content of the play.[6]

This gravitation towards anonymised writing and authorial dissolution articulates with his comments on *Pravda* (1985), co-written with Howard Brenton: 'The most interesting thing about collaboration, then, became the creation of a tone which is neither [Brenton's] nor mine, but which is a third person's, who is sometimes laughingly called Howard Hare.'[7]

The point we wish to emphasise here is that Hare's reflections on the development of his practice from the 1970s onwards reveal a remarkable and doggedly persistent vision of theatre's potential capacity to deliver unmediated expression of content in a way that elides or even transcends the artifices that conventionally suture dramatic writing, authorial style and stage aesthetics. The assertion of the primacy of content in the creative processes of play-making perhaps reaches its apotheosis in an observation from 2005: 'for a political artist, the subject matter chooses you'.[8] It is unsurprising, then, that Hare has made increasing use of the public lecture as a way of corroborating this vision: the lecture, after all, is both a form of direct address to an audience and a mode of self-presentation that entirely dispenses with actorly interposition in the communication of content. Given this, it is worth examining Hare's remarks on lecturing before considering the intimate correlation between his lectures and his own recent theatrical practice.

'Background murmuring'

In his introduction to *Obedience, Struggle and Revolt*, a collation of his speeches published in 2005, Hare laments the ambiguity of the word 'lecture'.[9] On the one hand, a lecture is the presentation of a prepared text for the purpose of instruction; on the other, it is a sustained reprimand or admonishment. In other words, lecturing oscillates between the cool presentation of an argument, a position, a body of knowledge, and a trenchant harangue. Hare is particularly conscious of this ambiguity, as a writer who has placed politics at the centre of his work for almost four decades. For some, his work is coolly analytical, dispassionately laying out the structure of our social life; for others, his work is full of violent accusations, political bias and deliberate provocation. One is clarity; the other rhetoric.

This tension between studied exposition and eviscerating polemic finds full expression in two of Hare's landmark lectures: 'The Play Is in the Air' and 'Don't They Know What a Play is?'[10] The former, Hare's first public lecture, was delivered to a theatre conference at King's College, Cambridge, in 1978; the latter was addressed to the Annual Dinner of the Fabian Society, the reformist think tank affiliated to the Labour Party, in 1993. As their published titles indicate, both lectures assert a no-nonsense ontological conviction about what a play *is* (and, by implication, what it isn't). Both, too, from their respective vantage points at the start of the Thatcherite and New Labour ascendancy, take advantage of the occasion of the lecture to upbraid the audience for its perceived reluctance to acknowledge how theatre might best negotiate changing political realities.

'The Play Is in the Air' offers a memorable example of Hare's blending of elucidation with provocation in the lecture format. It takes as its starting point his decision to speak publicly for the first time: as he admits, in a remark that echoes his rationale for collaborative writing, 'I used to turn down all invitations to speak in public, because I didn't want an audience to hear the tone of my voice' (p111). Hare proceeds gradually to identify two reasons for his recent change of attitude. First, he holds that public speaking will enable him to better engage his audience in dialogue, to take the pulse of its sentiments and convictions: 'I have been trying in the last few months to put my ear to the ground and find out what a particular section of my audience is thinking and feeling' (p112). If the seductive fiction and emotional intensity of theatrical performance can potentially lead spectators to '[commit] the sin of assuming that the playwright means what he says' (p113), his inference is that the cool disquisition of the lecture offers a more direct and felicitous mode of communication where the sincerity of the speaker can be taken for granted. Second, Hare uses the lecture to explode his audience's state of denial: he castigates university students for their nostalgia and quietism, defends his own approach to the arbitration of political critique in his recent plays and, above all, corrects his listeners' possible misapprehensions about the viability and efficacy of Marxist (and specifically Brechtian) drama in the current political climate. The content of the lecture embarks on a rhetorical demolition of the aesthetics and preoccupations of Marxist drama which, for Hare, are driven by a dogmatism that makes its truth-claims both inauthentic and wholly irrelevant to the contemporary spectator. His playwrighting, counter to this, attempts to place individual suffering within a broader historical canvas in order to make sense of its provenance and significance. The published title of the lecture is taken from its most resounding and indeed quasi-metaphysical passage in which he argues that a play is not comprised of text or actors, nor of the opinions and ideological convictions of the playwright, but, instead, 'is what happens between the stage and the audience . . . The play is in the air' (p118). Hare's first lecture is thus notable for its impassioned breach with Marxist writing, and for its attempt to reach out to his audience in an act of communion while simultaneously castigating it for its abdication of political responsibility. Hare himself records, with pithy resignation, that his speech solicited what he describes as an 'unanswerable interjection' from one irate and heckling audience member: '"Did Piscator die for this?"' (p111).

Hare's Fabian lecture was delivered in a markedly different political context: a glittering dinner attended by the Shadow Cabinet eighteen months after the Labour Party's fourth successive electoral defeat and shortly after the opening of the National Theatre's production of *The Absence of War*, the third and final play of Hare's trilogy. In one sense, this lecture offers a fiery riposte to a very different kind of heckling: leading Labour politicians – Roy Hattersley, Gerald Kaufman and Peter Mandelson – had reviewed the production in the national press and described it, in Hare's view misleadingly, as a straightforward theatrical re-enactment of Labour's disastrous 1992 election campaign. The lecture itself was subsequently published in the *Fabian Review*, in early 1994, with the title 'Don't They Know What a Play Is?' This headline accusation derives from Hare's contention that politicians strategically attacked the play for its factual inaccuracies while wilfully ignoring its deeper critique of an ascendant political culture dominated by image consultants, focus groups and spin doctors.

'What chiefly preoccupies Hare', John Bull has noted, 'is the analogy between public life and acting'.[11] This observation establishes the terms for an understanding of Hare's grievances as set out in this explosive confrontation between playwright and Labour leadership. Hare's procedure in the lecture was systematically to contest the political appropriation of the play by arguing that *The Absence of War* is not a species of documentary drama but a 'classic play about leadership . . . a tragedy, parallel to reality' (pp18, 19). George Jones, the fictional Labour leader, is posited as a tragic protagonist because he is compelled to make a Faustian 'pact with respectability' (p19) in order to attract more voters to the Party. The intractable problem presented by the play is described by Hare as follows: 'if a man makes this pact, if he smothers his real character, the passion of his character, how and when may he ever break out?' (p19). Hare's own decision to 'break out' and speak the truth in public is thus directly responsive to politicians' inability or unwillingness to do the same: 'the play presents a political universe in which for all sorts of seemingly good reasons politicians have decided that it is too dangerous to speak in public of what they really feel' (p20). Jones's disastrous attempt at unscripted oration during the set-piece election rally in *The Absence of War* – his desperate endeavour to supplant bombastic rhetoric with heartfelt and unmediated truth-telling – thus reveals the ethical vacuum at the heart of contemporary political culture. In this context, it's pertinent to note that, in 1995, Hare was invited by the *Observer* newspaper to report from the Conservative Party Conference that year, and his comments about the then Prime Minister are revealing: 'In the process of becoming a more practised speaker [John Major] has indeed mislaid the very likeability which once made him so attractive to the public. Although his style of speaking is infinitely more polished, although, in fact, it is considerably less *embarrassing*, overall you are saddened to see that he has become a man soured by the sheer nastiness of what he has endured at the hands of others, and mostly in the last few years.'[12] In Hare's discourse, polished speakers are morally suspect while unrehearsed speech signifies raw integrity. While a distrust of acting in public life is thematised as content in *The Absence of War*, Hare's Fabian lecture instantiates a direct counter to this, bursting through the conspiracy of silence and denial, and aggregating moral authority in the process. The distrust of acting, rhetoric and theatricality that is manifested in both play and lecture sets the terms for much of his playwrighting in the 1990s and beyond in which he attempts more fully to integrate the modalities of the lecture in those plays that engage with pressing political issues.

To be sure, the widely divergent contexts of these two pivotal lectures – addressed to university students and a Labour government-in-waiting – reflect Hare's increasing public profile over the fifteen years that separate them. Yet, in both, he attempts to define the political content and resonance of his work, and to play with the ambiguities of the lecture format – shifting effortlessly from exposition to excoriation in equal measure. On the one hand, his lecturing style is gentle, self-deprecating, witty and urbane, a modest presentation of self that gives the impression that the content can speak unimpeded. On the other, Hare has an acute sense of occasion and, as we have seen, his speeches are often deeply *performative*. He sometimes relishes the opportunity directly to accuse his audience, as demonstrated in both of these examples, but also in the lecture published as 'What Asian Babes? What Nazis?', delivered to 'an executive dining club' for senior media figures, which begins self-deprecatingly ('Playwrights don't get out much') and ends by lacerating his audience for their failure of nerve and responsibility (*Obedience*, pp127, 134–8).

Such ambiguity is reminiscent of other slippages in the vocabulary of performance. The word 'perform', of course, means both to *do* something (as in a high-performance engine) and to *pretend to do* something (performing

Othello). The word 'act' carries the same ambivalence. In his introduction to *The Anti-Theatrical Prejudice*, Jonas Barish notes how, almost alone of the arts, the words associated with theatre have accrued a negative connotation when used to refer to other things: theatrical, melodramatic, histrionic, stagey.[13] We might also add to that list the phrase 'acting up', which Hare uses wittily to title his memoir of the time spent performing *Via Dolorosa*.

The OED tells us that the earliest usage of 'lecture' as 'a discourse given before an audience upon a given subject, usually for the purpose of instruction' comes in 1536. Its admonitory meaning is first cited in 1600, and its verb form 100 years later.[14] In other words, the 'secondary' meaning that Hare laments in his introduction to *Obedience, Struggle and Revolt* came, historically, hard on the heels of the 'primary'. Indeed, the primary wasn't even primary. The first citation of the word is from 1398, where the word is a synonym for 'reading'. There is, then, a slippage in the word from an act of reading, to an act of speaking, to an act of rhetoric.

Jacques Derrida's early analyses of philosophers like Husserl, Saussure, Plato, Rousseau and others showed repeatedly the tremendous difficulty involved in trying rigorously to keep speaking apart from rhetoric, to maintain the latter's secondary and minor status.[15] When J. L. Austin wishes to insist that acting be marginalised in his discussion of speech acts, he employs an extravagant rhetoric – such uses are not serious, 'hollow', 'void', 'parasitical' upon 'ordinary' uses – that perhaps emphasises rather than diminishes acting's power and significance.[16] Hare is part of a distinguished tradition, then, when he remarks that one derogatory definition of the word 'lecture' has 'spilt over and infected the other five' (*Obedience*, p1).

In *The Truth in Painting*, Derrida fastens on a short section of the *Critique of Judgement* where Kant carefully excludes from his consideration of the aesthetic those aspects of art objects that are merely 'decoration, adornment, embellishment' and not 'an intrinsic constituent' to its aesthetic completeness.[17] Derrida puts pressure on this attempted exclusion and watches the determination of the aesthetic unravel as he does so. If we weren't familiar with Hare's little-disguised contempt for such academic theorising,[18] we might even see a small acknowledgement of this in his description of the value of giving lectures: 'I have found it useful, for the last quarter century, to decorate the writing of plays and films with a kind of commentary – call it background murmuring, maybe, in the form of public address' (*Obedience*, p1). The twin questions of whether the infectiously rhetorical can keep distinct from the lucid address and whether Hare's lectures merely decorate his plays will becomes particularly significant when discussing his 1998 one-man play, *Via Dolorosa*.

Via Dolorosa

The play has its origins in Hare's brief visit to Israel and Palestine in November 1997, under the auspices of the Royal Court's International Department. The plan had been that he and two other writers (an Israeli and a Palestinian) would then write plays about the period of the British Mandate in Palestine between 1922 and 1948. On his return, Hare announced that he wanted instead to write 'a monologue for myself to perform'.[19] This monologue describes Hare's visit to the region and is, in many ways, a lecture rather than a play, though this distinction, as we shall see, is embattled.

Why did David Hare decide to write his play in this form? The answer comes towards the end of the play itself. Visiting Yad Vashem, the Holocaust Museum in Jerusalem, Hare is appropriately humbled by the experience. 'The only false notes in the museum', he claims, 'are hit by works of art. Sculpture and painting. They seem superfluous. In every case the gesture seems inadequate. What is a painting, a painting of a starving man? What is a painting of a corpse? It's the facts we want. Give us the facts.'[20] In his memoir of the time spent performing Via Dolorosa, Hare describes meeting Robert Hughes, the eminent art historian, who apparently supports his view: 'All Holocaust art is terrible. There are certain subjects that are so monstrous, so huge that art needs to keep out of them' (p227).

In 'Why Fabulate?', a lecture given to the Royal Geographic Society in 1999, Hare elaborated on this theme:

> I became convinced that honour could only be done to complicated questions of faith and belief by dropping the familiar apparatus of playmaking and instead resolving to appear in my own play. As an outsider, a half-informed visitor, I despaired of writing fiction which relied on conventional scenes. Because I knew that English actors bearing machine guns and challenging each other at guard-posts or wearing yarmalkas, or pressing their wrongly-proportioned bodies against the wire of refugee camps, would, almost by definition, introduce an element of falsity which would pollute the subject matter.
>
> (*Obedience*, p78)

This remarkable passage reveals a profound anti-theatricality that organised the production of Via Dolorosa and has, for the most part, continued to organise his dramaturgy ever since. An easy riposte might be to suggest that indeed a 'half-informed visitor' might well be cautious before making grand statements about the Middle East, and that indeed 'conventional scenes' are rarely to be recommended, but it is clear that Hare thinks the problem goes deeper. It would seem that no matter how well informed is the writer, nor how good and appropriately proportioned the actors, the very fact of fiction will 'pollute' the attempt. Elsewhere, Hare asserts that 'it is the facts that must illuminate the great subjects. In these areas artifice is often not just unhelpful, it too easily becomes obnoxious' (*Acting Up*, p74). In this formulation, the theatre is polluting, obnoxious, infectious.

In fact, this summary is misleading. Hare's anti-theatricality is to theatre's *artifice*, and he believes that there is an alternative and vital function for the theatre. The passage from 'Why Fabulate?' concludes: 'I determined to stand . . . making myself the vessel of the show in order better to direct people's attention to the material itself' (*Obedience*, p78). Consistently in his non-dramatic statements, Hare has proposed a political view of theatre's role founded in the theatre's special ability to scrutinise the world and make us witnesses of it. 'It puts things under a microscope and people learn for themselves' writes Hare early in the rehearsal process (*Acting Up*, p21); midway through the New York run of the play, he returns to his theme, writing that 'the whole purpose of public art is that an act of communal discernment be made' (p220). Later in 'Why Fabulate?' he hymns 'the sheer seriousness and intensity [. . . of] theatre's special scrutiny' (*Obedience*, p77).

For Hare, theatre's political purpose is to portray the world, without artifice, and then permit an audience to scrutinise that portrait. He is scornful of those he calls the 'aesthetes' (Beckett being a frequent target)[21] and it is striking that he marginalises the aesthetic experiments of those writers he does admire, like Osborne and Pinter. Osborne was, of course, someone who brought new concerns, the attitudes and mores of an unrepresented generation, to the theatre but he was also a formal innovator in works like *The Entertainer* and *A Sense of Detachment*. At a celebration to mark Pinter's 70th birthday, Hare remarked that 'Pinter did what Auden said a poet should do. He cleaned the gutters of the English language, so that it ever afterwards flowed more easily and more cleanly' (*Obedience*, p. 177). One might just as plausibly see Pinter as a figure who drew our attention to the uncleanability of those gutters, laying bare language in all its aggressive opacity and rhetorical brutality. But the key word is 'flow': the theatre offers a flow of attention from auditorium to stage and then from stage to the world. It is a conviction that finds an eloquent expression in one of Hare's favoured registers of speech, the anecdote: 'There's a remark of Fiona Shaw's which is very brilliant but with which I *wholly* disagree; she said, "Theatre works by reflection not by representation." I believe theatre works by representation not reflection. Showing is what the playwright does, and Shakespeare's the greatest show-er of all; if he wants a mass murder he puts it *on* stage. He does it, and he doesn't brook any challenge to his vision.'[22] The theatre, for Hare, bears implacable witness to the world.

This important point entails a number of alterations to the way we might ordinarily see theatricality. In his diary, Hare describes being walked through the set for *Via Dolorosa*. Upstage there is a trench from which a model of Jerusalem will rise. Hare is particularly pleased with the wooden planking that creates a bridge across this void; the bridge itself is a 'point of command' from which one can powerfully address the auditorium. Immediately, he shudders to think of the consequences should this mighty weapon fall into the hands of an actor: 'I wouldn't trust one or two of our more prominent actors on this platform. You'd have to scrape them off the ceiling at the end of the show' (*Acting Up*, p41). The implication is clear: some actors lack the humility to allow themselves to be a powerful conduit for the depiction of the world embodied in the play. Given such a theatrical opportunity, their barnstorming tendencies would emerge, creating a barrier of artifice between audience and the world.

It is clear throughout Hare's work that he admires and respects actors, but his work on *Via Dolorosa* reveals a profound mistrust of their talents. This is, of course, most evident in his decision to efface their contribution altogether and perform the piece himself. His desire to efface their distorting presence reveals itself in a series of asides that seem to imply the complete dematerialisation of the actor. One persistent motif in the book is his discomfort with actors' bodies. As the rehearsal period takes its toll on Hare's health, he finds himself constantly exchanging tips and experiences with other actors: at one point he risks becoming 'a classic thundering bore – or actor, as one might call it' (*Acting Up*, p28). Later, he reports telling the director Jonathan Kent that 'I had turned myself into a Total Actor. I could talk about myself and my health obsessively for hours on end' (pp53–4). The identification of actors with their failing bodies reveals an anxiety about the material interposition of human physicality in the prized processes of theatrical scrutiny. He is careful not to dismiss all actors, recalling the Royal Court's 1970s belief 'that great actors somehow stand between the audience and the work itself', insisting that 'the chemistry great actors bring is more usually enrichment than obstruction' (p69). His attempt to capture great acting also reveals a search for an almost metaphysical immateriality in the theatrical moment: 'a feeling that the text is not just being spoken, but has melted right into the actor's being' (p70). Just as theatre is at its best when it can get over itself, actors are great to the extent that they efface their presence as actors.

The text, too, partakes of this dematerialisation. Early in the process, Hare announces his attitude to the text:

> I have two rules about the script itself. (1) Never write on it. (2) Never look at it. I have always believed the play should exist in an actor's head. Staring at bits of paper is the wrong action. (*Acting Up*, p22)

These rules suggest a wish to disavow his writing as writing. Elsewhere, it seems that he barely wishes to acknowledge their status as text at all, recalling the advice he has often given actors:

> I don't want you to be playing the line. I want you to be expressing an overriding feeling, and then to watch your mouth move independently underneath your forehead. Disconnect the line from your brain . . . And here I am, now doing it myself – concentrating on the feeling above the line, rather than the line itself.
>
> (p6)

In their way, these are not unusual sentiments, and variations of them will be heard in many rehearsal rooms, but, in the context of Hare's broader theatrical principles, they suggest that text, like the actor, should render itself invisible, immaterial, the better to let the audience through it. Indeed, it is hard to think of any uses of language in Hare's work that draw attention to themselves as language. His work is consistently characterisable by its appearance of transparency.

Describing what he wants to achieve in his performance, Hare writes 'I want a tone which is patient, lucid, clear like water, which – as I have said ten thousand times to actors – "just explains the facts with utter conviction"' (*Acting Up*, p19). This loosely recalls what Hare implicitly sees as the preferable definition of a lecture, a dialectic between 'an informed individual who, we hope, had thought long and hard about their own area of specialisation, and an audience which is ready honestly to assess what the speaker has to say' (*Obedience*, p5). In offering that definition, Hare is explicitly opposing the lecture to the harangue, to grand-standing, to self-promoting one-upmanship (pp3–4), to rhetorical self-assertion. In discussing the turn that his writing had taken in *Via Dolorosa*, Hare referred to it as a return to 'elucidation, instruction and enlightenment' (*Acting Up*, p29), all conventional virtues of any good lecture and less obviously key virtues of any good play.

It is clear, then, that the condition to which Hare strives in the theatre is that of the lecture. His anti-fictional convictions were reinforced by George Steiner, who 'confirmed that the appropriate approach to the subject matter was not to smother it in the sugar-ice of narrative convention' (pp75–6). We have heard the reverse of the position announced in the introduction to *Obedience, Struggle and Revolt*: the lectures are not a 'decoration' to his plays, they are the plays' ideal form. If anything, the dramaturgy is a decoration (and an obnoxious, polluting and infectious one at that) of the essential moral value of the lecture form. *Via Dolorosa* is, then, in many ways the apotheosis of his playwrighting, the point where he brings the theatre closest to the lecture. What remains unclear, though, is why Hare wanted *Via Dolorosa* to be a play at all. Given the seriousness of the subject, as he describes it, and the terrible phoneyness that ineradicably lurks in the theatre, why choose to perform it in a theatre? It would have been fairly easy for a writer of Hare's stature to find a suitably august occasion to deliver some thoughts on this subject as a lecture, where the risks of artifice are less apparent.

Hare seems unresolved about this point and nowhere is this clearer than in his profound uncertainty about the nature of his performance. His decision that his play could not be entrusted to an actor, and his desire to efface the actor's body, would incline us to believe that he considers himself not to be acting, that the whole endeavour is somehow to go beyond pretence. He declares early in the diary that 'I decided the only way of my being true to my subject would be by rejecting enactment altogether' (*Acting Up*, p75). He sternly reprimands someone who flatters his acting: 'bear this in mind: I still can't *act*. I perform' (p181). Very near the end of the book he quotes Simon Callow's perceptive description of Hare's performance as 'somehow the antithesis of acting . . . almost a war with acting' (p270). It is not clear whether he approves of Callow's verdict and elsewhere in the book he gives the strong impression of being rather prickly with people – from Jonathan Miller (p82) to his own wife, Nicole Farhi (p41) – who casually (and perhaps tactlessly) suggest that he isn't really acting at all.

At other times he is quite insistent on the opposite. He cites several people, from Harriet Walter to Mike Nichols (p203), who praise his acting; he describes the diary as an attempt 'to make the reader feel what it is to be an actor' (pp192–3). When the critic Ben Brantley claims he has a gauche and awkward physical stage presence, Hare rejoins, 'It's acting, Ben. I'm acting' (p161).

The possibility floated briefly throughout the diary is that being real – in the theatre – may simply be another style, another rhetoric. When he recalls the directorial note 'everything must look as if it comes from David and no one else' (p37) or he approves of an actor because of her 'essential quality which a regular actor cannot provide. She seems "real"' (p68) that 'as if' and that 'seems' remind us that reality in the theatre involves theatrical artifice, that the lecture can never be freed of rhetoric. Hare probably wishes to be both acting and not-acting at the same time. In *Via Dolorosa* he recalls meeting a poet and a director, the former believing you should merely write as well as you can and the latter insisting that a writer must think of their audience. 'If only', muses Hare, 'a play could be half-play, half-poem!' (p35).

What emerges from Hare's theatrical ambivalence is a resonant political vision of theatre's function which privileges content over form, the lecture over play-making. It is a principle that has continued to govern his writing, most notably in the verbatim and semi-verbatim plays *The Permanent Way* (2003) and *Stuff Happens* (2004), in which the theatrical means are pressed into the service of a deep social realism, a determination to bring the world into the theatre for scrutiny.

It is a profoundly materialist theatre, rejecting aesthetic experiment in favour of making visible historical processes and social structures. Achieving it, however, involves the theatre denying its own materiality, communicating somehow beyond the written text and the body of the actor. There is a fascinating contradiction at the heart of Hare's political dramaturgy, revealed most strongly in the relationship between his lectures and his playwrighting, between a persistent materialist analysis which we would associate most readily with the Royal Court and a theatrical metaphysics which we'd be more likely to identify with Artaud. This may explain the particular power and force of his great play, *Racing Demon* (1990), in which metaphysics and economics are brought most heartbreakingly into collision, and whose opening moments perhaps offer a minute vision of Hare's model of transcendent theatrical communication: a prayer.

NOTES

1. Catherine Itzin and Simon Trussler, 'David Hare: From Portable Theatre to Joint Stock . . . via Shaftesbury Avenue', *Theatre Quarterly* 5, 20 (1975–6), p113.
2. *Ibid.*, p112.
3. Georg Gaston, 'Interview: David Hare', *Theatre Journal* 45, 2 (May 1993), p214.
4. Jonathan Myerson, 'David Hare: Fringe Graduate', *Drama* 149 (Autumn 1983), p26.
5. David Bradby, Louis James and Bernard Sharratt, 'After *Fanshen*: A Discussion with the Joint Stock Theatre Company, David Hare, Trevor Griffiths and Steve Gooch', in David Bradby, Louis James and Bernard Sharratt (eds.), *Performance and Politics in Popular Drama: Aspects of Popular Entertainment in Theatre, Film and Television 1800–1976* (Cambridge: Cambridge University Press, 1980), p305.
6. Gaston, 'Interview: David Hare', p217.
7. Gaston, 'Interview: David Hare', p224.
8. Stephen Daldry, 'Platform Interview with David Hare', National Theatre, London, 4 October 2005.
9. David Hare, *Obedience, Struggle and Revolt: Lectures on Theatre* (London: Faber, 2005), pp1–8.
10. 'The Play Is in the Air', in *Obedience*, pp111–26, and 'Don't They Know What a Play Is?', *Fabian Review* 106, 1 (January/February 1994), pp18–20. All subsequent quotations from these lectures are cited in the text.
11. John Bull, *New British Political Dramatists* (London: Macmillan, 1984), p66.
12. David Hare, 'Requiem in Blue', *Observer Review*, 15 October 1995, p2.
13. Jonas Barish, *The Antitheatrical Prejudice* (Berkeley: University of California Press, 1981), p1.

14. 'lecture, *n*', and 'lecture, *v*', *Oxford English Dictionary Online*, 2006, Oxford University Press, http://dictionary.oed.com (accessed 2 November 2006).

15. Jacques Derrida, *Speech and Phenomena and Other Essays on Husserl's Theory of Signs* (Evanston, IL: Northwestern University Press, 1973); *Of Grammatology* (Baltimore: Johns Hopkins University Press, 1976); *Dissemination* (London: Athlone Press, 1981); *Margins of Philosophy* (Brighton: Harvester Press, 1982).

16. Quoted in Derrida, *Margins*, pp324–5.

17. Quoted in Jacques Derrida, *The Truth in Painting* (Chicago, IL: University of Chicago Press, 1987), p53.

18. See, for example, his Raymond Williams Lecture, delivered at the Hay-on-Wye Festival in 1989, published as 'Cycles of Hope' in *Writing Left-Handed* (London: Faber, 1991), pp1–23, and as 'Raymond Williams: "I Can't Be a Father To Everyone"' in Hare, *Obedience*, pp145–71.

19. David Hare, *Acting Up: A Theatrical Diary* (London: Faber, 1999), pxi.

20. David Hare, *Via Dolorosa; & When Shall We Live?* (London: Faber, 1998), p38.

21. Hare, *Acting Up*, pp260–1; Richard Boon, *About Hare: The Playwright and the Work* (London: Faber, 2003), p97. Hare also compared Beckett unfavourably with Osborne during the platform interview by Stephen Daldry, Royal National Theatre, London, 4 October 2005.

22. Duncan Wu, *Making Plays: Interviews with Contemporary British Dramatists and Their Directors* (London: Macmillan, 2000), p182.

SELECTED BIBLIOGRAPHY

PRIMARY SOURCES

Hare's personal papers, which include annotated typescript drafts of work, rehearsal scripts, schedules, production notes, correspondence, photographs and so on from 1968 to 1993, are held at The Harry Ransom Humanities Research Center at the University of Texas at Austin. A catalogue with a basic description of the material is viewable online at www.hrc.utexas.edu/research/fa/hare.scope.html.

Individual plays, teleplays and screenplays

(All published by Faber, London, unless otherwise stated; arranged alphabetically)

The Absence of War. 1993.
Amy's View. 1997.
The Bay at Nice and Wrecked Eggs. 1986.
The Blue Room: Freely Adapted from Arthur Schnitzler's La Ronde. 1998. With a 'Preface'.
The Breath of Life. 2002.
Dreams of Leaving: A Film for Television. 1980.
Enemies (adaptation of Gorky). 2006.
Fanshen. 1976. With an 'Author's Preface'.
The Great Exhibition. 1972.
The Hours (adapted from the novel by Michael Cunningham). 2003.
The House of Bernarda Alba (adaptation of Lorca). 2005.
How Brophy Made Good. Gambit 17, 1971.
Ivanov (adaptation of Chekhov). London: Methuen, 1997. With an 'Introduction'.
The Judas Kiss. 1998.
Knuckle. 1974.
Licking Hitler: A Film for Television. 1978. With 'A Lecture'.
A Map of the World. 1982.
Mother Courage and her Children (adaptation of Brecht). London: Methuen, 1995.
Murmuring Judges. 1991. With an 'Author's Note'.
My Zinc Bed. 2000.
Paris by Night. 1988. With an 'Introduction'.
The Permanent Way. 2003.

Selected bibliography

Platonov (adaptation of Chekhov). 2001. With an 'Introduction'.
Plenty. 1978.
Racing Demon. 1990.
Saigon: Year of the Cat. 1983.
The Secret Rapture. 1988.
Skylight. 1995.
Slag. 1971.
Strapless. 1988.
Stuff Happens. 2004. With an 'Author's Note'.
Teeth 'n' Smiles. 1976. With a 'Note'.
The Vertical Hour: A Play. 2007.
Via Dolorosa; & When Shall We Live? 1998.
Wetherby. 1985. With an 'Introduction'.

Collected plays and films

The Asian Plays. 1986. (*Fanshen, Saigon: Year of the Cat* and *A Map of the World.*)
   With an 'Introduction'.
The Early Plays. 1992. (*Slag, The Great Exhibition* and *Teeth 'n' Smiles.*)
Heading Home. 1991. (With *Wetherby* and *Dreams of Leaving.*)
The History Plays. 1984. (*Knuckle, Licking Hitler* and *Plenty.*) With an 'Intro-
   duction'.
Plays: One. 1996. (*Slag, Teeth 'n' Smiles, Knuckle, Licking Hitler* and *Plenty.*) With
   an 'Introduction'.
Plays: Two. 1997. (*Fanshen, Saigon: Year of the Cat, A Map of the World, The Bay at
   Nice* and *The Secret Rapture.*) Also published as *The Secret Rapture and Other
   Plays* (New York: Grove Press, 1997). With an 'Introduction'.
Collected Screenplays. 2002. (*Wetherby, Paris by Night, Strapless, Heading Home,
   Dreams of Leaving.*) With an 'Introduction'.

Collaborations

Brassneck (with Howard Brenton). London: Methuen, 1974. With an 'Authors'
   Note'.
Deeds (with Howard Brenton, Trevor Griffiths and Ken Campbell). *Plays and Players*,
   25, 8 and 25, 9 (May and June 1978).
Lay By (with Howard Brenton, Brian Clark, Trevor Griffiths, Stephen Poliakoff,
   Hugh Stoddart and Snoo Wilson). London: Calder and Boyars, 1972.
Pravda: A Fleet Street Comedy (with Howard Brenton). London: Methuen, 1985.

Other work

Books

Writing Left-Handed. 1991. Collected essays.
Asking Around: Background to the David Hare Trilogy, ed. Lyn Haill. 1993.
Acting Up: A Theatrical Diary. 1999.
Obedience, Struggle and Revolt: Lectures on Theatre. 2005.

Journalism and other material, arranged by date

Letter to Graham Cowley and the Joint Stock Policy Committee, September 1980 (Modern British Theatre Archive, University of Leeds).

'Much of What They Write Is a Kind of Wail from the Far Shore of the English Male Menopause', *Guardian*, 30 January 1981, p11.

'Time of Unease', in Richard Findlater (ed.), *At the Royal Court: 25 Years of the English Stage Company* (Ambergate: Amber Lane Press, 1981), pp139–42.

'Green Room', *Plays & Players*, October 1981, pp49–50.

'I Still Have the Unfashionable Belief That Critics Should Try to See Plays as They Are, in Their Fullness, and not Concentrate Solely on Those Parts Which Flatter Their Prejudices', *Guardian*, 3 February 1983 (Arts section, p12).

'Nicaragua: an Appeal', *Granta* 16 (Summer 1985), pp232–6.

'Why I Shall Vote Labour', *Spectator*, 23 May 1987, p14.

'Just What Are We Playing at?', *The Sunday Times*, 12 December 1993, pp10–11.

'Don't They Know What a Play Is?', *Fabian Review* 106, 1 (January/February 1994), pp18–20.

'A Good Man Let Down by Third-Rate Colleagues', *Sunday Telegraph*, 2 April 1995, np.

'John Osborne: A Lifelong Satirist of Prigs and Puritans', June 1995, http://dspace.dial.pipex.com/town/parade/abj76/PG/pieces/john_osborne.shtml (accessed 8 February 2007).

'Requiem in Blue', *Observer Review*, 15 October 1995, pp1–2.

'Diary', *Spectator*, 18 May 1996, p9.

'The RSC Won't Put Them on the Main Stage, Directors Seem Frightened of Them: What's to Become of Britain's Living Playwrights?', *New Statesman*, 14 March 1997, pp38–40.

'David Hare's Campaign', *Daily Telegraph*, April 1997 (daily General Election campaign diary).

'Give Me Broadway's Jungle Any Day', *Guardian*, 25 June 1997, p15.

Programme Note to *Plenty*, revival by the Almeida Theatre Company at the Albery Theatre, 15 April 1999.

'Don't Panic', *Guardian*, 21 April 1999, p14.

'A Month of Bad Hare Days', *Observer Review*, 14 November 1999, p5.

'*Via Dolorosa* Revisited', *Guardian*, 28 October 2000 (four-page pull-out in *Saturday Review*: text of *Via Dolorosa*, introduced by Hare).

'Why Reality is the Lifeblood of Theatre', *Guardian*, 18 November 2000 (*Saturday Review* section), p3.

'Hot and Young', programme note to *Platonov*, Almeida Theatre, 30 August 2001.

'Chekhov's Wild, Wild Youth', *Observer Review*, 2 September 2001, p5.

'Don't Give up the *Today* Job', *Observer Review*, 23 September 2001, p15.

'Theatre's Great Malcontent', *Guardian*, 8 June 2002. http://www.guardian.co.uk/Archive/Article/0,4273,4428811,00.html (accessed 8 February 2007).

'An Act of Faith', *Guardian Weekend*, 13 July 2002, pp28–32.

'Made in the UK', *Guardian Review*, 24 January 2003, p5.

'Leading us up the Wrong Track', *Guardian Weekend*, 1 November 2003, pp36–7.

'Nothing Works in Blair's Britain', *Daily Telegraph*, 15 November 2003, pp21–2.

'Enter Stage Left', *Guardian Review*, 30 October 2004, pp4–6.

'David Hare's Guide to Reality', *Guardian Weekend*, 30 April 2005, p9.

'In Pinter You Find Expressed the Great Struggle of the 20th Century – Between Primitive Rage on the One Hand and Liberal Generosity on the Other', *Guardian*, 14 October 2005, http://arts.guardian.co.uk/features/story/0,,1592011,00.html (accessed 8 January 2007).

'Gorky's Play for Today', *Daily Telegraph*, 1 May 2006, www.telegraph.co.uk/arts/main.jhtml?xml=/arts/2006/05/01/ btgorky01.xml (accessed 10 May 2006).

'Universal Quality', *Guardian*, 24 June 2006, p14.

'On *Enemies*', programme note for the Almeida Theatre production, June 2006.

'Battle in the Bedroom', *Guardian* (G2), 5 July 2006, pp18–20.

'Brecht is There for the Taking', unsourced photocopy, nd, Faber archive.

Interviews and interview profiles, arranged alphabetically by interviewer

Ansorge, Peter. 'Underground Explorations No 1: Portable Playwrights', *Plays and Players*, February 1972, pp14–23.

—. 'Current Concerns', *Plays and Players*, July 1974, p19.

Billington, Michael. 'Broken Rules', *Radio Times*, 12 January 1980, p17.

—. 'A Knight at the Theatre', *Guardian Review*, 4 September 1998, pp2–3, 11.

Bloom, Michael. 'A Kinder, Gentler David Hare', *American Theatre*, November 1989, pp30–4.

Boireau, Nicole. 'Re-Routing Radicalism with David Hare', *European Journal of English Studies* 7, 1 (2003), pp25–37.

Boon, Richard. 'Platform Interview with David Hare on *The Permanent Way*'. National Theatre, 27 January 2004, www.nt-online.org/?lid=8304&cc=1 (accessed 9 February 2007).

Brooks, Richard. 'Two Lovers and a Lino Floor', *Observer*, 6 January 1991, p47.

Coveney, Michael. 'Worlds Apart', *Time Out*, 21–7 January 1983, pp12, 15–16.

—. 'Impure Meditations', *Observer*, 4 February 1990, p35.

Daldry, Stephen. 'Platform Interview with David Hare', National Theatre, London, 4 October 2005.

Dempsey, Judy. 'Interview', *Literary Review*, 22 August 1980, pp35–6.

Dugdale, John. 'Love, Death and Edwina', *Listener*, 15 September 1988, pp38–9.

Ford, John. 'Getting the Carp out of the Mud', *Plays and Players*, November 1971, pp20, 83.

Gaston, Georg. 'Interview: David Hare', *Theatre Journal* 45, 2 (May 1993), pp213–25.

Goodman, Joan. 'New World', *Observer*, 23 January 1983, p44.

Hassell, Graham. 'Hare Racing', *Plays and Players*, February 1990, pp6–8.

Hewison, Robert. 'View from the Top', *Sunday Times*, 11 January 1998, pp6–7.

Isaacs, Jeremy. 'The Director's Cut: David Hare. Jeremy Isaacs Talks to David Hare', BBC Television, 16 May 1989.

Itzin, Catherine, and Simon Trussler. 'David Hare: From Portable Theatre to Joint Stock . . . via Shaftesbury Avenue', *Theatre Quarterly* 5, 20 (1975–6), pp108–15.

Kellaway, Kate. 'He Says People Are Too Backward-Looking, But Wishes He'd Been a Black American in the Fifties . . .', *Observer Review*, 3 August 1997, pp6–7.

Lawson, Mark. 'Making Mischief', *Independent Magazine*, 16 October 1993, pp48–54.

Lubbock, Tom. 'The Theatre-Going Public', BBC Radio 3, 13 April 1986.

McFerran, Ann. 'End of the Acid Era', *Time Out*, 29 August 1975, pp12–15.

Merlin, Bella. Unpublished interview with David Hare. March 2004.

Summers, Alison. 'David Hare's Drama, 1970–1981: An Interview', *Centennial Review* 36, 1992, pp573–91 (interview originally conducted in 1981).

Tynan, Kathleen. 'Dramatically Speaking', *Interview*, April 1989, pp80, 128, 130.

Walsh, John. 'Sound and Fury: David Hare on the Limits of His Art', *Independent Arts and Books Review*, 14 November 2003, p4.

Wolf, Matt. 'The Prime of David Hare', *American Theatre* 16, 1 (January 1999), pp64–6.

Wroe, Nicholas. 'The *Guardian* Profile: David Hare. Makeover Artist', *Guardian*, 13 November 1999, http://books.guardian.co.uk/departments/artsandentertainment/story/0,103076,00.html#top (accessed 26 February 2007).

Wu, Duncan. 'David Hare', in *Making Plays: Interviews with Contemporary British Dramatists and Their Directors* (London: Macmillan, 2000).

Wyver, John. 'Brenton and Hare', *City Limits*, 3–9 May 1985, p85.

(Unsigned). '*Via Dolorosa*: David Hare Interview', www.pbs.org/viadolorosa/davidhare_interview.html (accessed 9 February 2007).

SECONDARY SOURCES

Critical studies

Books and chapters in books

Boon, Richard. *About Hare: The Playwright and the Work* (London: Faber, 2003).

Bradby, David, Louis James and Bernard Sharratt. 'After *Fanshen*: A Discussion with the Joint Stock Theatre Company, David Hare, Trevor Griffiths and Steve Gooch', in David Bradby, Louis James and Bernard Sharratt (eds.), *Performance and Politics in Popular Drama: Aspects of Popular Entertainment in Theatre, Film, and Television 1800–1976* (Cambridge: Cambridge University Press, 1980), pp297–314.

Bull, John. *New British Political Dramatists* (London: Macmillan, 1984).

Dean, Joan FitzPatrick. *David Hare* (Boston, MA: Twayne, 1990).

Donesky, Finlay. *David Hare: Moral and Historical Perspectives* (Westport, CT: Greenwood Press, 1996).

Fraser, Scott. *A Politic Theatre: The Drama of David Hare* (Amsterdam: Rodopi, 1996).

Homden, Carol. *The Plays of David Hare* (Cambridge: Cambridge University Press, 1995).

Oliva, Judy Lee. *David Hare: Theatricalizing Politics* (Ann Arbor, MI: UMI Research Press, 1990).

Page, Malcolm (comp.). *File on Hare* (London: Methuen, 1990).

Wu, Duncan. *Six Contemporary Dramatists: Bennett, Potter, Gray, Brenton, Hare, Ayckbourn* (New York: St Martin's Press, 1995).

Zeifman, Hersh (ed.). *David Hare: A Casebook* (New York: Garland, 1994).

Selected bibliography

Articles, reviews and websites

Aaronovitch, David. 'Tracking Truth', *Observer*, 15 February 2004, www.observer.
guardian.co.uk/comment/story/0,6903,1148420,00.html (accessed 3 December
2006).

Ansorge, Peter. 'David Hare: A War on Two Fronts', *Plays and Players*, April 1978,
pp12–16.

Ascherson, Neal. 'Whose Line is it Anyway?', *Observer*, 9 November 2003,
http://arts.guardian.co.uk/politicaltheatre/story/0,,1082019,00.html (accessed 3
December 2006).

Billington, Michael. 'The *Guardian* Profile: Sir David Hare', *Guardian*, 13 February
2004, p15.

—. '"A Five-Course Meal After a Diet of Candyfloss" – Hare Hits Manhattan',
Guardian, 1 December 2006, p9.

Brantley, Ben. 'Battle Zones in Hare Country', *New York Times*, 1 December
2006, http://theater2.nytimes.com/2006/12/01/theater/reviews/01hour.html?
ref=theater (accessed 3 December 2006).

Brown, Mick. 'Still Angry After All These Years', *Elle*, December 1988, pp40–5.

Coveney, Michael. 'Turning over a New Life: *P&P* Investigates the Background to
Fanshen', *Plays and Players*, June 1975, pp10–13.

Edgar, David. 'The Italian Job', *Guardian*, 26 October 2005, p1.

—. 'The Most Wonderful Initiation Ceremony', *Guardian*, 29 November 2006,
p25.

Golumb, Liorah Anne. 'Saint Isobel: David Hare's *The Secret Rapture* as Christian
Allegory', *Modern Drama* 33, 4 (1990), pp563–74.

Heilpern, John. 'About Our Special Relationship . . .', *Observer Review*, 3 December
2006, p15.

Hiley, Jim. 'The Wetherby Report', *Observer Magazine*, 10 March 1985, pp64–5.

Jack, Ian. 'Just the Ticket', *Guardian Review*, 31 January 2004, p7.

Lennon, Peter. 'Just Leave Me Alone', *Guardian*, 17 February 1996, p26.

Lister, David. 'Passion Is All for Ideologue of the Theatre', *Independent*, 21 March
1998, p3.

Morrison, Blake. 'Profile: David Hare: He Only Does It To Annoy', *Independent*,
30 April 1995, p25.

Myerson, Jonathan. 'David Hare: Fringe Graduate', *Drama* 149 (Autumn 1983),
pp26–8.

Peter, John. 'Meet the Wild Bunch', *The Sunday Times*, 11 July 1976, p34.

Riddell, Mary. 'This is No Parody President', *Observer*, 5 September 2004, p28.

Sierz, Aleks. 'To Each His *Via Dolorosa*', *Al-Ahram Weekly*, 5 February
2001, http://weekly.ahram.org.eg/1998/1948/396_via.htm (accessed 26 February 2007).

Sommer, Elyse. Review of *Skylight*, http://www.curtainup.com/skylight.html
(accessed 13 January 2007).

Sutcliffe, Thomas. 'Hearing the Voice of the People', *Independent Arts and Books
Review*, 16 January 2004, p5.

Taylor, Paul. 'The Man Who Likes John Major', *Independent*, 26 April 1995, p26.

Theatre Record 5, 9 (1985), pp415, 418, 420.

Theatre Record 8, 20 (1988), p1388.

Theatre Record 26, 19 (2006), p1041.

Wood, Gaby. 'Can David Hare Take Manhattan?', *Observer*, 12 November 2006, http://arts.guardian.co.uk/features/story/0,,1945835,00.html (accessed 26 February 2007).

General bibliography

Aird, Eileen M. *Sylvia Plath* (Edinburgh: Oliver and Boyd, 1973).

Althusser, Louis. *Lenin and Philosophy and Other Essays*, trans. B Brewster (New York: New Left Books, 1971).

Ansorge, Peter. *Disrupting the Spectacle: Five Years of Experimental and Fringe Theatre in Britain* (London: Pitman, 1975).

Barish, Jonas. *The Antitheatrical Prejudice* (Berkeley: University of California Press, 1981).

Bauman, Zygmunt. *Postmodern Ethics* (Oxford: Blackwell, 1993).

Boon, Richard. *Brenton the Playwright* (London: Methuen, 1991).

Bourdieu, Pierre. *Distinction: A Social Critique of the Judgement of Taste*, trans. Richard Nice (London: Routledge, 1984).

Brecht, Bertolt. *The Exception and the Rule*, in *'The Measures Taken' and Other Lehrstücke* (London: Methuen, 1977).

Brenton, Howard. *Plays: One* (London: Methuen, 1986).

—. *Plays: Two* (London: Methuen, 1989).

Buber, Martin. 'Elements of the Interhuman', in John Stewart (ed.), *Bridges Not Walls: A Book About Interpersonal Communication*, 6th edition (New York: McGraw-Hill, 1995).

Büchner, Georg. *The Complete Plays*, ed. and intro. Michael Patterson (London: Methuen, 1987).

Bull, John. *Stage Right: Crisis and Recovery in Contemporary British Mainstream Theatre* (London: Macmillan, 1994).

Buse, Peter. 'Mark Ravenhill', British Council, www.contemporarywriters.com, pp1–4 (accessed 19 April 2006).

Calder, Angus. *The People's War* (London: Jonathan Cape, 1969).

Cave, Richard Allen. *New British Drama on the London Stage 1970–1985* (Gerrards Cross: Colin Smythe, 1989).

Craig, Sandy. *Dreams and Deconstructions: Alternative Theatre in Britain* (Ambergate: Amber Lane Press, 1980.)

Cunningham, Michael. *The Hours* (New York: Farrar, Straus and Giroux, 1998).

de Beauvoir, Simone. *The Second Sex* (New York: Knopf, 1963).

Debord, Guy. *The Society of the Spectacle* (Detroit, MI: Black and Red Printing Co-operative, 1970).

Derrida, Jacques. *Speech and Phenomena and Other Essays on Husserl's Theory of Signs* (Evanston, IL: Northwestern University Press, 1973).

—. *Of Grammatology* (Baltimore, MD: Johns Hopkins University Press, 1976).

—. *Dissemination* (London: Athlone Press, 1981).

—. *Margins of Philosophy* (Brighton: Harvester Press, 1982).

—. *The Truth in Painting* (Chicago, IL: University of Chicago Press, 1987).

Didion, Joan. *The Year of Magical Thinking* (New York: Knopf, 2005).

Donadio, Rachel. 'The Irascible Prophet: V. S. Naipaul at Home', *New York Times*, 7 August 2005, www.nytimes.com/2005/08/07/books/review/07DONADIO. html (accessed 7 February 2007).

Dromgoole, Dominic. *The Full Room: An A–Z of Contemporary Playwriting* (London: Methuen, 2002).

Edgar, David. 'Reality Time'. Unpublished manuscript of keynote speech, 'Reality Time: A Conference about Factual Drama on Stage and Screen', Birmingham University, 1996.

—. 'Come Together', *Guardian*, 10 January 2005, p2.

Elsom, John. *Post-War British Theatre* (London: Routledge and Kegan Paul, 1976).

Eyre, Richard. 'Speech Impediments', *Guardian*, 21 February 2004, www.arts.guardian.co.uk/features/story/0,11710,1152652,00.html (accessed 2 December 2006).

— and Nicholas Wright. *Changing Stages: A View of British Theatre in the Twentieth Century* (London: Bloomsbury, 2000).

Faber Playwrights at the National Theatre (London: Faber, 2005).

Faith in the City: A Call to Action by Church and Nation (Archbishop of Canterbury's Commission on Urban Priority Areas, 1985).

Figes, Eva. *Patriarchal Attitudes* (London: Faber, 1970).

Findlater, Richard (ed.). *At the Royal Court: 25 Years of the English Stage Company* (Ambergate: Amber Lane Press, 1981).

French, Marilyn. *The Women's Room* (London: André Deutsch, 1978).

Friedan, Betty. *The Feminine Mystique* (New York: Dell, 1963).

Gallop, Jane. *Around 1981: Academic Feminist Literary Theory* (London: Routledge, 1992).

Garner Jr, Stanton B. *Trevor Griffiths: Politics, Drama, History* (Michigan: University of Michigan Press, 1999).

Gavron, Hannah. *The Captive Wife* (Harmondsworth: Penguin, 1970).

Gilbert, Sandra M. and Susan Gubar. *The Madwoman in the Attic: The Woman Writer and the Nineteenth-Century Literary Imagination* (New Haven: Yale University Press, 1979).

Gottlieb, Vera. 'Thatcher's Theatre – or, After *Equus*', *New Theatre Quarterly* 6, 14 (May 1988), pp99–104.

Greer, Germaine. *The Female Eunuch* (London: MacGibbon and Key, 1970).

Griffiths, Paul J. 'Christ and Critical Theory', *First Things* 145 (August/September 2004), pp46–55.

Griffiths, Trevor. *Through the Night and Such Impossibilities* (London: Faber, 1977).

Grillo, John. 'An Excess of Nightmare', *Gambit* 6, 23 (1973), pp18–24.

Grotowski, Jerzy. *Towards a Poor Theatre* (London: Methuen, 1976).

Hammond, Jonathon. 'Messages First: An Interview with Howard Brenton', *Gambit* 6, 23 (1973), pp24–32.

Harasym, Sara (ed.). *The Post-Colonial Critic: Interviews, Strategies, Dialogues* (London: Routledge, 1990).

Hart, Josephine. *Damage* (New York: Ballantine, 1996).

Hay, Malcolm and Philip Roberts, 'Interview: Howard Brenton', *Performing Arts Journal* 3, 3 (1979), pp131–41.

Hinton, William. *Fanshen: A Documentary of Revolution in a Chinese Village* (Berkeley: University of California Press, 1996). First published 1966.

Holbrook, David. *Sylvia Plath: Poetry and Existence* (London: Athlone, 1976).

Houseman, John. 'Today's Hero: A Review', *Hollywood Quarterly* 2, 2 (1947), pp161–3.

Hughes, Ted and Frances McCullough (eds.). *The Journals of Sylvia Plath* (New York: Ballantine, 1982).

Hughes-Warrington, Marnie. 'Hayden White', *Fifty Key Thinkers on History* (London: Routledge, 2001).

Innes, Christopher. *Modern British Drama: The Twentieth Century* (Cambridge: Cambridge University Press, 2002).

Itzin, Catherine. *Stages in the Revolution: Political Theatre in Britain since 1968* (London: Methuen, 1980).

— and Simon Trussler (ints.), 'Petrol Bombs through the Proscenium Arch', *Theatre Quarterly* 5, 17 (1975), pp4–20.

Jack, Ian. *The Crash that Stopped Britain* (London: Granta Publications, 2001).

Jong, Erica. *Fear of Flying* (New York: New American Library, 1973).

Kershaw, Baz. 'Curiosity or Contempt: On Spectacle, the Human, and Activism', *Theatre Journal*, 55 (2003), pp591–611.

Kramer, Mimi. 'Three for the Show', *Time*, 4 August 1997, pp70–1.

Lessing, Doris. *The Golden Notebook* (New York: Ballantine, 1962).

McGrath, John. *A Good Night Out* (London: Methuen, 1981), p98.

Madison, Gary B. and Marty Fairbairn. *The Ethics of Postmodernity: Current Trends in Continental Thought* (Evanston, IL: University of Northwestern Press, 1999).

Merlin, Bella. Interview with Max Stafford-Clark for the Royal National Theatre educational website (www.nationaltheatre.org.uk/education) on *The Permanent Way*, March 2004.

Millett, Kate. *Sexual Politics* (New York: Doubleday, 1970).

Mitchell, Juliet. *Psychoanalysis and Feminism* (New York: Pantheon, 1974).

Nixon, Rob. *London Calling: V. S. Naipaul, Postcolonial Mandarin* (Oxford: Oxford University Press, 1992).

Paget, Derek. '"Verbatim Theatre": Oral History and Documentary Techniques', *New Theatre Quarterly* 3, 12 (1987), pp317–36.

—. 'Acting a Part: Performing Docudrama', *Media International Australia Incorporating Culture and Policy* 104 (2002), pp 30–41.

Patterson, Michael. *Strategies of Political Theatre: Post-War British Playwrights* (Cambridge: Cambridge University Press, 2003).

Peacock, D. Keith. *Thatcher's Theatre: British Theatre and Drama in the Eighties* (Westport, CT: Greenwood Press, 1999).

Pike, Frank (ed.). *Ah! Mischief: The Writer and Television* (London: Faber, 1982).

Plante, David. *Difficult Women* (London: Victor Gollancz Ltd, 1983).

Plath, Sylvia. *The Bell Jar* (London: Faber, 1963).

—. *Letters Home: Correspondence 1950–1963* (New York: Harper and Row, 1975).

Rajan, M. S., V. S. Mani and C. S. R. Murthy. *The Nonaligned and the United Nations* (New Delhi: South Asian Publishers, 1987).

Ravenhill, Mark. *Plays: 1* (London: Methuen, 2002).

Reinelt, Janelle. *After Brecht: British Epic Theater* (Ann Arbor: University of Michigan Press, 1994).

Ritchie, Rob (ed.). *The Joint Stock Book: The Making of a Theatre Collective* (London: Methuen, 1987).

Roberts, Philip and Max Stafford-Clark. *Taking Stock: The Theatre of Max Stafford-Clark* (London: Nick Hern Books, 2007).

Rokem, Freddie. *Performing History; Theatrical Representations of the Past in Contemporary Theatre* (Iowa City: University of Iowa Press, 2000).

Rowbotham, Sheila. *Woman's Consciousness, Man's World* (Harmondsworth: Penguin, 1973).

Royle, Edward. 'Trends in Post-War British Social History', in J. Obelkevich and P. Catterall (eds.), *Understanding Post-War British Society* (London: Routledge, 1994).

Said, Edward. *Orientalism* (New York: Pantheon, 1978).

Saturday Review, BBC Radio 4, 17 January 2004.

Sierz, Aleks. *In-Yer-Face Theatre: British Drama Today* (London: Faber, 2001).

Soans, Robin. *A State Affair*, in Andrea Dunbar and Robin Soans, *Rita, Sue and Bob Too/A State Affair* (London: Methuen, 2000).

—. *Talking to Terrorists* (London: Oberon Books, 2006).

Spivak, Gayatri. 'Can the Subaltern Speak?', in Cary Nelson and Larry Grossberg (eds.), *Marxism and the Interpretation of Culture* (Chicago, IL: University of Chicago Press, 1988), pp271–313.

Stafford-Clark, Max. '"A Programme for the Progressive Conscience": The Royal Court in the Eighties' (interview with Tony Dunn), *New Theatre Quarterly* 1, 2 (May 1985), pp138–53.

Stewart, John and Milt Thomas. 'Dialogic Listening: Sculpting Mutual Meanings', in John Stewart (ed.), *Bridges Not Walls: A Book About Interpersonal Communication*, 6th edition (New York: McGraw-Hill, 1995).

Svich, Caridad. 'Commerce and Morality in the Theatre of Mark Ravenhill', *Contemporary Theatre Review* 13, 1 (2003), pp81–95.

Taylor, J. R. *The Second Wave: British Drama of the Sixties* (London: Methuen, 1978).

Teevan, Colin. Interview in *Metrolife*, 19 September 2006, p25.

Trussler, Simon (ed.). *New Theatre Voices of the Seventies* (London: Methuen, 1981).

Turner, Cathy. Unpublished interview with Howard Brenton, London, 17 January 2001.

Tynan, Kenneth. *Curtains* (London: Longman, 1961).

Wandor, Michelene. *Look Back in Gender: Sexuality and the Family in Post-War British Drama* (London: Methuen, 1987).

—. *Drama Today: A Critical Guide to British Drama 1970–1990* (London: Longman, 1993).

White, Hayden. *Tropics of Discourse* (London: Johns Hopkins University Press, 1978).

Wikander, Matthew H. *The Play of Truth and State: Historical Drama from Shakespeare to Brecht* (London: Johns Hopkins University Press, 1986).

Wilde, Oscar. 'The Critic as Artist', in *The Complete Works of Oscar Wilde* (London: Collins, 1990).

Zimmerman, Jens. '*Quo Vadis*? Literary Theory beyond Postmodernism', *Christianity and Literature* 53, 4 (2004), pp495–519.

INDEX

Cambridge Companions to...

AUTHORS

Shakespeare edited by Margareta de Grazia and Stanley Wells

Shakespearean Comedy edited by Alexander Leggatt

Shakespeare and Popular Culture edited by Robert Shaughnessy

Shakespearean Tragedy edited by Claire McEachern

Shakespeare on Film edited by Russell Jackson (second edition)

Shakespeare on Stage edited by Stanley Wells and Sarah Stanton

Shakespeare's History Plays edited by Michael Hattaway

Shakespeare's Poetry edited by Patrick Cheney

George Bernard Shaw edited by Christopher Innes

Shelley edited by Timothy Morton

Mary Shelley edited by Esther Schor

Sam Shepard edited by Matthew C. Roudané

Spenser edited by Andrew Hadfield

Wallace Stevens edited by John N. Serio

Tom Stoppard edited by Katherine E. Kelly

Harriet Beecher Stowe edited by Cindy Weinstein

Jonathan Swift edited by Christopher Fox

Henry David Thoreau edited by Joel Myerson

Tolstoy edited by Donna Tussing Orwin

Mark Twain edited by Forrest G. Robinson

Virgil edited by Charles Martindale

Edith Wharton edited by Millicent Bell

Walt Whitman edited by Ezra Greenspan

Oscar Wilde edited by Peter Raby

Tennessee Williams edited by Matthew C. Roudané

August Wilson edited by Christopher Bigsby

Mary Wollstonecraft edited by Claudia L. Johnson

Virginia Woolf edited by Sue Roe and Susan Sellers

Wordsworth edited by Stephen Gill

W. B. Yeats edited by Marjorie Howes and John Kelly

Zola edited by Brian Nelson

TOPICS

The Actress edited by Maggie B. Gale and John Stokes

The African American Novel edited by Maryemma Graham

The African American Slave Narrative edited by Audrey A. Fisch

American Modernism edited by Walter Kalaidjian

American Realism and Naturalism edited by Donald Pizer

American Women Playwrights edited by Brenda Murphy

Australian Literature edited by Elizabeth Webby

British Romanticism edited by Stuart Curran

British Theatre, 1730–1830 edited by Jane Moody and Daniel O'Quinn

Canadian Literature edited by Eva-Marie Kröller

The Classic Russian Novel edited by Malcolm V. Jones and Robin Feuer Miller

Contemporary Irish Poetry edited by Matthew Campbell

Crime Fiction edited by Martin Priestman

The Eighteenth-Century Novel edited by John Richetti

Eighteenth-Century Poetry edited by John Sitter

English Literature, 1500–1600 edited by Arthur F. Kinney

English Literature, 1650–1740 edited by Steven N. Zwicker

English Literature, 1740–1830 edited by Thomas Keymer and Jon Mee

English Poetry, Donne to Marvell edited by Thomas N. Corns

English Renaissance Drama, edited by A. R. Braunmuller and Michael Hattaway (second edition)

English Restoration Theatre edited by Deborah C. Payne Fisk

Feminist Literary Theory edited by Ellen Rooney

Fiction in the Romantic Period edited by Richard Maxwell and Katie Trumpener

The Fin de Siècle edited by Gail Marshall

The French Novel: From 1800 to the Present edited by Timothy Unwin

Gothic Fiction edited by Jerrold E. Hogle

The Greek and Roman Novel edited by Tim Whitmarsh

Greek and Roman Theatre edited by Marianne McDonald and J. Michael Walton